Reconstructing Education

RECONSTRUCTING EDUCATION

Toward a Pedagogy of Critical Humanism

Greta Hofmann Nemiroff

BERGIN & GARVEY

NEW YORK • WESTPORT, CONNECTICUT • LONDON

Library of Congress Cataloging-in-Publication Data

Nemiroff, Greta Hofmann.
  Reconstructing education : toward a pedagogy of critical humanism
/ Greta Hofmann Nemiroff.
    p.   cm.
  Includes bibliographical references (p.   ) and index.
  ISBN 0-89789-266-6 (alk. paper). — ISBN 0-89789-267-4 (pbk. :
alk. paper)
    1. Dawson College. New School. 2. Free schools—Québec
(Province)—Montréal—Case studies. 3. Critical pedagogy—Québec
(Province)—Montréal—Case studies. 4. Education, Humanistic
—Québec (Province)—Montréal—Case studies.   I. Title.
LE5.M6625N47   1992
370.11′2′0971427—dc20   91-33944

British Library Cataloguing in Publication Data is available.

Library of Congress Catalog Card Number: 91-33944
ISBN: 0-89789-266-6 (hb)
        0-89789-267-4 (pb)

First published in 1992

Bergin & Garvey, One Madison Avenue, New York, NY 10010
An imprint of Greenwood Publishing Group, Inc.

Printed in the United States of America

The paper used in this book complies with the
Permanent Paper Standard issued by the National
Information Standards Organization (Z39.48-1984).

10 9 8 7 6 5 4 3 2 1

Copyright Acknowledgments

  The author and publisher are grateful for permission to reprint from the following sources.
  Reprinted by permission of Greenwood Publishing Group, Inc., Westport, CT, from
Education under Siege by Stanley Aronowitz and Henry A. Giroux. Copyright © 1985 by
Stanley Aronowitz and Henry A. Giroux.
  Reprinted by permission of Greenwood Publishing Group, Inc., Westport, CT, from *A
Pedagogy for Liberation* by Ira Shor and Paulo Freire. Copyright © 1987 by Ira Shor and
Paulo Freire.
  John Dewey, *Experience and Education* (London: Collier Books, 1938). Reprinted by
permission of Kappa Delta Pi, an International Honor Society in Education.
  Kathy Presner, "The Development of New School Academics: 1974–1987,"
unpublished paper (Montreal: Dawson College, November 1987), pp. 2–3.
  New School Annual Reports, Dawson College, Montreal.
  Margo Ford-Johansen, interview, 1984, and *New School Annual Report: 1981–82*, pp.
65–66, 80.
  Patrick Powers, interview, 1984, and *New School Annual Report: 1984–85*, p. 49.
  Vivianne Silver, interview, 1984.
  Shirleen Schermerhorn, interview, 1987.

To all New School students,
past, present, and to come.
You are what it is all about.

Though the world cannot be changed
by talking to one child at a time,
it may at least be known.

Grace Paley
Later the Same Day

Contents

Illustrations

Acknowledgments

THE PREPARATION FOR THIS BOOK would not have been possible without a grant from the Programme d'aide à la recherche sur l'enseignement et l'apprentissage (PAREA) of the Direction de la recherche et du développement, Service des études et du développement des collèges of La Direction générale de l'enseignement collégial (DGEC), Gouvernement du Québec, for 1987–1989. I must also mention the generosity of my colleague Cathy Fichton for her share in the extension of the grant for a second year.

I would like to acknowledge the contributions of these individuals to my work: Pat Powers, my codirector at the New School of Dawson College in Montreal, who was most generous with his friendship, encouragement, and time for the duration of this project; the students in my research group of 1987, especially Kathy Presner, Lyla Simon, Linda Ferch, and Heidi Quinsey, whose work was a great help to me; Stanley Nemiroff, who was most helpful with resources for my research and with incisive critiques of my text; my friend and colleague Frances Davis, whose need for absolute clarification helped me in the final draft of this book; Bruno Geslain of the Professional Development Service at Dawson College, who never paused in his encouragement of this project; Janice Bernath at Dawson College, whose detailed questions helped me to clarify my theoretical perspective and helped her to produce very accurate diagrams; Dina Saikali, who proofread and critiqued it; Debra Martens, who created the index; and finally Rina Marchei, whose organization of my home gives me the freedom to think and write.

The greatest thanks must go to the staff and students who have given their presence to the New School, many of whom have generously contributed their experiences and words to this study. Their experiences are inextricably woven into the fabric of the school's evolution.

PART ONE
THE EVOLUTION OF AN EDUCATIONAL PHILOSOPHY

Introduction

THE NORTH AMERICAN INSTITUTIONALIZATION of the training of educators has resulted in the formation of some epistemologically questionable discrete categories with which to formulate the educational experience. These categories are theoretical/educational foundations; curriculum development; pedagogy/educational psychology; and the social, historical, and comparative contexts in which formal education takes place.

While each category is instantly recognizable as a part of the whole, this division—which is reproduced through territorial divisions within higher education—does not reflect the reality in which teaching and learning are experienced by educators and students. Rather than experiencing teaching and learning in discrete categories, participants are involved in a dynamic process in which educational philosophy (whether overt, informal, or invisible), subject matter, pedagogy, and the context in which this activity is taking place are dynamically and mutually informing. While these four elements of education cannot be ignored, they also cannot be separated.

Educational theory is often presented in a manner divorced from the specificity of its praxis and its possible application. Indeed, theory has often been articulated after a praxis has been seen to "work." However, the criteria of "working" are not always articulated, and within state-run educational systems it is probably accurate to assume that the criteria for a praxis which "works" may be those which work in the interest of the state and a power elite who most benefit from the structures and system of rewards built into educational systems.

Pedagogy is not always regarded as a complex, intermeshed series of preoccupations but is often reduced to the positivistic ruminations of social scientists in the field of education, whose work is often funded by the state, and by organizations that share the state's interests in performing quantitative rather than qualitative analyses. Quantitative analysis, often highly speculative and based on a minuscule sample of subjects, is frequently funneled through the channels of learned journals juried by the like-minded into the big business of textbook publishing, where, through large sales, it can be recycled through schools of education to provide "valid" criteria for the provision of good education. Certainly excellent quantitative analysis has been done; however, the tendency to adhere to numbers rather than to risk a well-articulated philosophical position is endemic to educational systems and institutions.

Since curriculum choices are usually defended as the guardians of "standards," much discourse on curriculum is based on the desire for standardization either through assiduous attention to the tired old patriarchal monologue of a great "canon" approach in many of the disciplines, or through the technological enthusiasms of an avant-garde that foresees infinite possibilities for standardization through the use of computer-assisted learning. The latter has the additional virtue that neither computers nor their software is unionized, and they enjoy no employer-paid benefits other than repair contracts.

All curricula, however, deserve a detailed scrutiny of the sociopolitical contingencies that have historically contributed to their construction, the educational philosophies underlying their choice, and the pedagogical practices attached to them. Curriculum must always be examined with the understanding that it will be presented to particular groups of students, each of whom arrives with a historical, social, political, gender, and class identity. Students also arrive with particular psychological dispositions and needs that must be addressed both through the theoretical construction upon which curriculum formation is based and through a pedagogy that takes into account the complexity of each person individually and in interaction within a group. In the reconstructed pedagogy that I am proposing in this book, theory and praxis have a mutually informing and re-forming function in the ongoing project of education for individual and group empowerment.

The experience of the New School of Dawson College in Montreal, which provides a case study for this book, is based on an overt articulation of educational philosophy, the ongoing modification of the philosophy, and reaffirmation of its basic values. While students' and staff's concerns have changed since its beginning in 1973, it has remained faithful from its founding to the present to the precepts of humanistic education in its broadest form. On the other hand, it has also elaborated and added pedagogical concerns beyond the original articulation of its philosophy of humanistic education.

While much pedagogical theory has been developed for elementary and secondary education, there is remarkably little written on appropriate pedagogy for young people at the crucial ages of seventeen to twenty-five, when most North Americans are expected to take the necessary steps to find their place in the adult world. It is my contention that these formative years, when young people must go out into the world and separate from home, family, and known values, are of great importance and are a period of crisis. In our heterogeneous society they must find the strength to confront conflicting cultural and moral values, to make appropriate choices for themselves, and to find within this melée a place for themselves. Most people of this age have already tried drugs, love, and "McJobs." Now they have to look to the future, a frightening prospect at a time when drug and alcohol use may become problems, love becomes more complex and painful, and work becomes detached from the notion "This is just for now" and instead becomes "This may be the rest of my life." Many will begin to think of having children—if they do not already have them. They will have to respond to an increasingly divided world, rife with wars, pollution, and global injustice. It is not surprising that there is much less pedagogical analysis of their needs than of the needs of children and young adolescents. Their issues are quite overwhelming, and there are clearly no single solutions that can be offered in lofty solitude by educational theoreticians.

While the praxis described in this book is based on a seventeen-year experience of a particular educational setting, its ideas and theories are applicable—in part, if not in toto—to all forms of education, all age groups, and both formal and informal education. It is inherent in the application of critical humanism that theory and praxis must always interact in specific contexts with one another and with the contingencies relative to a clientele with specific needs.

When student-centered education is mentioned, often some "expert" will languidly state that "that was all fine for the sixties," but that we are currently in pursuit of something called a "competitive edge" so that we can "win" the economic war with our neighbors on this planet. People tend to dismiss educational ideology formulated in the 1960s as a kind of "doing your own thing" that "didn't work." In some ways, our schools have regressed to the joyless resourcelessness that produced a massive problem of illiteracy that characterized so much education in the 1950s and the early 1960s. A close analysis of educational critiques of that era reveals multiple theories, many of which may be of great relevance to education today. Rather than being neglected, these theories must be retrieved, reevaluated, and, where appropriate, applied within our schools.

One popular theory of the 1960s was humanistic education, which addresses the "whole learner" as a psychological entity rather than a student of a particular subject at a particular time. The humanistic educators had many valid recommendations to make about pedagogues and pedagogy, although their ignoring of the students' socioeconomic realities flawed the usefulness of their theories as sole underpinnings for a pedagogy.

The 1970s and 1980s saw the development of critical pedagogy from the writings of Paulo Freire through a second generation of educational philosophers. Here attention was paid to contextualizing the students within their sociopolitical situations and engaging with them in an epistemological "interrogation" regarding their educational needs and how to fulfill them. While critical pedagogy situates learners and teachers in their social contexts and helps them to develop intellectual strategies for empowerment, it does not take into account the many individual and systemic psychological factors that also inform learners' relationships with learning and the teachers' mode of teaching.

The experience of the New School of Dawson College, a community college program in Montreal, has shown that both these educational ideologies include factors necessary for good learning, but that neither takes sufficient account of the learners and the contexts of their learning, or of the teachers' engagement in a particular pedagogy. Our developing philosophy and pedagogy have led us to a cross-referential praxis that I have called "critical humanism," which contains elements of both the ideologies alluded to above. Critical humanism also draws on progressive education, existentialist theories, feminist pedagogy, and values education. It is an eclectic learning model based on a dialectical process, which ensures that it will always be in a state of ongoing modification and change. While its basic premises are clear and can be realized in most contexts without radical modification, its praxis is situationally attentive. This book, then, examines a body of educational ideology and posits a new ideology based on a synthesis of other ideologies. The ideology of critical humanism has been refined through the praxis of the New School of Dawson College since 1973. For this reason, the experience of the New School will be treated as an illustrative case study of how this ideology and praxis have dialectically developed.

The first names of respondents in most quotations from New School students have been changed. It is only when direct quotations from faculty and/or students cite both first and family names in their attributions that they derive from the people named.

In the hope that there are still educators who are interested in formulating and practicing alternatives to the status quo, I have ended with some cautionary remarks regarding the creation of alternative educational settings and strategies for their survival. These cautionary statements are a record of experience and should be no deterrent to those educators who are prepared to throw caution to the winds and get on with alternative educational projects that may draw on the theoretical framework of critical humanism. The educational engagement envisaged in this project presupposes that the educator has an immense curiosity, an ability to tolerate creative chaos, and the need to effect change—a risky enterprise, perhaps, but a rewarding one.

1

The Educational Context
in Quebec

We must be very, very critical every time we speak about emancipatory education, liberatory or liberating education. We must repeat
always that we are not meaning with these expressions that in the inti-
macy of a seminar we are transforming the structures of the society.
That is, liberating education is one of the things which we must do
with other things in order to transform reality. We must avoid being in-
terpreted as if we were thinking that first we should educate the people for being free, and after we could transform reality. No. We have to
do the two simultaneously, as much as possible. Because of that, we
must be engaged in political action against the dehumanizing structures of production.[1]

IN ORDER TO BE RENDERED UNDERSTANDABLE, discussion of educational theory and practice must give notice of the sociopolitical context that
informs their structure and patterns. This is especially important in the case
of public education, which is totally dependent on the state for its funding.
Consideration of the context of the New School must thus be made in terms
of its particular situation. The New School addresses the varied needs of a
minority community with negligible political power (English-speaking
Quebecers) within the larger Quebec society, which is undergoing fundamental changes and stresses internally and within the troubled confedera-
tion of Canada. A brief overview of this complex political context should
help readers to situate the New School's experiences, theories, and practices and to assess their applicability to their particular situations.

From 1944 to 1959, Quebec was ruled by a right-wing government under
the leadership of Premier Maurice Duplessis, who worked closely with the

highly influential and powerful Roman Catholic Church. All public education was, and still is, confessional, with Catholic children going to schools
in the Catholic system and Protestants and "others" going to schools in the
Protestant system. While the Catholics had both English- and French-
language schools, the "others" schools were all English-language. Although
there was always opposition to Duplessis, his death in 1959 significantly
weakened his party and brought about the beginnings of a "quiet revolution" to secularize and modernize what had been a largely rural and work-
ing-class population. The early 1960s is usually referred to as the "quiet
revolution" because, over the next thirty years and without warfare, the
province of Quebec was to become a modern industrialized "nation" with a
large urban population, a complex educational system, and a complicated
infrastructure.

Until the "quiet revolution," the two linguistic communities had totally
different educational systems. While there were both English and French
universities, the French population had an additional tier of education between high school and university, the collèges classiques. These "classical
colleges," mainly run by religious orders, catered to the children of the elite
and some children of the less wealthy classes whose academic skills earned
them scholarships. There were far more men's classical colleges than wom-
en's; for women, there was a system of free "schools of the domestic arts"
whose purpose was to train them to be wives and mothers. In 1964, the
Quebec government established its first Ministry of Education in order to
centralize control over education within the government. Soon after, it established the Royal Commission on Education, under the aegis of Monsi-
gnor Alphonse Parent, to address the educational situation in Quebec and
to bring recommendations to the minister of education.

In 1965, the Parent Commission reported its findings to the minister of
education in what came to be called the *Parent Report*. This document was
critical of the existing educational system, claiming that Quebec was in the
throes of an educational crisis that was "worldwide." Everywhere "administrative and pedagogical procedures" were being questioned and "more or
less radical reforms" applied.[2] Furthermore, the *Parent Report* maintained
that the educational system was not preparing people for the future. At
times it is difficult to ascertain if the writers characterized the "crisis" as the
necessity to provide an appropriate "modern education" to a changing society, or if the crisis they perceived was manifested by the questions and challenges the "quiet revolution" was posing to the old order.

Whichever crisis its authors considered the more pressing, the *Parent Report* recognized the need to meet the demands of an increasingly heterogeneous population at a time of great technological change and economic
growth. In order to achieve this end, the *Parent Report* recommended that
the French and the English communities follow the same educational se-
quence and that a postsecondary echelon of education between high school

and university be established through the creation of a community college system, significantly different from community college systems elsewhere in North America. The Quebec system is known as the CEGEP system (for Collèges de l'enseignement général et professionel, Colleges of General and Professional Education). The CEGEPs are open free of charge to students after they have completed eleven years of schooling. They offer two-year preuniversity programs that are necessary for admission into the Quebec university system. They also offer three-year professional training in a large assortment of social, medical, technical, and artistic career programs.

While the *Parent Report* recognized the need to democratize education and change society, it was also concerned with preserving the positive aspects of Québecois heritage and culture while recognizing the needs of youth today. The authors articulated their ideas in this way:

In the present cultural crisis and in the social evolution of our civilization, what should be the goals of education, what direction should be given to pedagogical reform? In more concrete terms: what degree of diversity and of specialization should we seek in education? . . . Behind these questions the point at issue is the concept of a human ideal in the context of modern society.[3]

The *Parent Report* advocated a "broader and more varied humanism," to be integrated into an increasingly automated and impersonal society. This was considered to be so important that it should be "the major preoccupation of both teachers and programmes of study."[4] The report affirmed that educators must be aware of the worldview of the students, which was often very removed from that of their teachers. Educators were urged to foster "the unity of civilization and the universal needs of the human person . . . [as the] . . . guiding principle for that general education henceforth required by everyone."[5]

While this liberal approach was supported in the *Parent Report*, it also defined as the school's primary task the need to "instill a passion for the truth and a respect for intelligence."[6] This implies a somewhat limited notion of "one" truth and of what comprises "intelligence." Teachers must instill in students a passion for truth and intelligence, bearing in mind that anything which "stands in the way of these virtues sins against the intelligence and deflects education from its primary objective."[7] Indeed, the *Parent Report* went further in suggesting that schools must "mould character" while opening the mind and training the intelligence in ways that make up for "parental inadequacy." Schools should not promote individualism but "intellectual culture, moral and even religious training . . . must be given social dimensions." Feelings of communal solidarity were "essential in modern society," not only because democracy requires of everyone an active participation in the public sphere but also because "modern man is more and more called upon to work in teams and in groups . . . in industry, smooth human relations have become almost as important as technical knowledge."[8]

In the French community, there was already an infrastructure of classical colleges, many of which were immediately transformed into public, nondenominational French-speaking CEGEPs and some of which remained open as private CEGEPs. The last "schools for the domestic arts" closed in 1967, and in that year various French CEGEPs opened around Quebec. It took the English community until 1969 to open its first CEGEP, Dawson College. Eventually there were forty-one public CEGEPs in Quebec, four of which are English-speaking, and numerous private ones as well.

The founders of Dawson College, an anglophone CEGEP, were responding to the same kinds of social forces as their French compatriots, and they thought that the "timing was right for the creation of a college which promised to be innovative." They wanted to create a community of teachers and students with student parity and the participation of all staff in the decision-making process.[9] In its first year, this modus operandi, according to its first director general, was stressful and "rife with ambiguity," but the founding group of employees believed these conditions to be worth the trouble. Between 1969 and 1973, the college's registration almost tripled, as did the number of faculty and other employees. In 1973–1974, Dawson College was obliged to expand its physical plant to three other campuses as well as rented satellite facilities spread across Montreal. This decentralization of facilities led to a muted sense of community and significant intraprogram competition for resources. With the change in scale, Dawson experienced difficulty in maintaining its morale. The original vision of a participatory community began to dissipate:

Participatory democracy seems to require a higher level of sophistication and selfless responsibility than most people can muster all the time. Some seem to meet these requirements for one episode and then subside to "average frailty." Others sustain this level of behaviour for . . . years but may finally collapse physically.[10]

Scale and early burnout also made it difficult for Dawson College to live up to its original slogan, "Dawson Is Students." There was increasing theft and student vandalism, and many Dawson teachers were not able to perform

at their best in the Dawson setting. Some wished to have more student-centered classes, but . . . did not know or learn how. . . . A few . . . refused to accept the institutional commitment and stubbornly refused to adjust their practices to the Dawson approach. . . . And there were many teachers who periodically faced the dilemma of trying on the one hand to respond to student individuality and expressed need[s] and, on the other, to the demands of their disciplines and courses or their own perceptions of student needs.[11]

It was at this juncture of expansion and disillusionment that a humanities teacher, Guy Millisor, and one of his classes met the challenge of imagining an "ideal" CEGEP. They had concluded that it was virtually impossible to ensure a high level of participation and commitment in a large, diffuse, and alienating community. They claimed that a strong feeling of individual self-worth was a necessary condition to motivate students' willingness to contribute to a group. They judged the structures solidifying at Dawson to be unconducive to strengthening people's self-esteem or helping them to build community. They became so confident of the correctness of their theories that they took advantage of Dawson's expansion plans to present a proposal for a "new school" preuniversity arts program that was accepted in 1973 by the Board of Governors of Dawson College. Dr. Paul Gallagher, director general at the time, recorded his impression of this proposal:

It would have to have its own separate facilities, almost certainly non-institutional in character, and its own operating budget to ensure its freedom to pursue its own priorities; its programs would meet college diploma requirements but would be organized distinctively with clusters of courses and an emphasis on workshops rather than formal classes and institutional timetables; it would place great emphasis on "community" participation and mutual help and trust among its members; most significantly, it would give concurrent emphasis to affective and cognitive learning.[12]

The founding proposal identified humanistic education as the New School's essential ideology, and it included several assumptions in the proposal to the college's Board of Governors:

1. Pedagogy: Teachers must "*trust* that students want to learn and tell their students that they do so trust." They must help students develop feelings of self-worth, encouraging them to continual personal growth. Above all, they must "approach learning situations as a learner, jointly pursuing goals and pedagogy with the students" in a manner that precluded the teachers "taking over."

2. Student responsibility: They must find matters of relevance, "real and important to themselves," to their purposes.

3. Community: Group discussion was to be the way in which the community examined assent and dissent. Through this "new methodology" they would achieve self-actualization by means of a more "open exploration of the inner self through exposing and nurturing unrevealed talents and values" originating in each student.

4. Curriculum: It would focus on the inner self, exploring new ways of learning. Students were to develop a social conscience and make social contributions to some "field of social betterment." They were also to be encouraged to self-expression in aesthetic and creative ways, developing "a philosophy of life" and learning that would enable them "to live an examined life."

5. There was to be a dissolution of distinctions between school and other learning.

The home, community, school, and other places would all be recognized as sites of learning where students could pursue the objective of intellectual, emotional, and ethical personal growth.[13]

The original proposal was very particular regarding the site of the New School. Since it was to be "noninstitutional," its first buildings were lovely decaying mansions on what was then called Embassy Row (Rue Wilder Penfield) in Montreal. Some of these buildings, however, were not in school zones, and none of them had the enclosed staircases required for school buildings. Because of strictly applied building and fire codes, the school was forced to move seven times between 1973 and 1975, in and out of a total of six buildings. From 1975 to 1988 the New School occupied two specially designed floors of Dawson College's rented administration building, a renovated "heritage" commercial building near the harbor in Old Montreal. Since the autumn of 1988, the New School has occupied a pleasant attic in one of the wings of Dawson's permanent campus, the recently renovated mother house of the Congregation of Notre Dame in the Westmount district of Montreal.

The New School opened its doors in the fall of 1973 to approximately 160 students. Its original plan had been to expand to accomodate 1,000 students in science and technology as well as preuniversity arts. However, because of cutbacks the school was soon reduced to 140 students (1974–1980), then to 100 (1980–1987). It has dwindled to 75 since the 1988 move into close proximity with the rest of the college.

Several factors might account for the decline in student population. While the New School's humanistic ideology was easily understood and attractive to students in the 1970s, its approach is not overwhelmingly attractive to the individual materialism fostered in the 1980s, although the school has always drawn students who are in opposition to the regular system of education and are looking for deeper human values and relationships. So suspicious are current students of a humanistic environment that prospective students often express the opinion that this could not really be a school—it's too comfortable. Indeed, they will frequently choose the anonymity of regular college programs on the assumption that this must be *real school*. The proximity to the rest of the college has meant that our students sometimes transfer to the regular college programs, buckling under pejorative remarks of peers or of teachers who indicate to them that the New School is not a *real* school, and they should see if they can "cut it" in the "real world out there." Most of these people have little idea of what actually happens in the New School and are suspicious of nonconformity. However, while some students "transfer out" to other college programs, just as many "transfer in" from more conventional college programs.

Staffing considerations also contribute to a periodic downward spiral. The CEGEP system is unionized, and all staffing is done on the basis of student numbers and teacher seniority. In 1983, the CEGEP teachers, along with other members of the public sector, lost a long and bitter strike against the government. There was a loss of trust and morale, and teachers endured a bitter seven years of frozen pay and a 13 percent increase in work load. Many teachers decided they were not ready for more than "working to rule," and the New School depends on extreme goodwill. As a result of several resignations to take "easier" teaching loads within the college, we became dependent on those teachers with low seniority who were being "bumped" into our program against their will. While many of them are excellent teachers for and devoted to the school, the constant struggle of training a new staff, which is increasingly fragmented between departments, has eroded staff morale. Moreover, student-faculty relationships tend to be less intense than they were at the school's inception. The teaching corps is aging while the students' ages remain constant. There is a larger emotional gap between the preoccupations of faculty and students, as faculty deal with their own children, marriages/divorces/relationships, debts, burnout and fear of burnout, medical problems, and the infirmities of aging.

It must also be said that while times are getting worse throughout North America, the English-speaking community in Quebec has the specific problem of being an aging population in numerical decline matched by lessening public influence, as French nationalism becomes increasingly institutionalized. Many young English-speaking people do not anticipate remaining in Quebec, and many English-speaking teachers feel trapped until retirement within a situation of declining student numbers and resources in a society that is less interested in investing in education than in attracting capital to finance some form of future sovereignty and to help defray its growing deficit. Postsecondary education is underfinanced and undercapitalized in both the French- and English-speaking sectors. Many young nonfrancophones do not feel they will have an equal opportunity in Quebec, and so their sojourn in CEGEP is often just a station on their way out.

This means they are reluctant to overinvest in a place where it is difficult for them to stay but that they are loath to leave for the great unknown. Increasing numbers of students come from new immigrant families or from families that have suffered a high degree of disorganization and/or have become dysfunctional due to parental drug and alcohol abuse, mental illness, divorce, or economic oppression. Many students live on their own in relative poverty, aided sometimes by the state and usually by part-time jobs. Each year a greater percentage of our students work for up to thirty hours per week away from the school, which limits their availability to create a community.

It must be admitted, however, that current students are suspicious of the notion of community in a way our original groups of students were not. When we surveyed their attitudes in 1984, we discovered that students do not share the belief of our "first generation" 1970s New Schoolers that no one over thirty could be trusted. On the contrary, they are much more likely to invest trust in teachers than in one another. However, with faculty "slotted" and only peripherally available to the New School, it is very difficult to provide the students, many of whom have had no real models of constancy in their own lives, with the needed intensive access to and attention from their teachers.

These trends do not identify our student body as a specifically disadvantaged self-selecting group. Indeed, in a 1988 report on the entire CEGEP system, it was pointed out that only 59 percent of students who enter CEGEPs receive a diploma, and that the rate of dropout and failure has been constantly increasing. This particular report established a correlation between dropouts/failures and the amount of time the students spent on outside jobs: Students who work more than twelve hours per week run a considerable risk of not completing their credit load each term.[14] Some educators argue that many students do not *need* to work for their room and board; while this may be true, most students are expected to earn their spending money, and it is my observation that their needs expand to more than the amount available. Going out to a bar on Saturday night can cost more than $100, and while it is easy to argue in principle that this is not a "need," to young people trying to become adults in a confusing society that exhorts them to be good consumers, this spending money is perceived as more immediate to their sense of identity than their schoolwork, which, at best, can only promise long-deferred gratification.

In 1991, the New School is still managing to attract some excellent students and some fine faculty; our message still transmits itself, but with difficulty. Yet, when we attend educational conferences and hear educators discussing their "ideal" educational environment, it appears to be one that takes the individual's cognitive and affective needs into account, is very demanding of commitment from teachers, and possesses some vision of possibility—a world helped toward "betterness" through this process. These notions were somewhat present in the original *Parent Report*. They are present in a 1990 governmental report, *Pedagogy as a Major Challenge in Higher Education*,[15] published by Quebec's Superior Council of Education. Our experience has shown that it is difficult to maintain such ideals in a situation where the structural nature of the educational system is not conducive to their realization.

Ironically, as the educational system moves toward increasingly rigid centralization of power in the government and its administrators in individual colleges, and as each collective agreement sews faculty into ever more limited mobility, the publicly articulated philosophy of the system continues to elaborate an ideology in total opposition to the reality in which the educational system is deeply entrenched. The actual practices of the CEGEP system become narrowed rather than broadened, with the aid of a technology that produces increasingly refined cost controls calibrated to classroom activities. These constraints, which eventually demarcate limits to praxis, are not auspicious for alternative programs. Indeed, while there were six such programs in the CEGEPs in 1980, the New School is the only remaining alternative program in the entire CEGEP system in 1991. We are told that eighteen years is almost six times as long as the average educational "experiment."

As the following chapters describe the ideology and praxis of the New School, the reader must bear in mind that this program is totally dependent on the state through its parent institution, Dawson College. As the last alternative CEGEP program, it can be snuffed out with great ease on the argument of declining resources. Our survival has depended on our ability to reconcile our ideology and practice with an institutional methodology developed to implement the norms of the state. It is a difficult and narrow line to walk: being true to ourselves, convincing authorities that we can offer "equivalent education" to our students, and not jeopardizing our students' future educational acceptability in the process. At the end of this book, I will discuss some of our strategies for staying alive; I will also identify some problems to which we have found only the most imperfect solutions.

NOTES

1. Paulo Freire and Ira Shor, *A Pedagogy for Liberation* (South Hadley, MA: Bergin & Garvey, 1987) p. 167.

2. Alphonse-Marie Parent, chairman, *Report of the Royal Commission of Inquiry on Education* (Quebec: Government of the Province of Quebec, 1965), pt. I, vol. 1, ch. 1.

3. Ibid., p. 11.

4. Ibid.

5. Ibid., p. 14.

6. Ibid.

7. Ibid.

8. Ibid.

9. Paul Gallagher and Gertrude MacFarlane, *A Case Study in Democratic Education: Dawson College* (Montreal: Dawson College, n.d., c. 1976), pp. 21–23.

10. Ibid., p. 288.

11. Ibid., pp. 250–51.

12. Ibid., pp. 165–67.

13. Guy Millisor, "An Abstract of the Original Proposal for the Foundation and Development of the New School of Dawson College," unpublished document (Montreal: Dawson College, August 1973), pp. 5-6.

14. Conseil des Collèges, *La réussite, les échecs et les abandons au collégial: L'état et les besoins de l'enseignement collégial. Rapport 1987–1988* (Québec: Gouvernement de Québec, 1988).

15. *La pédagogie, un défi majeur de l'enseignement supérieur* (Québec: Conseil Supérieur de l'Éducation, 1990). Title translated by the author.

2

Popular Educational Theories of the 1960s and 1970s

Every age but ours had its model, its ideal. All of those have been given up by our culture: the hero, the gentleman, the knight, the mystic. About all we have left is the well-adjusted man without problems, a very pale and doubtful substitute. Perhaps we shall soon be able to use as our guide and model the fully growing and self-fulfilling human being, the one in whom his potentialities are coming to full development, the one whose inner nature expresses itself freely, rather than being warped, repressed, or denied.[1]

WHILE THE *PARENT REPORT* CERTAINLY REFLECTED some of the preoccupations of contemporary North American educational critics, it was also informed by the tradition of Christian humanism that was struggling for survival in an increasingly secular society. During the mid-1960s to mid-1970s, anglophone institutions in Quebec, however, were enormously influenced by British and American radical educational critics. Schools were considered very influential institutions that determined not only the level of skills attained by students in prescribed curricula but also *what* students would value and *how* they would live their future lives.

Many educational critiques were fueled by the various movements of empowerment—most specifically the black movement, the women's movement, the peace movement, and movements of various identifiable national or cultural groups for autonomy and recognition. The most visible sites for educational critique were the universities. They provided locales for the organization of political action and the articulation of critiques of education under capitalism.

At the time a very popular book among university students and some educators was Jerry Farber's *The Student as Nigger*. Farber's central contention was that the student in the American classroom was like the "nigger" under slavery: "For one thing damn little education takes place in the schools. How could it? You can't educate slaves; you can only train them. . . . For students, as for black people, the hardest battle isn't with Mr. Charlie. It's with what Mr. Charlie has done to your mind."[2] To Farber, school "mould[s] [the students] in its image, stunting and deadening [them] in the process,"[3] thus ensuring the continuation of the capitalist hegemony.

Other writers agreed with Farber's general critique, some in less charged language. *The Little Red Schoolbook,* widely read in the early 1970s, had a more "liberal" and genteel reading of society than Farber's: "You can't separate school from society. You have to change one to be able to improve the other. But don't let this put you off. . . . Every little thing you change in school may have results in society."[4] *The Little Red Schoolbook* was concerned with arriving at a level of student motivation based on real feelings of interest, not on a system of academic bribery. It dismissed the newly fashionable audiovisual aids as devices used to "persuade students to work on things that don't interest them at all or that will be completely useless to them after they've left school. . . . This is called 'motivation.' A better word for it might be 'bait.'"[5] Liberal school reform was considered hypocritical, encouraging students to participate in unimportant decisions while excluding them from deciding on the "real and difficult changes . . . which give more and more people power to decide more and more for themselves."[6]

Academic readers and textbooks on radical and alternative education produced during this period provide a critique of the educational system not dissimilar to that in the more popular press: "We define schools as institutions that require students at specific ages to spend most of their time attending teacher-supervised classrooms for the study of graded curricula."[7] Contemporary schools were characterized as locales for the systematic processing of students with rigid curricula and criteria for judging the students' success. This critique is not significantly different from some of the critique implicit in the *Parent Report*.

As in any revolutionary movement, numerous popular texts were read not only by the most revolutionary members of the society but also by many educators who judged the educational system to be unsatisfactory and wanted to find solutions. Often revolutionary texts were included in education courses, where they were very popular among students who enjoyed seeing their own painful school experiences attacked by writers who were sufficiently respected to be included on course lists in faculties of education. These texts primarily addressed elementary and secondary education, although there was some work on university-level education. Since community colleges had not really developed as a major force in postsecondary education by the early 1960s, they were hardly touched by this educational critique. Many of the radical analyses and blueprints for change *were* partially adopted in schools and universities in an unenthusiastic spirit of reform that frequently undermined the purpose of these changes. Many of the works of the time not only vilified the school systems for oppressing, boring, underutilizing, and misguiding the young but also promulgated a romantic Blakean vision of the essential goodness of the child and ultimately the human adult, who had to be freed from the shackles of knowledge—or perhaps of education:

> If the doors of perception were cleansed every
> thing would appear to man as it is, infinite.
>   For man has closed himself up, till he sees all
> things thro' narrow chinks of his cavern.[8]

Since this Blakean vision had a strong effect on alternative education during the period of the New School's founding, it is instructive to examine two very popular works of the time: A. S. Neill's *Summerhill: A Radical Approach to Child Rearing*[9] and George B. Leonard's *Education and Ecstasy*.[10]

Neill begins his book with a quotation from William Blake:

> Children of the future Age
> Reading this indignant page,
> Know that in a former time
> Love! sweet Love! was thought a crime.[11]

This was an appropriate apostrophe for Neill, because he believed that honest and disinterested love of children was the only thing that would rescue them from leading truncated lives at best and very destructive ones at worst. His book is an account of the boarding school, for children from ages five to sixteen, that he founded in England in 1921. Neill claims that he and his wife created in Summerhill a school that would fit the child, as opposed to the usual institution, which children were contorted to fit. He views the "natural" child as "innately wise and realistic"; this child will *naturally* develop as far as his or her capacities allow if he or she is free from adult interference.[12]

Neill asserts that Summerhill is a happy place where teachers rarely lose their tempers, and he emphasizes that the creation of happiness is its pedagogical objective:

I hold that the aim of life is to find happiness, which means to find interest. Education should be a preparation for life. Our culture has not been very successful. Our education, politics, and economics lead to war. . . . New world wars threaten, for the world's social conscience is still primitive.[13]

Neill claims that this necessary condition for the preparation for life is provided at Summerhill through ensuring the maximum freedom for all children there:

> Summerhill is possibly the happiest school in the world. We have no truants and seldom a case of homesickness. We very rarely have fights—quarrels, of course, but seldom have I seen a stand-up fight like the ones we used to have as boys. I seldom hear a child cry, because children when free have much less hate to express than children who are downtrodden. Hate breeds hate, and love breeds love. . . . Summerhill is a school in which the child knows that he is approved of.[14]

Although the child is steeped in approval and love at Summerhill, Neill is emphatic that the school is not overly permissive: the children are treated as responsible beings insofar as they are ready for particular responsibilities. The child is permitted to do as he or she pleases "in things that affect him [or her]—and only him [or her]."[15] Since the objective of his school is to bring out the best inclination in each of the students, Neill fervently believes that, left to their own devices, children will choose what is most meaningful for them to know.[16] The criteria of what is worth knowing to an individual should be set by that person, even if that person is a child:

> The function of the child is to live his own life—not the life that his anxious parents think he should live, nor a life according to the purpose of the educator who thinks he knows what is best. All this interference and guidance on the part of adults only produces a generation of robots.
>
> You cannot make children learn music or anything else without to some degree converting them into will-less adults. You fashion them into accepters of the *status quo*.[17]

Neill had published numerous books on education before, but it was *Summerhill* that brought him recognition. *Summerhill* was an immensely popular book, selling over 200,000 copies a year between 1960 and 1970. Perhaps this was because of the period in which it was published.[18] In the early days of the New School, when people were very well acquainted with Neill's notion of a "free school," strangers would insist that the New School was a "free school" where "anything goes." To our detractors, this statement hid the usual prurient expectations of "sex, drugs and rock and roll"; to prospective students it often indicated that they were anxious for an escape from the thralls of the regular school system as well as from their parents' control. Frequently we would begin presentations to parents and/or students with the words "This is not a free school." It seemed to us then, and it seems even more so in the light of further educational analysis, that Neill's (and Blake's) hopes for the "New Jerusalem" coming forth from an environment of love were somewhat naive, given the complexities of the contemporary world. On the other hand, whether through coincidence or through emulation, we did arrive more or less at a model of governance within the school similar to Neill's:

> Summerhill is a self-governing school, democratic in form. Everything connected with social, or group, life, including punishment for social offenses, is settled by vote at the Saturday night General School Meeting.
>
> Each member of the teaching staff and each child, regardless of his age, has one vote. My vote carries the same weight as that of a seven-year old.[19]

Neill not only sees self-government as a necessary educational aspect of progressive education, but he claims that "You cannot have freedom unless children feel completely free to govern their own social life." To him, one such meeting can have more curriculum value than a whole week's "curriculum of school subjects." He also describes a problem similar to one we have had perennially with self-governance at the New School: the conflict between the needs of the individual and those of the community at large, and the various ways in which these sometimes conflicting needs may be mediated.[20]

Summerhill is an anecdotal book describing an interesting school from the point of view of its founder. Being in more or less the same position (I am one of the founding teachers of the New School), I can well understand the desire to "sell" the institution, perhaps even to convince the reader of its rightness. Certainly Neill makes his solutions sound commonsensical and workable. However, nowhere does he address the issue of social class or acknowledge the fact that the students in his school by and large come from families sufficiently privileged to afford the fees of private education. He does not speculate on its "portability" to less rarefied environments. I do not think there are any schools modeled absolutely on Neill's Summerhill on this continent thirty years after the publication of his immensely popular book. Perhaps the fact is that Summerhill was very dependent on the particular vision of Neill. Nonetheless, this does not mean that positive aspects of the school cannot be integrated into other places. It would have been more helpful to other educators, however, if Neill had presented a tighter and more reasoned philosophical rationale for his practices.

Reading *Education and Ecstasy* is somewhat like listening to an enthusiastic conversation where all explanation is self-referred. It is a rambling conversational book in which numerous people and publications are quoted without benefit of footnotes or bibliography. The main argument of the book is that schools dam "up the flood of human potentialities," children sit about waiting for "something to happen!" and "It is as cruel to bore a child as to beat him."[21] The author believes the situation to be remediable. Ways "can be worked out" to help average students learn what is needed in less time and more pleasurably, to provide a "new apprenticeship for living," to make the task of teaching better for teachers, and to ensure that education will become a "lifelong pursuit for everyone." In fact, Leonard claims, "Education, at best, is ecstatic."[22]

Leonard defines good learning as change, and education as the process that changes the learner. By monitoring the change within learners, the teacher can assess further directions for specific courses and human interactions. What can save education from passivity and boredom is the fact that learning "involves interaction between the learner and his environment, and its effectiveness relates to the frequency, variety and intensity of the interaction." While he does not really demonstrate in what way learning can become ecstatic, Leonard tends to see true learning as the

pursuit of the ecstatic moment. At its best, its most effective, its most unfettered, the moment of learning is a moment of delight . . . the varieties of ecstasy are limitless . . . the skillful pursuit of ecstasy will make the pursuit of excellence not for the few, but for the many, what it never has been—successful.[23]

The main arguments for the possibility of achieving numerous moments of ecstasy are developed in a rambling section of the book devoted to human potential. Here numerous luminaries from fields as diverse as religion and neurology are quoted without any sources cited. There is an amorphous section of anecdotes about children in various situations as well as some autobiographical recounting. The book focuses exclusively on the American experience of the time, from a standpoint divorced from the socioeconomic realities of children's lives. The author admits that "ecstasy is one of the trickier conditions to write about," and it is especially difficult for him to show how "moments of ecstasy" in learning can become sufficiently compelling, for example, to obviate the difficulties of memorization, which comprises an important part of studying languages or sciences. Even when Leonard lists the possibility of learning various "skills" for creating a better world, there is a suspect hype to his expression. He advocates the learning of the following:

. . . delight, not aggression; sharing, not eager acquisition; uniqueness, not narrow competition.
. . . heightened awareness and control of emotional, sensory and bodily states and, through this, increased empathy for other people (a new kind of citizenship education).
. . . how to enter and enjoy varying states of consciousness, in preparation for a life of change.[24]

The biographical note on Leonard does not indicate that he has ever taught, although he has written and "consulted" on education.

At the beginning of the CEGEPs, some teachers, counselors, and administrators in the English colleges were impressed by this book, which they circulated among their colleagues. Often its heightened language, even more than the laissez-faire position of Neill, was reflected back to the New School in people's expectations of our objectives. Were we after ecstasy, and in what way? How did the students cope with the hard stuff like writing term papers? We often found ourselves responding to the expectations of our critics on the basis not of our own articulation of our philosophy but of the movement of educational hype in the heady 1960s and 1970s, when people hoped and thought that education could save the world.

Some radical analyses of education were especially optimistic about alternative education's becoming a quiet revolutionary social force, moving toward a more open society in which social class distinctions, racism, religious bigotry, the unjust distribution of resources, and the boundaries of nation-states would all disappear. Rational and flexible decision making would prevail throughout society.[25] One writer even alluded to the songs of Bob Dylan: "Education has a new role to play. The times they are a-changing."[26] The founders of an organization called New Nation Seed Fund, whose purpose was to help alternative libertarian schools survive, described the most desirable methodology:

> The schools are kept small so that persons can have access to one another. Relationships replace arbitrary discipline. The absence of coercion makes room for morality and ethics, and these in turn foster the humane relations which alone are the proper setting for the growth of the young.[27]

The ideas expressed by writers popular in the late 1960s and early 1970s surfaced in many institutions in many Western countries. In response to these critiques, numerous official commissions were formed to evaluate educational systems. Their conclusions were often dissimilar and did not always result in systemic reforms, in changes in educational institutions, or in the creation of new institutions. However, it is clear that most educational critics were concerned with articulating a philosophy of education in which growth, and not just the acquisition of facts, was an important factor; acknowledging that growth is a holistic phenomenon in which there are personal, intellectual, spiritual, and social factors; differentiating legitimate curriculum inquiry from indoctrination; pruning from standard curriculum methods those subjects and works which were no longer relevant to students' lives; making school an integral and relevant part of society; breaking down the social barriers between students and between students and teachers; empowering students and giving them greater freedom, with a view to making them responsible citizens in a freer society; and regarding education as a facilitative force in improving the society through helping students to become more authentic as individuals and in relation to the society at large.

Perhaps it was due to the slowness of systemic change within established educational institutions that during the 1960s, numerous alternative schools emerged in North America. Some of these were "free schools," some were community-supported schools with strong parental participation and accountability structures, and some eventually became part of public school systems' desperate efforts to keep young people in school.

In the 1960s the federal government, private foundations, corporations, and community groups poured massive amounts of money and energy into efforts to change the public school system. The gloomy statistics documenting the shortcomings of public schools in the education of minority students highlighted the poor fit between school offerings and the needs and goals of many students. . . . beginning in the late 1960s, the Ford Foundation assisted efforts at a new kind of reform involving smaller, more experimental, more tentative efforts to improve education.[28]

While most of these alternatives in Canada and the United States were at the elementary and secondary levels, there were some alternative programs within postsecondary institutions. Although these alternatives were usually organized on variously and vaguely articulated educational philosophies, their guiding force was that they were "alternative" to the existing mainstream education provided at the elementary and secondary levels by the state, and at postsecondary levels by the state and private institutions.

The founders of the New School shared many of these views. They believed schools to be overcontrolling, disconfirming of the individual, and generally a pernicious force in society. They found in humanistic education a solution that would provide a better and more interesting school environment as well as the tools for basic social change. Their notion of social change was based on individual changes of attitude that resulted from personal growth, rather than on radical social change resulting in the global redistribution of power and resources. It would take changing times, years of experience, and the work of many students and teachers to elaborate the New School's educational philosophy beyond the premises of contemporary educational critiques and the tenets of humanistic education, to the education of critical humanism.

NOTES

1. Abraham H. Maslow, *Towards a Psychology of Being*, 2d ed. (New York: Van Nostrand, 1968), p. 5.

2. Jerry Farber, *The Student as Nigger* (Richmond Hill, Ontario: Simon and Schuster of Canada Ltd., 1970), pp. 98, 100.

3. Ibid., p. 90.

4. Soren Hansen and Jesper Jensen with Wallace Roberts, *The Little Red Schoolbook*, trans. from the Danish by Berit Thornberry (New York: Pocket Books, 1971), p. 251.

5. Ibid., p. 33.

6. Ibid., p. 251.

7. Everett Reimer, "An Essay on Alternatives in Education," in *The Radical Papers: Readings in Education*, ed. Harold W. Sobel and Arthur E. Salz (New York: Harper & Row, 1972), p. 160.

8. William Blake, "The Marriage of Heaven and Hell," in *The Portable Blake*, ed. Alfred Kazin (New York: Viking Press, 1955), p. 258.

9. A. S. Neill, *Summerhill: A Radical Approach to Child Rearing* (New York: Hart, 1960).

10. George B. Leonard, *Education and Ecstasy* (New York: Dell, 1968).

11. Blake, p. 116.

12. Neill, p. 4.

13. Ibid., p. 24.

14. Ibid., p. 8.

15. Ibid., pp. 348–49.

16. Ibid., pp. 26–27.

17. Ibid., p. 12.

18. Lawrence A. Cremin, "The Free School Movement: A Perspective," in *Pygmalion or Frankenstein? Alternative Schooling in American Education*, ed. John C. Carr, Jean Dresden Grambs, and E. G. Campbell (Reading, MA: Addison-Wesley, 1977), p. 225.

19. Neill, pp. 44, 47.

20. Ibid., pp. 52–54.

21. Leonard, pp. 1, 9, 14.

22. Ibid., p. 16.

23. Ibid., pp. 18–22.

24. Ibid., pp. 132–33.

25. Ibid., pp. 168ff.

26. Charles Weingartner, "Communication, Education, and Change," in *The Radical Papers: Readings in Education*, ed. Harold W. Sobel and Arthur E. Salz (New York: Harper & Row, 1972), p. 207.

27. George Dennison, Paul Goodman, Nat Hentoff, John Holt, and Jonathan Kozol, "New Nation Seed Fund," in *The Radical Papers: Readings in Education*, ed. Harold W. Sobel and Arthur E. Ross (New York: Harper & Row, 1972), pp. 208-9.

28. Richard I. Foster, "Matters of Choice: A Ford Foundation Report on Alternative Schools," in *Pygmalion or Frankenstein? Alternative Schooling in American Education*, ed. John C. Carr, Jean Dresden Grambs, and E. G. Campbell, Reading, MA: Addison-Wesley, 1977), pp. 160–61.

3
Early Philosophical Roots of Humanistic Education

WHILE THE ORIGINAL PLANS FOR THE NEW SCHOOL may have sprung from a critique of the current educational system, the school was founded on the notion that all education should be people-centered and process-centered rather than simply information-centered. True education was to evolve from the self-perceived needs of the students, and it should develop from an understanding of why they wanted to learn certain things, why certain types of knowledge might be important for them personally, rather than simply as a means to another and distant end, such as institutional prerequisites, or some distant privilege that might accrue to the holder of specific and privileged knowledge. The crucial factors in any educational undertaking were the learners: Who were they? What did they want to know? Why did they want to know? How did they want to go about learning?

This educational project had to operate with a working model of the human personality and the exercise of freedom. Because the school had a commitment to social change, learning at the New School would involve balancing personal needs and freedoms with the need to live and work collaboratively with others.

The New School was founded on philosophical premises that had their roots directly in the works of Maslow, Rogers, Brown, Moustakas, and other humanistic psychologists and philosophers. However, there were other sources for the original development of the New School's educational philosophy: Dewey, the existentialists, the values-clarification philosophers and educators, and feminist and black theorists. Later, the New School would become influenced by work in critical pedagogy and peace education. Numerous teachers, administrative assistants, and students who passed through the school were influential in shaping its philosophy. The New School's philosophy develops continually in a dialectical and dialogical manner: ideological position to praxis to experience to feedback to discussion to modulation of ideological position to further development of praxis to experience to feedback, and so on. Although over time the philosophy has become more elaborated, its basic premises of individual and group empowerment remain constant.

The educational point of departure to prepare young people to better their society mentioned in the founder's "Abstract of the Original Proposal" was the development of a strong self-concept. Indeed, it was considered an essential condition for appropriate and productive interpersonal relations. The development of the self was considered to be a function of education:

While we as a society devote much energy to teaching the students to think logically about such matters as solid geometry, number systems etc., explicit training of the student in methods of processing information about himself and others in his inter-personal world is almost totally lacking. The development of a collection of hypotheses about oneself, the *self-concept*, is largely haphazard and the product of unexamined and unverbalized experience. Lacking the necessary skills for seeking and processing information about ourselves, is it any wonder that few of us can construct relatively clear and unambiguous accounts of our goals, aspirations, values, traits and abilities? And in the absence of learned skills necessary to the understanding of inter-personal interaction, is it any wonder that many individuals are confused about their relationship to self or to others?[1]

This critique of education echoes a similar critique made by the American educational philosopher, John Dewey, almost half a century earlier:

The history of educational theory is marked by opposition between the idea that education is development from within and that it is formation from without; that it is based upon natural endowments and that education is a process of overcoming natural inclination and substituting in its place habits acquired under external pressure.[2]

It is not coincidental that there should be this parallel between an early progressive educator and more contemporary proponents of the human potential educational movement, because there are parallels between the two movements. Certainly the second was informed by the first. The progressive education movement began in protest against the narrow formalism and inequities of public education around 1890 in the United States, peaked in the 1920s and 1930s, and collapsed in the years after World War II. Like humanistic educators, progressive educators saw schools as levers of social reform, education as an instrument for individual self-realization or growth and as a site for people to learn how to adjust to the rapid changes taking place in their world.[3] John Dewey, who was the chief articulator of the movement's aspirations, saw education as an essential factor in the growth of individuals. This growth was to be achieved through controlling an environment "conducive to having experiences that lead to growth." Teachers must use all aspects of the surroundings "so as to extract from them all that they have to contribute to building up experiences that are worthwhile."[4]

Dewey's concept of growth, however, was much more focused than what was to become the prevailing notion of the humanistic psychologists who succeeded him in the 1960s and 1970s. To him, "Growth in judgement and understanding is essentially growth in ability to form purposes and to select and arrange means for their realization."[5]

Dewey saw education as a means of helping people grow, of helping them experience freedom, or of giving them power. Growth, to Dewey, had specific characteristics related to understanding objective information and making wise choices on the use of that information. Giving people power did not include the notion of "power over." Dewey's concept of power is expressed in the phrase "power as a means to"—it describes the individual's being enabled to act wisely on his/her own behalf. Freedom must never be seen as an end in itself, because "shared cooperative activities are the normal source of order." To Dewey, freedom from restriction could be prized only as a means to power: "power to frame purposes, to judge wisely, to evaluate desires by the consequences which will result from acting upon them; power to select and order means to carry chosen ends into operation."[6]

Because of his emphasis on "freedom/power to," Dewey was convinced that the learner must participate "in the formation of the purposes which direct his activities in the learning process." There was

no defect in traditional education greater than its failure to secure the active cooperation of the pupil in construction of the purposes involved in his studying. But the meaning of purposes and ends is not self-evident and self-explanatory. The more their educational importance is emphasized, the more important it is to understand what a purpose is; how it arises and how it functions in experience.[7]

To Dewey the learner's experience (what would be called "relevance" by later critics) was an essential point of departure for undertaking to learn something. However, he emphasized that this preliminary connection was only the first step in a learning process. It had to be followed by a progressive development into fuller and richer and more organized forms. "It thus becomes the office of the educator to select those things within the range of existing experience that have the promise and potentiality of presenting new problems which by stimulating new ways of observation and judgement will expand the area of further experience."[8]

Dewey did not believe that all experiences were automatically educative.

In order to be educative, they had to "tend both to knowledge of more facts and entertaining of more ideas and to a better, a more orderly arrangement of them." He saw learning as a progression from the first personal experiential connection to a more "objective" sense of reality, thence to the capacity for self-control.[9] To Dewey, freedom was ultimately to be found in the fullest exercise of self-control or in a modulation "toward a more objective intellectual scheme of organization." He warns that such organization is not an end in itself but a means "by which social relations, distinctively human ties and bonds, may be understood and more intelligently ordered."[10]

Some existentialist writers on education share some of Dewey's concern with issues pertaining to freedom. Because the human situation is "essenceless," humans are "confronted in every waking moment by phenomenal situations to each of which there are numberless responses we could give."[11] Clearly they must learn to make choices. Van Cleve Morris, in his book *Existentialism in Education,* traces the process through which people must go before they are ready to enter the realm of choice. Drawing on other existentialist philosophers, Morris claims that when people realize how utterly arbitrary the fact of their individual existence is, they undergo an "encounter with nothingness":

The encounter with nothingness, seemingly so unpromising as a starting problem in philosophical discourse, is in fact the test we should be willing to take as a demonstration of our worth in the world. It is not nothingness but the encounter with nothingness which provides the vehicle for our humanness to exhibit itself. . . . Nothingness, after all, is not a foregone conclusion; it is only a possibility.[12]

However, this state of consciousness, while causing individuals their moments of darkness and alienation, can end not in despair but in the knowledge that one may create "the project of living one's life in such as way as to be deserving of something better than nothingness and obliteration; to confront nothingness, to deny nothingness, by filling it up with a life that ought never to be lost or annihilated."[13] This project is particularly difficult to realize because there are so many claims on people's attention and desires. Creating a raison d'etre is a difficult task of education. In order to learn a truly valuable subject matter, individuals must consider themselves "worthy" of the knowledge. To achieve this end, they must recognize their own irreplaceability as well as their own "belongingness" in society. Very often people develop a false sense of affiliation through the arbitrary descriptions imposed by others: nationality, class, race, gender, creed. These are not essential characteristics, nor can they be chosen at birth. Rather, they are simply classifications, "facticités," as de Beauvoir called them, that must be replaced by chosen values as we attempt to infuse our lives with a sense of meaning and purpose. The creation of values is the task of the learner:

I am the starter of the value-making process, but as such I myself have no base to stand on that can tell me which values I should start making. In this role, then, I discover that I am the originator, the inventor, the *creator* of values. . . . In the act of choosing, man brings values into being.[14]

There are necessary conditions for constructing a meaningful life: freedom, the awareness of one's own freedom, and the understanding of one's personal responsibility in valuing and choosing action appropriate to one's freedom and life. People who choose not to address these conditions of meaning are often relegated to a personal and moral numbness; on the other hand, choosing to choose—recognizing one's possibilities of creating a life of meaning—creates the possibility of living in good faith and authenticity. Finally, if individuals should strive for authenticity in their life's experience and moral positioning, then an authentic society is also desirable and possible. In view of the need for freedom in establishing authenticity, freedom from moral or material coercion is essential to the maintenance of an authentic society.[15]

The task of education for the existentialist is a complex one in our imperfect world where the human striving for authenticity must perforce take place within the dramatic tensions of variably coercive social institutions like the family and the school. While Dewey defined the child as having various innate dispositions to be encouraged by the educator, the existentialist will not acknowledge the possibility of innate dispositions: rather, the objective is "to be aware of the possibility of being disposed this way or that. It is to be aware that one is the author of his own dispositions!" Learners may become fully aware of themselves as the shapers of their own values and lives. Through their own efforts and unique ruminations, they may posit what "a human being ought to be," thus moving beyond "mere intellectual discipline, beyond mere subject matter, beyond mere enculturation, beyond mere 'fundamental dispositions,' to the . . . zone of value creation."[16]

It is important to bear in mind that exercising freedom to choose one's ideas and taking responsibility for them do not exist in an emotional vacuum. There is always an affective level to each thought, each choice. In fact, in humanistic education as practiced at the New School, the feelings related to choices are an integral part of the data examined before making choices. This is not the trivial "if it feels good, do it" school of thought. Rather, it is based on the recognition that in order to make authentic choices, people must understand their emotional roots and their impact upon themselves and others. These insights must be weighed along with all other values that people may wish to attribute to any situation.

Being aware of their feelings is important not only as people make choices of value but also as they learn. It is important for learners to appropriate knowledge, to filter it through their own emotional as well as "factual" and experiential understanding in order to comprehend it in a way that informs their lives with authenticity. This means that in order to achieve authenticity, learners must subject the proffered knowledge to an epistemological analysis which takes into account its meaning, signification, social context, and emotional connection to them. Through this process, their knowledge becomes unique and transformed into a meaning that informs their lived (and only) lives.

There is an inherent paradox in supporting the role of the teacher as agent of awakened awareness in the learner while at the same time acknowledging the individual's need to achieve awareness of himself/herself as a single and unique subjectivity in the world. This problem arises continually at the New School; later I will discuss this in detail. Suffice it to say here that neither Dewey nor Morris comes to terms with these issues: Who really knows the "true" dispositions of the learner that should be encouraged by the teacher? How can a teacher awaken a student to his or her own unique subjectivity without influencing the content of the learner's perception? In both cases the teacher must respect the learner's autonomy while precipitating active involvement in what may become a painful moment of insight for the learner.

NOTES

1. Lee Sechrest and John Wallace, Jr., *Psychology and Human Problems* (Columbus, OH: Charles E. Merrill, 1967), p. 223. Quoted in Guy Millisor, "An Abstract of the Original Proposal for the Foundation and Development of the New School of Dawson College" (Montreal: Dawson College, August 1973), p. 25.

2. John Dewey, *Experience and Education* (New York: Collier Books, 1938), p. 17.

3. Lawrence A. Cremin, "The Free School Movement: A Perspective," in *Pygmalion or Frankenstein? Alternative Schooling in American Education*, ed. John C. Carr, Jean Dresden Grambs, and E. G. Campbell (Reading, MA: Addison-Wesley, 1977), p. 225.

4. Dewey, pp. 34–40.

5. Ibid., p. 84.

6. Ibid., pp. 63–64.

7. Ibid., p. 67.

8. Ibid., pp. 73–75.

9. Ibid., p. 82.

10. Ibid., p. 83.

11. Van Cleve Morris, *Existentialism in Education: What It Means* (New York: Harper & Row, 1966), p. 46.

12. Ibid., p. 27.

13. Ibid., p. 29.

14. Ibid., p. 40.

15. While some of these ideas derive from Morris, I have also brought together ideas from other existentialists: Camus, Sartre, Kafka, and de Beauvoir.

16. Morris, pp. 110–11.

4

Theoreticians and Theories of Humanistic Education

> I think of the self-actualizing man not as an ordinary man with something added, but rather as the ordinary man with nothing taken away. The average man is a human being with dampened and inhibited powers.[1]

ABRAHAM MASLOW

SOME OF THE NEW SCHOOL'S ORIGINAL BASIC TEXTS were descriptive antischool works popular at the time of its inception: books, broadsides, magazines, and campus newspapers. However, there were significant theoretical texts provided for our consideration on humanistic education, as articulated by Carl Rogers and Abraham Maslow. Many of the first teachers at the New School had taken part in political action in the black movement, the anti-Vietnam War and the peace movements, the women's movement, and the gay rights movement; we were familiar with Marxist analyses of society. We clearly saw the function of class in determining our students' perceptions and choices. In a college as ethnically, racially, and socially diverse as ours, it is undeniable that ethnicity, class, gender, and race are strong determinants of our students' interests, behavior, and aspirations, of their interrelationships at school, and of conditions where self-actualization can take place.

Abraham Maslow criticizes the educational system for having as its chief concern efficiency, "that is, with implementing the greatest number of facts into the greatest possible number of children, with a minimum of time, expense and effort."[2] He argues that education should not be "extrinsic" (for various signifiers of status) but "intrinsic," for the pleasure of knowing more about oneself and one's full potential as a human being:

The ideal college would be a kind of educational retreat in which you could try to find yourself; find out what you like and want; what you are and are not good at. People would take various subjects, attend various seminars, not quite sure of where they were going, but moving toward the discovery of vocation, and *once they found it*, they could make good use of technological education. The chief goals of the ideal college, in other words, would be the discovery of identity, and with it, the discovery of vocation . . . part of learning who you are, part of being able to hear your inner voices, is discovering what it is that you want to do with your life.[3]

Maslow clearly saw growth as the objective of education, and he named the highest form of growth "self-actualization." The self-actualized person must be "in a state of good psychological health" with basic needs satisfied, and a life's work or "mission in life" that is of intrinsic value to him/her. Maslow identifies as necessary conditions for self-actualization the satisfaction of a "hierarchy of needs," beginning with people's needs for basic biological survival and moving upward to needs for security, belongingness, dignity, love, respect, and esteem. Self-actualization is a development of the personality that frees the person from neurotic problems so that she/he is able to come to terms with the real issues of the human condition. To Maslow self-actualization was not a static state but a dynamic lifelong process.

Growth is seen then not only as a progressive gratification of basic needs to the point where they "disappear," but also in the form of specific growth motivations over and above these basic needs . . . basic needs and self-actualization do not contradict each other any more than do childhood and maturity. One passes into the other and is a necessary prerequisite for it.[4]

Maslow also believed that under optimum conditions, "There seems no intrinsic reason why everyone shouldn't be this way [self-actualizing]. Apparently, every baby has possibilities for self-actualization, but most get it knocked out of them."[5]

While Maslow liked to speculate that self-actualization was available to all people, his own studies of people he considered self-actualized convinced him that although they were exceptional, they did not have a life free of dilemma. Their problems were those of isolation, detachment, and fear of overshadowing others. Maslow also posited that men and women might experience self-actualization differently. In a letter, he claimed that because our culture disconfirms feminine modes, "our conceptions of the universe, of science, of intelligence, [and] of emotion are lopsided and partial because they have been constructed by man. . . . If only women were allowed to be full human beings, thereby making it possible for men to be full human beings." However, Maslow also thought that the closer both men and women came to self-actualization, the more similar they would become, each having all the human qualities.[6]

In order for people to achieve self-actualization, they must be prepared to take increased responsibility for their lives. To achieve this end, they must develop coherent value systems. Maslow identified the following as key principles regarding the need for values:

1. All humans, including children, need a coherent value system.
2. Lack of a value system in the larger culture breeds certain forms of psychological disorder.
3. Individuals will crave and search for a coherent value system.
4. People prefer having *any* value system, however unsatisfying, to none at all—that is, complete chaos.
5. If there is no adult value system, then a child or adolescent will embrace the value system of peers.[7]

While several of these principles are corroborated by our experience at the New School, what is significant here is that Maslow's and then Rogers's theories paved the way for the development of further work on values clarification which in turn were integrated into humanistic education. The issue of values and valuing as a central factor in education has developed incrementally from Dewey onward. Maslow was to become increasingly concerned with what he considered a crisis in and collapse of traditional values in his society. Because there were no "readily available" values to replace them,

a very large proportion of our artists, novelists, dramatists, critics, literary and historical scholars are disheartened or pessimistic or despairing, and a fair proportion are nihilistic or cynical. . . .

[We are in] a chaos of relativism. No one of these people now knows how to defend and validate his choice. This chaos may fairly be called valuelessness.[8]

Educational settings can create the optimum circumstances for self-actualization for "psychologically healthy" students by encouraging them to experience joy, refresh their aesthetic consciousness, control impulses, and find meaning in their lives. Maslow acknowledged that often young people, living in pathological states of passivity and drug and alcohol dependency, do not come from situations of great biological, social, or psychological deprivation. He described their state as a "cognitive and spiritual sickness," and attributed it to the lack of transcendent meaning in their lives. This meaning must come from an appreciation of more abstract qualities like truth, beauty, and justice. Once these values are internalized, the boundaries of the self will extend beyond the constricting personal sphere of interests to include the whole world:

We would have a great flowering of a new kind of civilization. People would be stronger, healthier, and would take their own lives into their hands to a greater extent. With increased personal responsibility for one's personal life, and with a rational set of values to guide one's choosing, people would begin to actively change the society in which they lived.[9]

Finally, Maslow believed that if teaching were carried out in a way that stressed personal discovery, this would encourage learners to have "peak-experiences, illuminations, the sense of mystery, and of awe" in the process. He considered the appropriate circumstances to be "certainly one of the pressing tasks for professional educators."[10] Indeed, Maslow was convinced that the "power of the peak-experience could permanently affect one's attitude to life." It could "prevent suicide . . . and perhaps many varieties of low self-destruction, [such as] alcoholism, drug-addiction, and addiction to violence."[11]

Maslow's answer to the existentialists' "nothingness" is that the only way to avoid a sense of meaninglessness is to create one's own meaning, to get in touch with the marvels of the world through cultivating autonomy, independence of culture and environment, a continued freshness of appreciation, a *Gemeinschaftsgefühl*, good personal relations, and a good sense of humor. He was not, however, advocating the search for "ecstasy" in Leonard's sense of the quest. For Maslow, the way to arrive at meaning and purpose in our imperfect world was to undertake the discipline and struggle toward self-actualization.

CARL ROGERS

Carl Rogers characterized the traditional classroom as a locus where only the intellect is valued, in which authoritarian rule is the accepted policy, with the teacher as powerful possessor of all the knowledge and the student as obedient recipient. There is no place for emotions in the traditional classroom. Teacher-student and student-student trust is at a minimum in such a repressive environment. Rogers's response to the conventional educational setting and methodology was to develop a theory of "person-centered education" where cognitive skills may be combined with better knowledge of self and of interpersonal behavior: "When students perceive that they are free to follow their own goals, most of them invest more of themselves in their effort, work harder, and retain and use more of what they have learned than in conventional courses."[12] One of Rogers's deepest criticisms of education was of the mistrust of the student implicit in the prevalent regimentation of almost every part of the student's school life: "at the very age when he should be developing adult characteristics of choice and decision making, when he should be trusted on some of those things, trusted to make mistakes and to learn from those mistakes."[13]

To critics who insisted that if left to their own devices, students would choose not to do anything, Rogers responded that those students who naturally become interested in esoteric subject matter should be encouraged in that direction. However, "there ought to be a place, too, for the emotional learnings, for getting to know oneself better as a feeling person."[14]

Rogers was very critical of contemporary education in America. Indeed, toward the end of his life he became even more critical, claiming that the educational system was

suffering from many elements of a crippling sort: the decreased financial resources, the dwindling enrollment, the tangled web of law and bureaucratic regulations that so often dehumanizes the classroom, a dangerous right-wing attack that aims to prevent freedom of thought and choice, and boredom, frustration, rage and despair on the part of many students.[15]

In order to understand the full application of Rogers's theories of education, it is important to understand his model of the "functioning person." To Rogers the dysfunctional person lives in continual fear of himself and the external world. Most of his hypotheses regarding functional people derived from his therapeutic model or goal. In this sense he was unlike Maslow, who derived his notion of self-actualized people by studying people whom he considered self-actualized de facto as a result of his familiarity with them or with their accomplishments and attitudes. The process of therapy through which Rogers's client became "functioning" acquainted him with "elements of his experience which have in the past been denied to awareness as too threatening, too damaging to the structure of the self." By experiencing these feelings fully and intensely, the client realized that these feelings were part of himself/herself, and that by accepting them he/she no longer needed to fear them but could choose to develop with or from them as a functional person.[16]

The characteristics found in the functional person are the following: she/he is open to experience; she/he lives in an existential fashion. This means that she/he will not live in anxiety about those things she/he cannot control and will not try to impose a rigid structure on experience. The person will "find his[her] organism a trustworthy means of arriving at the most satisfying behavior in each situation."[17] While Rogers claimed the person should do what "feels right," he did not suggest impulsive action. He indicated that this "feeling" should be arrived at after factors in a situation had been weighed; it should be the controlling factor. The functional person is creative; Rogers claimed that all people are by nature creative, but that they are blocked from their creativity by fears and social norms. Rogers was careful to emphasize that this paragon was hypothetical. He confirmed that the more open a personality is, the more likely the person is to live in flux: "The most stable personality traits would be openness to experience, and the flexible resolution of the existing needs in the existing environment."[18]

While Rogers was not simplistic enough to think that people in fact have absolute freedom, his solution to the freedom/determinism debate was somewhat glib and dismissive: "The fully functioning person . . . not only experiences, but utilizes the most absolute freedom when he spontaneously, freely, and voluntarily chooses and wills that which is absolutely determined."[19] Rogers acknowledged the function of social-environmental or genetic-deterministic factors that might limit personality development. However, his focus as an educator was on the "self-deterministic" because he claimed that environmental and genetic limitations could often be stretched or transcended. In the learning situation, it is only "the person himself who is able to understand those factors that have contributed to who he is, and to choose his own future."[20]

Rogers believed that awareness of formative factors in their backgrounds could help people make realistic and sensible choices for their lives. However, although people could transcend some of these inhibiting factors, Rogers did not believe in absolute free will, at the same time claiming that the denial of the significance of personal choice, a view he attributed to the strictest behaviorists, was "totally unrealistic."[21]

One way in which people wanting to live the fullest versions of their lives may express their free will is in the search for authenticity. The person who has embarked upon such a search "values communication as a means of telling it the way it is, with feelings, ideas, gestures, speech, and bodily movement all conveying the same message." This person must be willing to engage in "painful honesty" and to pay the price of this honesty rather than to resort to "tactful generalities."[22] The person who has reached this level of development has worked out feelings of incongruence that arise when "experience is quite discrepant from the way he has organized himself," when he dares to be aware of what he is experiencing without defending against it.[23]

The means by which people may arrive at the congruence that characterizes functionality is through what Rogers calls the "valuing process." Here people must rid themselves of "introjected" and often highly contradictory values from various formative sources through analyzing the sources of those values and the affect attached to them. This means "restoring contact with experience" unmediated by others' introjections. Rogers claimed that rigidly held values are a result of insecurity. The mature person must have flexibility in valuing and be willing to test values with an eye toward either self-correction or self-enhancement. While Rogers claimed he could not set down absolute patterns of value change, he did identify "value directions"[24] that move people in the way of personal growth and maturity; such people tend to move away from facades, pleasing others as a goal in itself, and "oughts." They value as positive "being real," self-direction, themselves and their own feelings, being in process, sensitivity to and acceptance of others, and deep relationships. They show an openness to inner and outer experiences and are open to their own inner reactions and feelings as well as those of others and the realities of the world."[25]

Like Maslow, Rogers believed that people can actualize themselves with or without therapy, by being "acceptantly aware of what's going on within" and constantly changing to increasing complexity on the basis of this awareness.[26] However, Rogers did not articulate for his "functional" person the total transcendence or the attainment of peak experiences that Maslow claimed for self-actualized people. The fundamental difference here is that to Maslow peak experiences were an end in themselves, while to Rogers they formed an epiphenomenon, a possible result of becoming functional.

Rogers developed coherent and elaborated educational theories and practices that focused on helping people become self-actualized, mature, and functional. True education, to Rogers, was the "facilitation of change and learning"; he advocated a reliance on process rather than on the transmission of prepackaged knowledge as the only sensible goal for contemporary education. To Rogers, the key element in this process was the quality of the personal relationship between facilitators and learners.[27]

Here the teacher is referred to as a "facilitator" and shares with all participants the responsibility for the learning process. The students, facilitated through shared responsibility, develop, alone or with others, their own program of learning based on their self-perceived cognitive and affective needs. While the humanistic educator is very important in initiating the class and helping it get started, this leadership role should decline as the class progresses, allowing the students to lead themselves and use the teacher as a resource person. The teacher becomes part of the class, sharing his/her experiences, feelings, and skills with the students as they require them.[28]

Rogers carefully outlined the qualities necessary to facilitate real learning: "The facilitator is a real person, being what she is, entering into a relationship with the learner without presenting a front or a façade." Part of this realness is expressed in a sense of "puzzlement," where the facilitator has the obligation to express ignorance or lack of understanding. The facilitator must also "prize" the other person's feelings and opinions and hold the belief that the other person is fundamentally trustworthy. This prizing or acceptance of the learner "is an operational expression of her essential confidence and trust in the capacity of the human organism." Empathic understanding is a necessary quality. Here the facilitator "has the ability to understand the student's reactions from the inside, has a sensitive awareness of the way the process of education and learning seems to the student."

Finally, the facilitator must be willing to live in uncertainty where only what she/he discovers in the process of facilitating will guide her/him along the way.[29] Rogers was fully aware of the doubts these criteria would raise in the minds of potential facilitators: they may feel incapable of fulfilling the demands of "unleashed curiosity"; will they have the academic resources? Do they have the courage, creativity, tolerance, and humanity to accept such a responsibility?[30]

Rogers moved from identifying appropriate facilitative attitudes to identifying appropriate facilitative behaviors. The facilitator is instrumental in setting the initial mood or climate of the group; helps to elicit or clarify the purposes of individuals and the group; relies upon the motivation of each student to implement those "purposes which have meanings for him"; tries to organize and make available appropriate resources for learning; identifies himself/herself as a flexible resource to be utilized by the group; in responding to expressions in the group, accepts and addresses both the cognitive and the affective attitudes in direct relation to their presence in the group; becomes increasingly integrated as a member of the group; takes the initiative in sharing feelings and thoughts with the group without imposing them; and continually endeavors to keep aware of and accept his/her own limitations.[31]

Consistent with his philosophy of the person, Rogers had great faith that teachers who really want to become facilitators in this manner will learn how to do it: "We've also had experience enough to know that some people who are not particularly skilled but who possess some basic attitudes can be trained in relatively short intensive periods to become much more skillful as facilitators of communication."[32] Rogers believed in and provided experiential training for numerous teachers and leaders in order to ease their learning the skills of facilitation.

Having identified key factors in facilitative attitudes and behaviors, Rogers outlined pedagogical methods that enhance personal growth. An emerging curriculum, always connected with their self-perceived needs, would motivate students to work on issues that are real to them. Humanistic education values the continuing process of learning rather than objectively verifiable products. There is an ongoing process of self-, mutual, and group evaluation. Students are empowered in every facet of the learning process, they are motivated toward self-discipline and accountability within groups. Rogers argued that this kind of learning is deeper, proceeds more rapidly, and becomes more internalized by the students than the learning acquired in the traditional classroom. He suggested the use of contracts to give learners both security and responsibility; students who do not desire this kind of learning should always have other options in a course. He suggested that all learning be presented as an inquiry, with each learner a full participant. Rogers was also very partial to the use of simulation in teaching, arguing that it provides

the student with first hand experience of various processes which occur in real life: with decision-making based upon incomplete and changing information, made urgent by deadlines; with the difficulties of communication, the sometimes disastrous results of misunderstandings and crossed messages, or the discrepancy between verbal communication and actual behavior; with the handling of interpersonal relationships in negotiation, bargaining, and "deals."[33]

Rogers supported programmed instruction for the "functional learning of subject matter" that requires step-by-step application. His only proviso was that programmed learning should be presented as a fairly limited means to learn and should never take the place of creativity in learning.

On the more affective level, Rogers believed the basic encounter group to be an excellent locus for learning. If it is properly handled, it should result in increased self-understanding, more independence in the individual, and an increased comprehension and acceptance of others.[34] The group should start with little imposed structure; the leader's function is essentially facilitative in that she/he clarifies or guides the group process when necessary.[35] Rogers described the kinds of processes found in encounter groups, many of which are used in bands at the New School. "In such a group, after an initial "milling around," personal expressiveness tends to increase. This also involves an increasingly free, direct and spontaneous communication between members of the group." As this process develops, people drop their facades and reveal deeper and previously hidden aspects of themselves. The spontaneous feedback they give and receive from others informs their growth, as a result of which many participants learn to become more facilitative in groups.[36]

A sine qua non of Rogerian education is self-evaluation and group evaluation of both the facilitator and the learners. This is an essential step to ensure that learners take responsibility for pursuing the aims they set for themselves in their contracts and that facilitators are continually learning.

BROWN AND MOUSTAKAS

Both Maslow and Rogers came to humanistic theory and education through their work as psychologists. They had an important influence on numerous educators who wrote on pedagogy and ideology of the person. Two such educators who became influential in the literature of humanistic education were George Isaac Brown and Clark Moustakas.

George Isaac Brown wrote on applications of humanistic education in *Human Teaching for Human Learning,* in which he differentiated between healthy and sick societies:

A sick society at worst could totally turn on itself in a blazing necrophilic orgy of self-destruction. A healthy society learns from its mistakes and allows its members to grow toward authenticity, communication and productivity. It makes available a continuing choice between the tranquillity of reflection and the excitement and gratification of individual and group creative endeavor.[37]

In the next paragraph, Brown gives a "Cook's tour" of the history of education (beginning with Socrates) in order to prove that education has had a profound effect on "human powers" and the formation of history. He claims that his country, the United States, is "at a new threshold. Simultaneously emerging in our time are a number of approaches to the extension of human consciousness and the realization of human potential."[38] Brown coined the term "confluent education" to describe the process that he believed would bring human consciousness and society to further heights: "Confluent education describes a philosophy and a process of teaching and learning in which the affective domain and the cognitive domain flow together, like two streams merging into one river, and are thus integrated in individual and group learning."[39]

Brown presented various civic goals that could be met by confluent education. By addressing the students' feelings, one could accord them more power, which would increase their sense of freedom and consequent responsibility. While he did not elaborate on how this is done, Brown claimed that "Gestalt-therapy experiments were especially productive in teaching the relationship between freedom and responsibility."[40] He also believed that properly conducted confluent education could stabilize students' reactions to injustice and frustration. If the intellect and emotions did not work in concert, there could be a veritable "volcano" of feeling that would result in revolution. Properly managed, these feelings and thoughts could be channeled into "innovative action."[41] The third civic goal of confluent education was "Americanism and Patriotism." Here Brown revealed a highly individualistic bias: the individual comes before the state, but properly developed individuals will naturally see the value of tolerance and a free society as well as the evils of a totalitarian state. "Concern for preserving the freedom of our country must permeate the very being of every citizen."[42] Brown articulated what he considered to be the necessary conditions to succeed at these somewhat questionable goals:

The ideal pedagogical condition is where a learner, fully possessed of feelings of personal adequacy as an explorer in the universe of experience, finds the adventure of new experience a prospect of challenge and excitement. Thus he learns. And he thirsts for yet more experience. He feels most alive when he is learning, whether what he learns be pleasant or unpleasant. This kind of vitalized learning involves both affective and cognitive dimensions. That is, the learner learns as a whole person, with both mind and feeling.[43]

The tautological quality of Brown's argumentation here gives a good sense of the shallowness of his ideas as well as the vagueness of his pedagogical advice. The reader should not be taken in, however, by the blandness of his assurances that confluent education can stem the tide of revolution by turning people to the promise of innovation. This cannot be construed as benign when one realizes that he was writing in the America of the early 1970s, a country with numerous riots in its major cities that were precipitated by the "frustrated" and oppressed (a word Brown never used) citizenry. It is disheartening to realize that he was advocating the use of humanistic education for social control, and ultimately to ensure that civic power remains in the hands of conservative self-interests, which, in turn, maintain the social institutions that regulate the access of the "frustrated" population to those resources they need and want.

At the inception of the New School we used the terminology of "confluent education" primarily because it was used by the director as well as our community facilitator, the latter having been educated in the University of Massachusetts program on humanistic education. However, the concept was presented extracontextually, without the benefit of Brown's jingoism and paradoxical use of a pedagogy of empowerment to derail people's carrying through what they felt they wanted to do, if that something were revolution. Later, we dropped the term because it was so specialized that nobody outside of our small community understood it. We found it more useful to talk of "holistic education" because it broadened the scope of learning to include the social, political, aesthetic, spiritual, and physical development of the person along with the affective and cognitive aspects that, taken alone, become somewhat amorphous categories.

Clark Moustakas, writing in 1972, was much more focused on notions of the self and of personal growth. He tried to come to terms with the notion of self. On the one hand, people could never consciously know, define, or categorize themselves, though they could get somewhat in touch with the self through its expressions of uniqueness and universality. The self was also the source for all growth.[44] Moustakas differentiated between the self and the personality. The personality was more available to people:

Every person is born a unique individual and remains so throughout his life. Even when the development of personality has been thwarted and the potentialities of the self are unfulfilled, a certain core of quality intrinsic to one's inner nature persists and stamps a mark of individuality on the person.[45]

He also believed that the individual is born with personal integrity that can be stifled but never completely destroyed.[46]

Moustakas's model of the human, then, includes an elusive self that is sometimes expressed insofar as the personality is allowed to develop in keeping with the person's innate integrity. The way in which the self can grow is through the expression of its "being," which is the form, pattern, or context of individuality. It is "the experience of oneself as a totality, as a whole, in the immediate presence. In the being experience there is no sense of time or direction, or separation of self from other. There is a complete absorption, self-involvement, and fullness."[47] Although being is a necessary condition for growth, it does not "necessarily lead to changes in development." Rather, it is found through each person's "absorption in an activity where there is sheer satisfaction in perceiving, contemplating, sensing, listening and expressing complete experience."[48]

If being is the organizing factor that allows the innate self to develop into a person, self-actualization or personal growth can be called "becoming." Moustakas did not believe that all experience and learning necessarily lead to growth or becoming. Only "true" or "significant" experiences can lead to self-actualization. The experiences that lead there must be consistent with the person's aims and touch a person in such a way that "being and becoming merge into the self."[49] The kind of experience that touches the "core of one's being" must comprise "an underlying unity and distinctiveness. . . . [and] . . . involve expressions of self which unify or integrate one's intrinsic nature with an immediate state of being and a process of becoming or growth."[50]

One may well ask how one knows that an experience is contributing to growth of the real self when the self is so inaccessible and the clues are so ephemeral. Moustakas said that, first of all, the person must know what he/she wants even if that knowledge is unconscious. It might also be a rational and studied desire. It must be the affirmative expression of the self related to something of intrinsic worth to the individual, something the individual perceives himself/herself as "needing."[51]

Like the other writers discussed here, Moustakas was convinced that freedom to grow and develop automatically brings with it the element of responsibility in an individual's life. The primary responsibility is that the self be consistent with the self's innate tendencies. From this process, a sense of others' needs will emerge and lead to a sense of responsibility.[52]

A central quality is needed to work all these elements together into the highest possible personal growth. There must be a unifying pattern of the self that imbues the person with a sense of wholeness and "integrates thought and feeling and gives coherence to everything the individual does. . . . The unity itself, the harmony of one's own life seems to come from an increasing capacity to find in the world that which also obtains within the depths of one's own being."[53]

Moustakas did not seem to be sure whether the self is an innate and elusive primordidal structure within each individual, or whether it is the unifying pattern that gives growth to our personalities. It may be both. Since he attributed a rather mystical function to the self, his philosophy of the person is not clear.

Convoluted as his definitions are, they eventually bring Moustakas to education, which he called "the world of the learner," where personal meaning and involvement become expressed through individual interests and concerns.[54] He also emphasized that the presence of values must continually be acknowledged and analyzed in learning situations.

To Moustakas, the growth of the learner or group of learners depended strongly on the atmosphere created by the teacher, or "nurturer." The teacher must set the tone by demonstrating concern with "the becoming nature of each member in the group" as well as with his/her own personal growth. The teacher reveals his/her own beliefs and attitudes openly, rather than depending on a position of authority or an externally ascribed role.[55] The teacher must listen with respect and acceptance, making elaborations where necessary; must learn to listen beyond the surface for the "real" person; must not impose himself/herself on the learner but must allow the learner's point of view to emerge and evolve; must create an environment of mutual acceptance, trust, and love. Like Rogers, Moustakas emphasizes the "realness" the teacher must convey through a firm belief in the potential of the learner. Teachers must also support individuals without minimizing the feelings of the group and acknowledge the fact that the process of self-exploration implies risk-taking.[56]

Moustakas attributed great importance to intra-teacher relationships. Because he advocated continuous self-searching on the part of the teacher, he described the best atmosphere for the teacher's growth to be "in an atmosphere of affection where the terrors of loneliness are assuaged and the impulse freely to link hands with others is strengthened."[57] He acknowledged that it is difficult to get teachers to trust one another and advocated their openly discussing their possible mistrust and doubt about the process. He emphasized that if teacher evaluation or any pressure were associated with the development of intra-teacher relationships, the teachers would not respond with trust or openness.

While teachers can create optimum environments and facilitate well, the "actual nature and substance of learning" evolved from the students' individual choices.[58] For this reason,

The educational situation which most effectively promotes learning is the one in which (a) the uniqueness of the learner is deeply respected and treasured and (b) the person is free to explore the relationships, ideas, materials, and resources available to him in the light of his own particular interests, potentialities, and experience.[59]

Ultimately, effective teachers must become learners by initiating processes that will affect them as well as the students.[60]

In the first year of the New School our staff development meetings were the locus of endless discussions about the nature of the self. There did not seem to be agreement on much other than that it was ephemeral. Moustakas's model of the self was never brought to our attention. Where he was perhaps most influential on the founders of the school was in his emphasis on staff development, on creating an atmosphere of trust and safety. At most times in our history we have been able to do this; on the occasion when this trust was severely undermined, it took years to rebuild a comparable environment. The notion of teachers learning through teaching has always been an operant value and practice of the school; frequently in their written academic profiles and contributions to the *Annual Report* teachers express their personal objectives for learning through teaching.

VALUES CLARIFICATION

The issue of values and valuing is crucial to the philosophical and educational views of the existentialists and the humanistic educators. Because of the importance of people's ascertaining their own unmediated values in order to make appropriate choices for themselves and thus achieve meaning, or self-actualization, or mature functioning in their lives, it became obvious that it would be useful to develop ways of helping people to articulate, evaluate, judge, and perhaps change their values and priorities. Only with this kind of clarification could people responsibly express their freedom and choose wisely for themselves.

Various educators, philosophers, and psychologists have worked on means of rendering values and values choices dynamic to learners. Values clarification, by means of various exercises and "strategies," would help people to turn confusion and conflict "into decisions that are both personally satisfying and socially constructive."[61] Consequently, a comprehensive methodology of group and classroom techniques was developed to facilitate the learning of seven broadly defined value skills:

1. Seeking alternatives when faced with a choice
2. Looking ahead to probable consequences before choosing
3. Making choices on one's own, without depending on others
4. Being aware of one's own preferences and valuations
5. Being willing to affirm one's choices and preferences publicly
6. Acting in ways that are consistent with choices and preferences
7. Acting in those ways repeatedly, with a pattern to one's life.[62]

Drawing on the work of both Dewey and the humanistic psychologists, researchers in values clarification developed seven processes of valuing in an educational setting:

1. Prizing and cherishing—supporting the learners' articulating what they value

2. Publicly affirming—creating a situation where the learners must take public positions on their values

3. Choosing from alternatives

4. Considering consequences

5. Choosing freely from one's own feelings and proclivities

6. Acting—encouraging the learner to act on the basis of his or her cherished values, thus closing the gap between saying and doing

7. Acting with a pattern—helping people eliminate behavior patterns that are contradictory to their beliefs.[63]

This sevenfold valuing process was refined by Howard Kirschenbaum. His new schema, "the valuing process," is much more sophisticated and initiated the process that linked the humanistic educators with the later critical educators. The central elements in his valuing process are feeling; numerous forms of thinking that include three kinds of critical thinking, logical thinking, creative thinking, and fundamental cognitive skills involving language use, mathematical skills, and research; communicating verbally and nonverbally with clarity and empathy, as well as seeking clarification and feedback; choosing freely by considering consequences, gathering data, setting goals, and planning; acting skillfully with competence, pattern, and consistency.[64]

Later in the same essay, Kirschenbaum indicated many imperfections in this complex schema, emphasizing that it is important to improve on it in order to make clear how values clarification fits in with, or in fact is, humanistic education.[65] There is no doubt that theorists of values clarification see it as an essential aspect of humanistic education.[66] Other points frequently emphasized in favor of values clarification are that it is a concrete, workable set of strategies; that the preoccupation is consistent with a democratic and pluralistic society; that it is pedagogically fairly easy to do, although teachers must be cautioned not to present themselves as values authorities; that, rather than a loss of subject matter, the use of this pedagogy enhances the students' understanding of subject matter; that it is useful to address a variety of issues and subjects; that it is not dangerous, involving only fairly low-risk exercises; that it is not meant to replace all other pedagogies, and it can often be used well in conjunction with them.[67]

Certainly the directions given for the use of values-clarification exercises sound somewhat like a primer of humanistic educational attitudes:

When using the activities and strategies for values-clarification, encourage a classroom atmosphere of openness, honesty, acceptance and respect. If students feel that something they say about their own beliefs and behaviour is going to be ridiculed by their peers or frowned upon by the teacher, they will not want to share their thought and feelings about value issues.

The teacher must help the class learn to listen to one another. One of the best ways he can do this is to be a model of a good listener himself. He can indicate by his verbal and nonverbal expressions that he is interested in what the students think, and will seriously consider their ideas and possibly be influenced by them.[68]

Despite the authors' strong arguments that values clarification is inherent in humanistic education, it does not necessarily follow that either their schemata or their exercises are sufficient to render an educational setting humanistic. Indeed, the methodology implicit in some of their exercises and in accounts of the structuring of classes in various disciplines, is somewhat antithetical to humanistic education. The central principle of humanistic education is that the concerns of the learners constitute the point of departure for all discourse in the learning environment. If this discourse and discussion indicate that a values-clarification approach would be helpful, then is the time to introduce appropriate exercises and techniques. However, it is clear from many of their examples that their approach is much more programmatic than the usual approach in humanistic education. They often organize their exercises or the structure of discourse a priori, without checking the immediate concerns of the learners.

Certainly, many "trainers" have designed repertoires of values exercises that they give in workshops to participants whose concerns they have no way of knowing in advance. These highly "portable" programs of values-clarification exercises have become a lucrative field where "professional development seminars" involving large groups of people are orchestrated. In many cases the program comprises a "bag of tricks" that can be done fairly effectively, even with people who do not intend to invest too much affect in the proceedings.

However, there is a significant qualitative difference between responding to hypothesized values conflicts and responding to those which emerge organically through group interaction. It is in the latter case that learners may happen upon insights of a sufficiently compelling nature to encourage them to attempt behavioral changes. Groups at the New School have made very good use of the kind of exercises developed by Simon and Kirschenbaum, but usually in response to specific concerns. Values-clarification exercises often cut through the defenses people construct in difficult situations; under the conditions mentioned above, they may offer the facilitator and learners a new and often more authentic way of relating to one another. It has been our experience that the best use of values clarification is when it emerges directly from the discourse within a group.

The works on values clarification to which I have referred are early works written around the time of the establishment of the New School. They are the works we consulted in learning how to use techniques appropriate to humanistic education in our teaching. While numerous works on the subject have been written since, there has been little real development of the theoretical premises on which the original writers based their claims. A work on values most relevant to our teaching at the New School has been the analysis of values and valuing processes with respect to gender undertaken by Carol Gilligan and by Mary Belenky and her group in their book *Women's Ways of Knowing*.[69] I shall refer to these theories later when I discuss the influence of feminism on the theoretical framework of education at the New School. Another potentially interesting field of values study in the future should be the emerging work on critical thinking and its application in education.

CRITIQUING THE 1960s AND 1970s

The period in which most of the humanistic educators were writing was an exciting one in which people felt they could solve the problems not only of school, but of society itself, with humanistic education. Various critiques soon emerged of what was often perceived as an environment of "excess" in which students were not "taught to do anything." The critiques tended to fall into several categories: the "back to basics" movement, which has slowly evolved into the dusting off of fairly arbitrarily chosen selections from the old, hackneyed, and white male Eurocentric "great works canon"; and the critical theorists, who maintain that in order to change schools [and then society], one must subject them to a sociopolitical analysis which takes into account the dominant conservative interests they protect, their place in society, and an epistemological analysis of the hegemonic nature of curriculum.

While critics acknowledge that there were some valuable innovations in the 1960s and 1970s which have left an "important residue," they claim that "The combination of the political backlash and a serious economic recession has worked to wipe out many if not most of the very modest and mild changes of the 1960s." This view usually leads to the perception that the current changes in social ethos and practice are a systemically repressive force:

Our consciousness has reverted and regressed to one involving scarcity, survival, competition, and stagnation. The language of growth, potential, daring, and challenge has become muted: a sense of infinite possibility has been replaced by timidity, expansiveness by caution, long-range thinking by the bottom line, visions by quotas. . . . Freedom has come to mean license to the powerful rather than liberation for the weak; equality is seen as the privilege of competing rather than the right to dignity; individualism has come to mean greed rather than moral autonomy; and community has come to be oriented around terms of class rather than terms of humanity.[70]

Jonathan Kozol was one of the first writers to offer a comprehensive critique of the humanistically oriented experiments of this period, as exemplified by the free school movement. His critique is essentially that free schools are the offspring of the disaffected educated white upper class, whose lives he characterizes as "passive, tranquil and protected" and dependent on "strongly armed police" and "well-demarcated ghettos." Having characterized the supporters of free schools in this way, Kozol claimed that "Free Schools . . . cannot, with sanity, with candor, or with truth, endeavor to exist within a moral vacuum." He also considered their existence to provide an "ideal drain on activism and the perfect way to sidetrack ethical men from dangerous behavior."[71] He claimed that these schools were not merely nonpolitical but actually "in many instances, conspicuously and intentionally anti-political."[72] Kozol visited numerous free schools in his country and observed practices that could not have been identical from school to school. Nonetheless, he often confused theory with practice, claiming that "Leather and wheat germ may appear to constitute a revolution in the confines of a far-removed and well-protected farm or isolated commune ten miles east of Santa Barbara," but that they do nothing for the disinherited poor.[73] Since the free schools met the aspirations of the white middle classes, Kozol considered them virtually incapable of meeting the aspirations of the poor:

How can the Free School achieve, at one and the same time, a sane, ongoing, down-to-earth, skill-oriented, sequential, credentializing and credentialized curricular experience directly geared-in to the real survival needs of colonized children in a competitive and technological society; and simultaneously evolve, maintain, nourish and revivify the "uncredentialized," "unauthorized," "unsanctioned" "noncurricular" consciousness of pain, rage, love, and revolution.[74]

Kozol dramatically attacked the narcissism that he related to the free school movement's emphasis on "relevance": "The Free School that shatters the mirror and turns to face the flames is the one that will not lose its consciousness of struggle or its capability for a continued process of regeneration. When we forget the enemy's name, we turn our guns upon each other."[75]

Kozol was even less enamored, however, with the American public school system. To him its goal was not to educate good people but to indoctrinate them as obedient citizens. He cited a telling quotation from the nineteenth-century American educator Horace Mann, who made it abundantly clear that schools were not only the best place to teach people to maintain the social order, but that the taxes paid for the maintenance of the schools were "the cheapest means of self-protection and insurance."[76] "The problem with public schools," Kozol claimed, "is not that [they] do not work well, but that they do."[77] In his critique, Kozol brought together two strains of the American education of his time: Public schools are there to maintain the social order, and the humanistic educational innovators are most dangerous not when they confine themselves to free schools but when their pedagogy is applied within the public system:

Their greatest contributions stand today in the same relationship to freedom as those of Einstein did to the preservation of life . . . [their works] are now being used by corporations such as I.B.M., Xerox and E.D.C. in order to develop the most clever methods ever known for teaching children how to phantasize a sense of freedom that does not exist.[78]

Kozol indicted the available schooling of his time: the mainstream public schooling for deceiving its clientele by passing off clichés of democracy and access while hypocritically maintaining the social status quo, thus implicating the oppressed in the creation of their own oppression; he indicted the free schools because they represent the interests and narcissism of a privileged class that nonetheless manages to acquire outside the schools those skills necessary to protect its status. These very skills are denied to the poor within the free schools, and they have no access to them through the informal education provided by their socioeconomic class.

NOTES

1. Quoted from Abraham Maslow's diary in Edward Hoffman, *The Right to Be Human: A Biography of Abraham Maslow* (Los Angeles: Jeremy P. Tarcher, 1988), p. 174.

2. Abraham H. Maslow, *The Farther Reaches of Human Nature* (New York: Penguin Books, 1966), p. 173.

3. Ibid., pp. 176–77.

4. Abraham H. Maslow, *Toward a Psychology of Being*, 2d ed. (New York: D. Van Nostrand, 1968), p. 25.

5. Hoffman, p. 174.

6. Ibid., pp. 192, 233-36.

7. Maslow, *Farther Reaches*, p. 363.

8. Abraham H. Maslow, *Religions, Values, and Peak-Experiences* (Columbus: Ohio State University Press, 1964), p. 8.

9. Maslow, *Farther Reaches*, pp. 180–88.

10. Abraham H. Maslow, "Humanistic Education vs. Professional Education," *New Directions in Teaching* 2, 3-10 (1970), 17–19.

11. Maslow, *Religions*, p. 75.

12. Carl R. Rogers, *Freedom to Learn* (Columbus, OH: Charles E. Merrill, 1969), p. 95.

13. Richard I. Evans, ed., *Carl Rogers: The Man and His Ideas* (New York: E. P. Dutton, 1975), p. 39.

14. Ibid., p. 42.

15. Carl R. Rogers, *Freedom to Learn for the 80s* (Columbus, OH: Charles E. Merrill, 1983), p. 17.

16. Ibid., p. 285.

17. Ibid., p. 286.

18. Ibid., p. 288.

19. Ibid., p. 295.

20. Evans, pp. 75–76.

21. Ibid.

22. Ibid., p. 158.

23. Ibid., p. 19.

24. Rogers, *Freedom to Learn for the 80s*, pp. 160–65.

25. Evans, pp. 265–66.

26. Ibid., p. 17.

27. Ibid., pp. 120–21.

28. Carl R. Rogers, *Carl Rogers on Personal Power* (New York: Delacorte Press, 1971), pp. 69–76.

29. Rogers, *Freedom to Learn for the 80s*, pp. 121–28.

30. Ibid., pp. 137–42.

31. Carl Rogers, *Freedom to Learn* (Columbus, OH: Charles E. Merrill, 1969), pp. 164–66.

32. Evans, p. 87.

33. Ibid., p. 139.

34. Ibid., pp. 141–42.

35. Ibid., p. 142.

36. Ibid.

37. George Isaac Brown, *Human Teaching for Human Learning: An Introduction to Confluent Education* (New York: Viking Press, 1971), p. 9.

38. Ibid., p. 10.

39. Ibid.

40. Ibid., pp. 227–29.

41. Ibid., pp. 229–33.

42. Ibid., p. 237.

43. Ibid., p. 233.

44. Clark Moustakas, *Teaching as Learning* (New York: Ballantine Books, 1972), p. 3.

45. Ibid.

46. Ibid.

47. Ibid., p. 6.

48. Ibid., p. 7.

49. Ibid., p. 11.

50. Ibid., p. 13.

51. Ibid., p. 16.

52. Ibid., pp. 18–19.

53. Ibid., p. 20.

54. Ibid., pp. 19–20.

55. Ibid., p. 26.

56. Ibid., p. 27.

57. Ibid., p. 36.

58. Ibid., p. 72.

59. Ibid., p. 73.

60. Ibid., p. 171.

61. Howard Kirschenbaum, "In Support of Values Clarification," in *Innovations in Education: Reformers and Their Critics*, ed. John Martin Rich, 3rd ed. (Boston: Allyn and Bacon, 1981), p. 272.

62. Merrill Harmin and Sidney B. Simon, "Values," in *Readings in Values Clarification*, ed. Howard Kirschenbaum and Sidney B. Simon (Minneapolis: Winston Press, 1973), p. 13.

63. Howard Kirschenbaum and Sidney B. Simon, "Values and the Futures Movement in Education," in *Readings in Values Clarification*, ed. Howard Kirschenbaum and Sidney B. Simon (Minneapolis: Winston Press, 1973), pp. 23–26.

64. Howard Kirschenbaum, "Beyond Values Clarification," in *Readings in Values Clarification*, ed. Howard Kirschenbaum and Sidney B. Simon (Minneapolis: Winston Press, 1973), pp. 105–06.

65. Ibid., pp. 107–08.

66. Kirschenbaum and Simon, *Readings*, is filled with articles that refer to values clarification and humanistic education almost interchangeably.

67. Kirschenbaum, "In Support of Values Clarification," pp. 275–76.

68. Sidney B. Simon, Leland W. Howe, and Howard Kirschenbaum, *Values Clarification: A Handbook of Practical Strategies for Teachers and Students* (New York: Hart, 1972), pp. 25–26.

69. Carol Gilligan, *In a Different Voice: Psychological Theory and Women's Development* (Cambridge, MA: Harvard University Press, 1982); Mary Field Belenky, Blythe McVicker Clinchy, Nancy Rule Goldberger, and Jill Mattuck Tarule, *Women's Ways of Knowing: The Development of Self, Voice, and Mind* (New York: Basic Books, 1986).

70. David E. Purpel, *The Moral and Spiritual Crisis in Education* (South Hadley, MA: Bergin & Garvey, 1988), pp. 15–16.

71. Jonathan Kozol, *Free Schools* (New York: Bantam, 1972), pp. 10–12.

72. Ibid., p. 95.

73. Ibid., p. 53.

74. Ibid., p. 58.

75. Ibid., p. 63.

76. Jonathan Kozol, *The Night Is Dark and I Am Far from Home* (New York: Bantam Books, 1975), quoted on pp. 4–5.

77. Ibid., p. 1.

78. Ibid., pp. 4–6.

5
Critical Pedagogy: Contributions and Limitations

SOME BASIC CONCEPTS OF CRITICAL PEDAGOGY

JONATHAN KOZOL IS KNOWN TO HAVE BEEN greatly influenced by his teacher at Harvard, Paulo Freire, whose theories of critical pedagogy, developed through his work in adult literacy with agricultural workers in his native Brazil, have influenced many educators. I will discuss Freire's philosophy further on. First, I would like to review some ideas that have become identified as the core of critical pedagogy. In reading the work of the critical theorists, it is important to bear in mind that they wish to "reappropriate" language by attributing very specific and radical meanings to words in common usage while developing their own specialized vocabulary. Although the critical thinkers are certainly not unanimous on all points, there is virtual consensus on the following:

1. The schools represent a powerful force of social, intellectual, and personal oppression.
2. The reasons for such oppression are rooted in the culture's history.
3. They represent a number of deeply held cultural values—hierarchy, conformity, success, materialism, control.
4. What is required for significant changes in the schools amounts to a fundamental transformation of the culture's consciousness.[1]

The points of major interest to the critical theorists may also be couched as questions in a "reinvigourated debate about education":

1. What will be the approach to social inequality or social transformation?

2. What will be the approach to social inequality in the education debate?
3. Will curriculum be concerned with traditional and religious values, or will issues of gender, race, and class inequality come to the forefront?
4. Will the curriculum reflect the ethnocentrism of our Western heritage, or will pluralism prevail through multicultural and global education?
5. Will vocational interests prevail, or can critical literacy and teaching be implemented?
6. Will the schools be controlled by central boards or teachers, administrators, and communities?[2]

Starting with Freire, the critical theorists have developed a particular vocabulary to describe a set of interrelated and widely shared concepts that have grown through the dialectical process of their discussion and writing. The first concept of importance is that of critical pedagogy:

Fundamentally concerned with the centrality of politics and power in our understanding of how schools work, critical theorists have produced work centering on the political economy of schooling, the state and education, the representation of texts, and the construction of student subjectivity . . . critical theorists generally analyze schools in a twofold way: as sorting mechanisms in which select groups of students are favored on the basis of race, class, and gender; and as agencies for self and social empowerment.[3]

While the New School's educational philosophy tended to focus primarily on the affective life of its students from 1973 to 1978, as the economy worsened, the economic and social situations and expectations of our students changed. Their situations forced us to enlarge the scope of our considerations. One danger in humanistic education is its isolation of the "self" as an entity beyond material consideration. In order to help our increasingly alienated students understand themselves as social beings, the teachers had to understand the students' individual living situations and their relationship to systemic oppression, and we had to implicate the students in critically examining their own living situations. While we have not relinquished the concepts of self-actualization and authenticity, it has become urgent to articulate that the feelings related to these concepts are grounded in and mediated by a socially constructed context.

When people are aware of the psychological, cultural, and socioeconomic determinants in their lives, they are enabled to negotiate the task of "inventing" themselves and their lives. The aim of the New School has always been an emancipatory one: to free people from the emotional shackles imposed by others' expectations of them and to help them achieve a high level of self-actualization that will result in personal happiness and reinvestment in their own and the global community. For this reason, we have always worked with the notion of emancipation (however restrained it originally was) as primordial to our educational objectives.

Since its inception, the New School has worked on both the affective and the conceptual levels, in the latter case with a methodology somewhat similar in essence to the critical pedagogy of Paulo Freire. It is difficult to identify the precise extent to which this tendency has been consciously adopted in the New School. While I recall reading Kozol's and Freire's work and hearing them speak in the early 1980s, other teachers' contributions are drawn from diverse intellectual and experiential sources. We have also drawn from the theoretical frameworks of women's studies, black studies, gay studies, and peace education—all of which are interrelated in that they address the emancipation of oppressed groups and advocate radical change in the distribution of power in the world. In order to meet our ideological objectives and our students' changing needs, we have had to combine some principles from these diverse sources with critical pedagogy into an elaborated form of humanistic education, which I have named "critical humanism." This educational philosophy addresses the issues of critical pedagogy simultaneously with the often eccentric or individual psychological dimensions that to date have been virtually ignored in the literature of critical pedagogy.

PAULO FREIRE

Freire's theoretical writings are most relevant to our situation. He clearly identifies the hegemonic nature of school knowledge, and how it effectively silences the masses:

In the culture of silence, the masses are mute, that is, they are prohibited from creatively taking part in the transformations of their society and therefore prohibited from being. Even if they can occasionally read and write . . . they are nevertheless alienated from the power responsible for the silence.
. . . Overcome by the myths of this culture, including the myth of their own "natural inferiority," . . . [illiterates] . . . do not know that their action upon the world is also transforming.[4]

While Freire considers knowing how to read a necessary condition to emancipation, it is not a sufficient one. The learners must develop a critical understanding of

the reasons behind many of their attitudes toward cultural reality and thus confront cultural reality in a new way. . . . The learners' capacity for critical knowing—well beyond mere opinion—is established in the process of unveiling their relationships with the historical-cultural world in and with which they exist.[5]

That is why

we can conclude that only a literacy that associates the learning of reading and writing with a creative act will exercise the critical comprehension of that experience, and without any illusion of triggering liberation, it will nevertheless contribute to its process.

And, of course, this is no task for the dominant classes.[6]

This creative act, also called "conscientization," is a form of "cultural production" as opposed to the standard "cultural reproduction" in schools. Although he is fully aware of the problematic situation of the dominant classes passing along learning to the dominated, Freire sees ways around this paradox. Literacy is an "eminently political phenomenon" to be analyzed through a theory of power relations and an understanding of social and cultural reproduction and production."

While our students are not totally illiterate, their critical skills as well as their ability to analyze texts are often blunted by eleven passive years within the state or private educational system. However, we have developed numerous methods of creating and structuring our learning groups toward the goal of collective cultural production.

By "cultural reproduction" we refer to collective experiences that function in the interest of the dominant groups, rather in the interest of the oppressed groups that are the object of its policies. We use "cultural production" to refer to specific groups of people producing, mediating, and confirming the mutual ideological elements that emerge from and reaffirm their daily lived experiences. In this case, such experiences are rooted in the interests of individual and collective self-determination.[7]

The educator is an important part of this process, and Freire is uncompromising in his statements on the purpose and role of the radical educator:

Educators must develop radical pedagogical structures that provide students with the opportunity to use their own reality as a basis of literacy. This includes, obviously, the language they bring to the classroom. To do otherwise is to deny students the rights that lie at the core of the notion of an emancipatory literacy. . . . It is through their own language that they will be able to reconstruct their history and their culture.[8]

Freire identifies as the best learning process a socially contextual one in which the learners situate themselves within their social context through a process of critical questioning. He argues that individuals must come to a critical consciousness of their "own being in the world." To him, both teachers and students are agents engaged in the process of questioning the dominant ideology and constructing and reconstructing meaning. This dominant ideology

lives inside us and also controls society outside. . . . Transformation is possible because . . . as conscious human beings, we can discover how we are conditioned by the dominant ideology. We can gain distance on our moment of existence. Therefore, we can learn how to become free through a political struggle in society.[9]

The natural result of the dominant ideology is the creation of a "curriculum" that comprises the transfer of the guiding principles of the dominant ideology to the dominated.[10] Concomitant with this transfer of the "formal curriculum" are elitist notions of "rigor" that must be countered:

We have to fight with love, with passion, in order to demonstrate that what we are proposing is absolutely rigorous. We have, in doing so, to demonstrate that rigor is not synonymous with authoritarianism, that "rigor" does not mean "rigidity." Rigor lives with freedom, needs freedom. I cannot understand how it is possible to be rigorous without being creative. For me it is very difficult to be creative without having freedom. Without being free, I can only repeat what is being told me.[11]

The first requirement for liberating education, to Freire, is that teachers and students both must be "critical agents in the act of knowing." Furthermore, teachers must be aware of a contradiction inherent in liberating education: unless the teachers are convinced of what must be changed, they cannot convince the students. On the other hand, although they are convinced of the value of their positions, they must respect students and not impose ideas on them.[12] Freire constructs a complex model of learning and knowing that assumes a priori learner motivation. He dismisses North American difficulties in inspiring student motivation.

I think it [motivation] is an interesting issue. I never, never could understand the process of motivation outside of practice, before practice. It is as if first I needed to be motivated and then I could get into action! Do you see? That is a very anti-dialectical way of understanding motivation. Motivation takes part in the action. It is a moment of the very action itself. That is, you become motivated to the extent that you are acting, and not before acting. . . . This book will be good if at the very moment in which the possible reader is reading, he or she is able to feel motivated because of the act of reading, and not because he or she read about motivation.[13]

In our experience in the New School, it is often difficult to motivate students to open the book. Reading a book, as a cultural act, frequently presents a technical difficulty that precipitates low self-esteem in the learners, for some of whom school has been the site of continual failure. Very often, by the time they have passed through elementary and secondary school, they have already labeled themselves "stupid." They are further reinforced by a popular adolescent culture in which, as a result of the often meaning-less reading to which students have been exposed in elementary and high school, they are rightfully suspicious of "book learning." The popular cul-ture of the society is very "thing oriented." The extremely concrete aspira-tions to own various signifiers of class or status reduce abstract or even "passionately applied" school learning to utter redundancy in the students' day-to-day lives.

While we may generate discussion with students on the nature of these values, on their previous education and the interests it represents, this dia-logue is not always sufficient to motivate them to overcome their fears and engage with reading and what it may bring them. Their sense of cultural ex-clusion, indeed, often makes them want to create a strictly adolescent culture, or to participate in a prepackaged culture that can give them imme-diate gratification with some illusion of meaning, control, and a sense of *Mittsein*. It is precisely because humanistic educators address the psycho-logical dimensions of a problem that cannot be fully addressed through the current analysis of critical pedagogy, that the New School is continually in-volved in the dialectical process of unifying the two strains of theory and developing from this process a pedagogy of critical humanism.

Freire, however, does give a very valuable account of a cycle of knowing, which he sees as having two definite and separate phases that are related to one another: "The first moment of the cycle . . . is the one of production, the production of new knowledge, something new. The other moment is the one during which the produced knowledge is known or perceived. One mo-ment is the production of new knowledge and the second is one in which you know the existing knowledge." Freire claims that in regular schools knowledge is far from the students. The teacher is simply a specialist at transferring knowledge, rather than someone with the qualities necessary for both phases in the cycle of knowing: "action, critical reflection, curiosity, demanding inquiry, uneasiness, uncertainty."[14]

This cycle of knowing is exemplified in the experience of reading by the reader's doing more than "walk on the words" or fly over them. "Reading is re-writing what we are reading. Reading is to discover the connections be-tween the text and the context of the text, and also how to connect the text/content with my context, the context of the reader."[15]

Liberating education is not just a question of methods or methodologies: "The criticism that liberating education has to offer emphatically is not the criticism which ends at the subsytem of education. On the contrary, the criticism of the liberatory class goes beyond the subsystem of education and becomes criticism of society."[16] Freire emphasizes the importance of dialogic method between students and teachers:

Dialogue is a moment where humans meet to reflect on their reality as they make and remake it . . . [it] seals the relationship between the cognitive subjects, the sub-

jects who know, and who try to know . . . dialogue is a challenge to existing domination. Also, with such a way of understanding dialogue, the object to be known is
not an exclusive possession of one of the subjects doing the knowing, one of the
people in the dialogue. In our case of education, knowledge of the object to be
known is not the sole possession of the teacher, who gives the knowledge to the
students in a gracious gesture. Instead . . . the object to be known mediates the two
cognitive subjects. . . . They meet around it and through it for mutual inquiry.[17]

A dialogic approach is inherent in humanistic education and has always
been used at the New School; what Freirean pedagogy adds is an enlarged
notion of "reality" that includes the political-social-economic context in
which the dialogue is taking place. Freire's education of liberation, which
must result in social class empowerment, concretely extends the humanistic
objective of self-actualization:

Even when you individually feel yourself most free, this feeling is not a social feeling, if you are not able to use your recent freedom to help others to be free by transforming the totality of society, then you are exercising only an individualist attitude
towards empowerment or freedom.[18]

Freire's work should be an invaluable inspiration and help to humanistic
educators. However, while the sociopolitical dimensions of knowledge and
the individual's relation to it are well addressed by Freire, his notion of the
"self" or a recognizably individual entity does not account for much of what
goes on at the affective level of people's lives:

The comprehension of the social is always determined by the comprehension of the
individual. In this sense, the individualistic position works against the comprehension of the real role of human agency. Human agency makes sense and flourishes
only when subjectivity is understood in its dialectical, contradictory, dynamic relationship with objectivity, from which it derives.[19]

While it is true that we know ourselves to a great extent in relation to the society in which we live and in terms of our relation to dominance, it is also
true that we may have understandings of the "real role of human agency"
that derive from other experiences: emotional, aesthetic, spiritual, or con-
templative, for instance.

Carl Rogers mentioned Freire in his chapter "The Person-Centered Approach and the Oppressed." He revealed that he considered the best work
on the education of the oppressed to be by Freire. Rogers clearly felt great
admiration for and identification with Freire's work: "*The Pedagogy of the
Oppressed* was first published in Portuguese in 1968 and translated into English in 1970. My book, *Freedom to Learn*, was published in 1969. There is
no indication that he [Freire] had ever heard of my work, and I had never
heard of his."[20]

Rogers compared his work with Freire's, saying that although he was very grounded in concrete example and Freire was extremely abstract, he found their principles almost "completely similar." He especially emphasized their common model of understanding and sympathetic facilitators who do not try to impose their ideas and values, but work from those of the learners. As the ideal Rogerian facilitator would, so does the Freirean teacher allow the learners to take over from him/her, Rogers also acknowledged that through the dialogical method, which provides for the critical consideration of the learners' lives, they begin to see themselves as transformers and to take steps toward change. However, Rogers hardly commented on the application of Freire's social collectivist vision to his own primarily individualistic model of human change. Rather, he applied his own theories to Freire's model by demonstrating how the emotions of individuals who feel powerless in groups may be turned to positive ends through a process of self-expression.

The import of Rogers's analysis is that facilitative attitudes of respect, openness, acceptance, and democratic choice within a group riddled with conflict can set in motion a process in which hostile and negative feelings are expressed, understood, and accepted. As a result of this, individuals are accorded recognition, and mutual trust begins to develop. Irrational feelings become defused by their expression and also by feedback from group members. Confidence grows individually and collectively, and trust forms. In this climate a group can move toward "innovative, responsible, and often revolutionary steps . . . which can be taken now, in an atmosphere of realism." Leadership within the group multiplies, constructive action is taken by individuals, and the group as a whole and individuals within it are able to take personal risks.[21] I do not know if Freire is aware of this work by Rogers. It would be interesting to know if Rogers's terminology would communicate clearly to him, and if Freire would agree with Rogers's causal association of unconditional positive regard and the consequently heightened self-esteem with the impulse toward transformative radical social action.

LATER THEORISTS OF CRITICAL PEDAGOGY

While it is the writings of Freire that I have found the most applicable to the ever-developing pedagogy of the New School, this pedagogy also includes numerous points of agreement and divergence with some of the key notions developed by the younger generation of critical philosophers. Many of them have built a structure of ideas and a vocabulary from the base of Freire's work.

The word "discourse" has been appropriated by the critical theorists to refer to a "family of concepts" composed of discursive practices that are governed by rules relating to the said, the unsaid, and the legitimation of the authority of voice. Dominant discourse is the "language" with which the power group defines reality.[22] The controlling ideology, structure, and dissemination of the dominant discourse are called the "hegemony." This pervasive class dominance depends on the active participation of the dominated for its perpetuation. The participation of the dominated is ensured by the creation of "consensual social practices, social forms, and social structures produced in specific sites such as the church, the state, the school, the mass media, the political system, and the family."[23]

Education is

an important social and political force in the process of class reproduction. By appearing to be an impartial and neutral "transmitter" of the benefits of a valued culture, schools are able to promote inequality in the name of fairness and objectivity. . . . The importance of the hegemonic curriculum lies in both what it includes—with its emphasis on Western history, science, and so forth—and what it excludes—feminist history, black studies, labor history, in-depth courses in the arts, and other forms of knowledge important to the working class and other subordinate groups.[24]

One way in which the hegemony asserts itself in schools is through a hidden curriculum that comprises "those unstated norms, values, and beliefs embedded in and transmitted to students through the underlying rules that structure the routines and social relationships in school and classroom life."[25] The notion of hidden curriculum is not exclusive to critical pedagogy. Since 1970 there has been significant research on the hidden content of schooling, on principles that govern the form and content of teacher-student relationships, and on the form in which subject matter is presented in books and from books to the students. Critiques of hidden curriculum have customarily focused on the inherent racism, sexism, and classism in most educational material and presentation. According to the critical theorists, hidden curriculum, as defined by the "liberal theorists," tends to be descriptive rather than analytical, with "little or no understanding of how the social, political, and economic conditions of society create either directly or indirectly some of the oppressive features of schooling."[26]

Radical perspectives on hidden curriculum, however, go beyond the merely descriptive to

explain the political function of schooling in terms of the important concepts of class and domination . . . [and to] . . . point to the existence of structural factors outside the immediate environment of the classroom as important forces in influencing both the day-to-day experiences and the outcomes of the schooling process.[27]

In order to transform education, curriculum theory will have to include fundamental questions regarding the "normative assumptions underlying its logic and discourse." It will also have to analyze the "structural 'silences' and ideological messages that shape the form and content of school knowledge."[28]

Frequently this kind of analysis lies at the bottom of learning group negotiations at the New School. We do not only try to discover the emotional base for students' interest in a topic; in establishing the contract for the group, we search for means of approaching a subject that cut through the customary appropriation of information and respond to the way in which the students and teacher contextualize the subject matter in their shared world.

Another important concept is that of cultural capital. Cultural capital represents ways of talking and acting; modes of style, moving, and socializing; forms of knowledge, language practices, and values.[29]

Certain linguistic styles, along with the body posture and the social relations they reinforce, lowered voice, disinterested tone, non-tactile interaction, act as identifiable forms of cultural capital that either reveal or betray a student's social background. In effect, certain linguistic practices and modes of discourse become privileged by being treated as natural to the gifted, when in fact they are the speech habits of dominant classes and thus serve to perpetuate cultural privileges.

Class and power connect with the production of dominant cultural capital not only in the structure and evaluation of the school curriculum but also in the dispositions of the oppressed themselves, who sometimes actively participate in their own subjugation.[30]

This certainly has been our experience at the New School, where many of our students come from immigrant and/or visible minority families whose parents have had very little formal education. Others are from Canadian-born families who for generations have lived on subsistence income either earned through labor or provided by welfare. Other students identify themselves as "system kids," who have lived in state-financed foster care or group homes for varying periods of their lives, usually due to various forms of abandonment. Their cultural capital puts them at a definite disadvantage in the mainstream educational system, where students from the milieu most likely to benefit from the dominant culture have inherited substantially different cultural capital that is reinforced and confirmed, while that of the "disadvantaged" is systemically devalued.

The state of affairs described above calls for a pedagogy of empowerment or "conscientization" whose major objective, according to Freire, is to provoke recognition of the world, not as a "given" world but as a world dynamically "in the making."[31] Conscientization is encouraged through the development of a pedagogy that "takes the notion of student experience seriously . . . [by] . . . developing a critically affirmative language that works dialectically, engaging the experiences that students bring to the classroom."[32]

This affirming pedagogy is related to the concept of voice, "the shared meanings, symbols, narratives and social practices of the community or culture in which dialogue is taking place." There are various voices in each educational interaction: the teacher's voice, which characteristically is the voice of the hegemony; the "school voice," which refers to the learned expectations of all learners; the students' voices, which are shaped by their prior experience and particular cultural and social history. It is often through the mediation of a "teacher voice" that the "very nature of the schooling process is either sustained or challenged." Thus, while the teacher's voice can be a tool of oppression, a teacher who is a "transformative intellectual" can change the nature of discourse, can confirm the students' experiences and roots, and can thus turn learning into an experience of empowerment. Together students and teacher live out the emancipatory possibilities of education.[33]

This search for and recognition of the unmediated voice is the cornerstone of empancipatory education exemplified in women's studies, black studies, gay studies, and peace studies. All of these areas of inquiry and pedagogy are predicated on the need to question the current epistemology on the basis of whose interests it serves and whose standards are being met. These fields (they are all fields of great interest in the New School) attempt to redefine the nature of knowledge through arriving at information and conclusions based on the subjective experience of people as well as on externally and empirically verifiable "facts." They are based on the primacy of the subject's self-definition as opposed to the hegemony in which primacy is always accorded to the definitions generated by the conservative self-interest of a ruling class.

Certainly the search for and confirmation of authentic voice is of central importance at the New School, where the student is recognized as the ultimate authority on his/her own life. This is true in the bands, the primary affiliative groups that form the backbone of the school (to be discussed in Part 2 of this book), where the many levels of self-definition are examined in themselves and in learning groups, where these levels of self-definition are examined through the mediation of other subject matter.

While much of what the "critical theorists" say is interesting and provoking, and even rings true, I find them frequently caught within a great contradiction, especially when, in the name of the accessibility of education and critical reflection to all, they develop a highly rarefied yet dense vocabulary that is dauntingly circumlocutory even to experienced readers like myself. By the creation of a specialized and often contrived vocabulary, and by the dubbing of even their most random ruminations with the catchword "discourse," they create a closed circuit of communication, totally removed from the ideology of their inspiration, Freire. The one positive aspect of their vocabulary, I suppose, is that it identifies their followers immediately, and one knows the general context of what will follow at the very outset.

The following paragraph from the work of Stanley Aronowitz and Henry Giroux illustrates the inaccessibility of much post-Freirean diction and its concomitant and tortuous mystification of the obvious.

Moreover, the concept of intellectual provides the theoretical groundwork for inter-rogating the specific ideological and economic conditions under which intellectuals as social group need to work in order to function as critical, thinking, creative human beings. This last point takes on a normative and political dimension and seems especially relevant for teachers.[34]

I am not, however, only faulting their form and the sociopolitical contradictions into which their choice of form has propelled them. It is their treatment of the "educator as intellectual" that concerns me, not so much in what they include as in what they omit. They choose four categories to use in analyzing the function of the educator as intellectual: "a) transformative intellectuals, b) critical intellectuals, c) accommodating intellectuals, and d) hegemonic intellectuals." This categorization is immediately followed by disclaimers regarding its completeness or the discreteness of these categories.[35]

The problem here is that they discount the importance of addressing individual students as a starting point in the educational process, and seem to believe that there is a level and leveling function of general "discourse" that will reach all students and move them somehow into the mode of being "agents" of transformation:

Making the political more pedagogical means utilizing forms of pedagogy that treat students as critical agents, problematizes knowledge, utilizes dialogue, and makes knowledge meaningful, critical, and ultimately emancipatory. In part, this suggests that transformative intellectuals take seriously the need to *give* [emphasis added] students an active voice in their learning experiences. It means developing a critical vernacular that is attentive to problems experienced at the level of everyday life, particularly as these are related to pedagogical experiences connected to classroom practice. As such, the starting point pedagogically *for such intellectuals* [emphasis added] is not with the isolated student but with collective actors in their various cultural, class, racial, historical, and gendered settings, along with the particularity of their diverse problems, hopes, and dreams. It is at this point that the language of critique unites with the language of possibility. That is, transformative intellectuals must take seriously the need to come to grips with those ideological and material aspects of the dominant society that attempt to separate the issues of power and knowledge. Which means working to create the ideological and material conditions in both schools and larger society that give students the opportunity to become agents of civic courage, and therefore citizens who have the knowledge and courage to take seriously the need to make despair unconvincing and hope practical. In short, the language of critique unites with the language of possibility when it points to the conditions necessary for new forms of culture, alternative social practices, new modes of communication, and a practical vision for the future.[36]

It appears here that one contradiction in which the authors find themselves is that under the rubric of "empowerment," they still perpetuate the notion of the balance of power being on the side of the "transformative intellectual." It is he or she who "gives" or bestows upon the students their "active voice." Consistent with their own notions of empowerment, should not the intellectual create a situation where the students' active voices come forward of their own volition? In the latter situation, however, the "intellectual" who must "come to grips" with the "ideological and material aspects of the dominant society" might find that the students do not speak in one voice but in many. The model suggested by the authors does not allow students the option to refuse "civic courage." In a world where people disappear for much less than public critiques of the state, it is trivializing to assume that all it takes is "knowledge and courage" to render "despair unconvincing and hope practical." It is difficult to imagine why they consider their particular use of social control and repression of individual differences and proclivities to be empowering. On the contrary, it seems to me that these authors apply a generalized patina of ideological purposefulness onto what may be, and in our society is almost destined to be, a group of individuals, each of whom is grounded in and repressed by particular experiences and contingencies that must be validated and addressed as part of the process of empowerment.

It is no coincidence that the "discourse" of critical pedagogy is essentially articulated by men. The emphasis on the "public sphere" and the ignoring of the "private affective spheres" are consistent with the acculturation of males in our society. Focusing on the interpersonal may render them uncomfortable and complicate their assertions of the empowering possibilities of their ideology. To date there appears to be little room in this pedagogical theory for the positive effect of a direct relationship with the student or for a refined and empathic knowledge of a particular student's life experience separated from the fairly crudely and statistically defined norms attributed even to gender, ethnicity, class, and race. All relationships with the students seem to be theoretically mediated by a complex and inaccessibly articulated educational theory that could lend itself to overt political posturing by the teacher, to be taken up with gusto by those students who have been trained that "doing well" in school consists of pleasing the teacher.[37]

THE LIMITATIONS OF CURRENT RESISTANCE THEORY

I wonder how this younger generation of critical theorists would address the resourcelessness of so many of our students at the New School. Certainly their theories are most useful in situating the way in which education traditionally reproduces the inequities within the society. It helps contextualize our students' preparation, many of the values they hold, and their highly variable sense of social participation and power. This theoretical base even helps contextualize the multitudinous sociogenic problems our students live and internalize into low self-esteem. However, there is nothing in their writing that is helpful in communicating change and the possibilities of personal growth to the individual and often very resistant student who clings tenaciously to the belief that winning Lotto Québec not only is possible but will resolve all of his/her problems in perpetuity.

The critical theorists address the issue of student resistance through a theory of resistance that questions "the processes by which the school system reflects and sustains the logic of capital as well as dominant social practices and structures that are found in a class, race, and gender divided society." Student resistance may arise from various causes, such as the monitoring of passion and desire, the creation of "dead time," and the reduction of interpersonal relationships "to the imperatives of market ideology." Even the bodies of the students become the site of authoritarian definition and control through prescribed times for ingestion, excretion, and so on. One way in which learners express their resistance is through choosing ignorance: refusing "to acknowledge that . . . [their] . . . subjectivities have been constructed out of information and social practices that surround" them.[38]

The theory of resistance rejects currently popular explanations of oppositional behavior by arguing that it has little to do with deviance and learned helplessness, and really arises from "moral and political indignation." It shifts the theoretical discussion to a "concept of resistance" that sees resistance as an active dialectical response to domination, which in itself is multidimensional. This response of resistance may become transformed by substituting analysis and consequent action for random behaviors.[39] Aronowitz and Giroux are careful to say that not all "oppositional" behaviors constitute politically based resistance, and it is incumbent on the teacher to analyze the source of the behavior through a "mode of inquiry that is self-critical and sensitive to its own interests—radical consciousness-raising and collective critical action."[40]

They emphasize that

When a theory of resistance is incorporated into radical pedagogy, elements of oppositional behavior in schools become the focal point for analyzing different, and often antagonistic, social relations and experiences among students from dominant and subordinate cultures. A radical pedagogy, then, must recognize that student resistance in all of its forms represents manifestations of struggle and solidarity that, in their incompleteness, both challenge and confirm capitalist hegemony. What is most important is the willingness of radical educators to search for the emancipatory interests that underlie such resistance and to make them visible to students and others so that they can become the object of debate and political analysis.[41]

One way in which such resistance may be transformed into a transcendent ideology of empowerment is through the "language of possibility." This language or pedagogy of possibility rests on a vision of collective human freedom:

An education that empowers for possibility must raise social questions of how we can work for the reconstruction of social imagination in the service of human freedom . . . the project of possibility requires an education rooted in a view of human freedom as the understanding of necessity and the transformation of society.[42]

The education toward possibility requires that teachers educate students to

take risks, to struggle with ongoing relations of power, to critically appropriate forms of knowledge that exist outside of their immediate experience, and to envisage versions of a world which is "not yet"—in order to be able to alter the grounds upon which life is lived.[43]

This means that the students' voices must be legitimated and the "cultural logic" of their subjectivity recognized.[44] Simon sees a contradiction in a pedagogy geared toward the empowerment of students that must "teach" them to use their voice while at the same time raising serious questions regarding the existing social forms. He identifies the dilemma this way: "How can we both legitimate the expression of a student voice and challenge at the same time those aspects of that voice which negate our educational/political vision?" Simon arrives at a solution to this dilemma by claiming that each person does not have one voice but a multiplicity of voices, and that the educator must encourage the kind of critical discussion which forces clarification and consequent radicalization.[45]

Aronowitz and Giroux identify various weaknesses in resistance theory that are certainly corroborated by our experience at the New School. They claim that some students see through the postures of the dominant school ideology but decide not to express themselves through rebellious behavior; indeed, sometimes students may be totally indifferent to the hypocrisy of schools. They also claim that resistance theory does not take sufficient account of gender and race. However, the criticism that is the most corroborated by our experience is that insufficient attention is paid by resistance theorists to "the issue of how domination reaches into the structure of personality itself." Aronowitz and Giroux claim that

Radical educators have shown a lamentable tendency to ignore the question of needs and desires in favor of issues that center around ideology and consciousness. A critical psychology is needed that points to the way in which "un-freedom" reproduces itself in the psyche of human beings . . . without a theory of radical needs and critical psychology, educators have no way of understanding the grip and force of alienating social structures as they manifest themselves in the lived but often non-discursive aspects of everyday life.[46]

In my opinion, some of the work done on motivation and aspiration by Maslow and Rogers can be well applied to developing a critical psychology and radical praxis in dealing not only with the rebellious but also with the indifferent. The techniques of values clarification developed by Kirschenbaum et al. can also be used to bring emotions to the surface and introduce them into the discourse of critical pedagogy. While we at the New School see the need for a more formalized psychology that takes into account the social/economic/political context of the student and the group, we have not to date collectively formulated an all-embracive theoretical base. Later, however, I will posit a learning model that addresses the synthesis of critical humanism.

Henry Giroux sees the application of the education of possibility as central to citizenship education, which he considers to be one of the necessary aspects of critical pedagogy. The basic factors in citizenship education for Giroux are the following:

The active nature of the student's participation in the learning process must be stressed; students must taught to think critically, and the development of a critical mode of reasoning must be used to enable students to appropriate their own histories; students must not only clarify certain values, but they must articulate why they are indispensable to the reproduction of human life; and through the above process, students must learn about the structural and ideological forces which influence and restrict their lives.[47]

At the New School we experience frequent resistance on the part of students to completing work they themselves have contracted to do, to considering insights suggested to them, or to ways in which the ideology of the school has become expressed through custom and practice. In reading the critical theorists, it is very clear to me that we have come to a modus operandi similar to that which they describe, with the exception that we also look into the possible psychological and personal reasons for individual behavior. We first try to find the roots of the resistance and to understand if they are individual or systemic. In either case, we attempt to address them by helping the student(s) arrive at a critical analysis of the ground for the resistance. Sometimes the resistance points to the need for basic changes within the school, which are discussed at community meetings and put into operation in ways arrived at by consensus or a vote. The student voice, with all that it implies regarding ethnicity, gender, race, and class, is primary in these deliberations. The deliberations are always based on a notion of possibility, and all solutions are seen as "in process," to be monitored with an eye to change. The contradiction referred to by Simon is one staff and students face continually. Our way of resolving it is ultimately to leave the behavioral choices to the people most affected, even if we are in basic ideological disagreement.

The problem with education for empowerment, from the point of view of an occasional dissident, is that as issues are worked out, it frequently is not possible to satisfy everyone. It is often very difficult for people to relinquish their "objective" visions of a situation or their choices and behavior in view of what they might regard as an individual's wrongheaded desire "not to know" and insistence on continuing a course of action that is generally regarded as disempowering. The ultimate sign of trust that a community can give at this particular juncture is the trust Rogers mentions as each person's ability to accept "what they do not wish to know" only when they are ready to. As well, one must learn to accept that there are people who tenaciously hold a totally different view of the universe from that of the critical humanistic educator; they do not wish to relinquish this point of view, and they should not be coerced to do so. There must be room for honest disagreement. While we can and should embark on a critical discussion and analysis with them, ultimately we must not only accept but also confirm their right to choices that may be contrary to the views of the rest of the community. This often can bring into focus the perennial dilemma of democracy: Where do individual rights end and collective rights begin? While there may be no answer out there in the cosmos for this question, by their regularly posing and discussing it, people's consciousness becomes raised and the issue becomes an important point of referral in our educational community.

Ultimately, the teacher must be the important link in providing an empancipatory education to learners. The critical theorists emphasize that critical teachers must be "transformative intellectuals" who are not only interested in individual student success but also are

concerned in their teaching with linking empowerment—the ability to think and act critically—to a concept of social transformation. Teaching for social transformation means educating students to take risks and to alter the grounds upon which life is lived. . . . [They must perceive the classrooms] . . . as active sites of public intervention, where students and teachers learn to redefine the nature of critical learning and practice outside the imperatives of the corporate marketplace.[48]

Teachers must also be willing to be "bearers of dangerous memory," keeping alive the memory of human suffering by recounting the history of the marginal, the vanquished, and the oppressed, and by actively opposing the hegemonic practice of "not naming" those things which challenge the status quo and suggest the elimination of the sources of human suffering by the realization of alternative possibilities for society.[49]

For Freire the function of a transformative intellectual is to "unveil" the reality hidden by the dominant ideology and to "dream about the reinvention of society."[50] Freire does not dwell on appropriate methodology to the same extent that some of his followers do. He claims that because "a liberating teacher will illuminate reality even if he or she lectures," what is important is that critical thinking must be animated, that the speech have a "certain dynamism" to "provoke critical attention" and "unveil reality."[51] Freire also believes that ideology precedes practice even while it informs it dialectically:

Teachers whose dream is the transformation of society have to get control of a permanent process of forming themselves, and not wait for professional training from the establishment. The more an educator becomes aware of these things, the more he or she learns from practice, and then he or she discovers that it is possible to bring into the classroom, into the context of the seminar, moments of social practice.[52]

Freire believes that it is only through a practice of such idealism that teachers can keep motivated:

Being engaged in a permanent process of illuminating reality with students, fighting against the opacity and obscuring of reality, has something to do with avoiding a fall into cynicism. This is a risk which we have as educators, to the extent we work, work, work!, and often see no results. Many times, we can lose hope. In such moments, there is no solution and we may become mentally bureaucratized, lose creativity, fall into excuses, become mechanistic. This is the bureaucratization of the mind, a kind of fatalism.[53]

All the critical theorists agree in principle that radical pedagogy must be informed by a "passionate faith in the necessity to create a better world" and needs a vision of possibility, a kind of "concrete utopianism" that is a result of "creative risk-taking, of engaging life so as to enrich it."[54]

It has certainly been our experience at the New School that the people who have managed to withstand the exhaustion and stress of continual self-criticism, the continual need to prepare to respond to the students' articulated needs, and the ongoing exposure to the pain of the students' lives are those who have approached the school with a transformative vision, and with a belief that schools may provide one locus where people can make a difference where they live and breathe. However, with increased human longevity and people's work lives ever lengthening, our society is being presented with the unprecedented human experience of teachers spending more than four decades in an occupation that demands great resources of energy. The question raised by the optimism of both Freire and Giroux is: Where does one get the stimulation necessary to maintain the passionate focus demanded by critical pedagogy?

NOTES

1. David E. Purpel, *The Moral and Spiritual Crisis in Education* (South Hadley, MA: Bergin & Garvey, 1988), pp. 19–20.

2. Harvey Holtz, Irwin Marcus, Jim Dougherty, Judy Michaels, and Rick Peduzzi, eds., *Education and the American Dream* (South Hadley, MA: Bergin & Garvey, 1989), p. 9.

3. Peter McLaren, *Life in Schools* (Toronto: Irwin, 1989), pp. 161–62.

4. Paulo Freire, *The Politics of Education: Culture, Power, and Liberation,* trans. Donaldo Macedo (South Hadley, MA: Bergin & Garvey, 1985), p. 50.

5. Ibid., p. 54.

6. Ibid., p. 17.

7. Paulo Freire and Donaldo Macedo, *Literacy: Reading the Word and the World* (South Hadley, MA: Bergin & Garvey, 1987), p. 142.

8. Ibid., p. 151.

9. Paulo Freire and Ira Shor, *A Pedagogy for Liberation: Dialogues on Transforming Education* (South Hadley, MA: Bergin & Garvey, 1987), p. 13.

10. Ibid., p. 77.

11. Ibid., p. 78.

12. Ibid., p. 133.

13. Ibid., pp. 4–5.

14. Ibid., pp. 7–8.

15. Ibid., pp. 10–11.

16. Ibid., p. 33.

17. Ibid., pp. 98–99.

18. Ibid., p. 109.

19. Freire and Macedo, p. 59.

20. Carl R. Rogers, *Carl Rogers on Personal Power* (New York: Delacorte Press, 1971), pp. 105–06.

21. Ibid., pp. 113–14.

22. McLaren, pp. 180–81.

23. Ibid., pp. 172–73.

24. Stanley Aronowitz and Henry A. Giroux, *Education under Siege* (South Hadley, MA: Bergin & Garvey, 1985), pp. 80–81.

25. Henry A. Giroux, *Theory and Resistance in Education* (South Hadley, MA: Bergin & Garvey, 1983), p. 47.

26. Ibid., p. 55.

27. Ibid., p. 47.

28. Ibid., p. 61.

29. McLaren, p. 190.

30. Aronowitz and Giroux, p. 82.

31. Freire, p. 106.

32. Henry A. Giroux, "Educational Reform and Teacher Empowerment," in *Education and the American Dream,* ed. Harvey Holtz and associates (South Hadley, MA: Bergin & Garvey, 1988), p. 182.

33. McLaren, pp. 230–36.

34. Aronowitz and Giroux, p. 31.

35. Ibid., p. 36.

36. Ibid., pp. 36–37.

37. The only full book I know of written by a female "critical pedagogue" is Kathleen Weiler's *Women Teaching for Change: Gender, Class, and Power* (South Hadley, MA: Bergin & Garvey, 1988). Although this work is filled with the jargon of critical pedagogy, Weiler discusses the affective dimensions of feminist education and, when she does so, her language perforce drops its jargon and she frequently refers to works outside the small canon of critical pedagogy.

38. McLaren, pp. 187–89.

39. Aronowitz and Giroux, pp. 104–5.

40. Ibid., p. 106.

41. Ibid., pp. 107–08.

42. Roger I. Simon, "Empowerment as a Pedagogy of Possibility," in *Education and the American Dream*, ed. Harvey Holtz and associates (South Hadley, MA: Bergin & Garvey, 1989), p. 135.

43. Ibid., p. 140.

44. Ibid., p. 141.

45. Ibid., p. 138.

46. Aronowitz and Giroux, pp. 103–04.

47. Giroux, *Theory and Resistance in Education*, pp. 202–3.

48. Giroux, "Educational Reform and Teacher Empowerment," p. 179.

49. Ibid., p. 180.

50. Freire and Shor, p. 36.

51. Ibid., p. 40.

52. Ibid., p. 47.

53. Ibid., p. 49.

54. Giroux, *Theory and Resistance in Education*, p. 242.

6

Reconstructing Pedagogy

WOMEN'S STUDIES HAS BEEN A PRESENCE in the New School curriculum since the school opened. This has been due only in part to my presence as director and teacher during a period when I have been researching, teaching, publishing, and giving talks within the field of women's studies, as well as participating in various projects of the women's movement. Each year there has been at least one other faculty member or external resource person who has worked from a feminist perspective. The objectives of women's studies are congruent with those of both humanistic education and critical pedagogy.

The first women's studies course in the United States was taught in 1965, and courses in women's studies have been taught in Canadian universities since 1970.[1] In both Canada and the United States the earliest articulation of women's studies usually included some of the following objectives: involving women in the women's movement through education; serving as a focal point for developing a body of knowledge about women; acting as an institutional base for the struggle against sexism; and providing a center of resources that could be tapped by the women's movement for the benefit of the community.[2] These objectives are clearly in line with many of the more fully articulated purposes of critical pedagogy spelled out earlier.

Other aspects of women's studies were also to prove important: women's studies must compensate for the absence of women from curriculum by building a body of research on women; it must ensure the understanding of patriarchy in its historical perspective and of the effects of socialization and sex-role stereotyping on women through a cross-cultural perspective; it must promote an understanding of women in history, of female sexuality, of the function of education as a codifier of sex segregation, of the function of the family vis-à-vis women in all cultures, of the relation of women to paid and unpaid work, and of the relationship between social movements and women.[3]

Added to the above list is the expectation that there will be an analysis of scholarship by and about women in both the traditional disciplines and in interdisciplinary forms. The structures and conditions of women's oppression as well as contrasting models for self-determination must be studied. Above all, it is considered essential to examine the relationships between the personal subordination of women and the broader social, political, and economic structures. Women's studies addresses the personal and systemic dimensions of women's experience in both its formal and its informal content by starting with the self as subject.[4] Women's studies legitimates life experience as an appropriate subject of analysis; it concerns itself with process as well as product, is multicultural, and explores interlocking systems of oppression based on sex, race, and class.[5]

While the above characteristics may not be true of every women's studies course, they do cover a wide cross section of concurrence among women's studies teachers. Concomitant with the creation of this field of study is the requirement for an epistemological shift by rephrasing and critiquing all the standard ways of developing questions, answers, and paradigms.[6] This developing epistemology rejects the dichotomous notion of cognitive/affective learning in favor of a theory of a continuum from the affective and unconscious levels of learning to the cognitive. Feminist epistemology recognizes that there are many ways of learning involving intuition, spiritual understanding, creativity, the body as knower, and sociopolitical contextualization. Women's studies cannot avoid touching on the personal dimensions of the lives of both the teacher and the student: "The premise that men dominate women, in however partial or subtle or brutal a way, lends a certain urgency to feminist investigations."[7] This urgency is experienced on the level of one's personal life: What does this mean for me? How will it affect my relationship with my lover, my brother, my father, my friends? It is also experienced in one's public-political sphere: How can I escape this domination? Will it affect my future success or my ability to attain my own goals?

Because women's studies not only has developed from the women's movement but also has grown inextricably with it, the emphasis on praxis and its role in social and intellectual transformation has charged it with a mission far beyond that acknowledged within traditional intellectual preoccupations.

Women's studies, then, has developed on the bedrock of an emancipatory philosophy affecting, at the very least, 51 percent of the world's population. From its very beginning it has emphasized the need for an epistemological analysis of the "knowledge" purveyed in schools. For this reason, women's studies must pressure institutions on the basis of compensatory education: analyzing current curricula and assuring that they are at least gender-fair. Because of the charged nature of its subject matter, in practice women's studies has always had to address the affective dimensions and to confirm the personal experiences and insights of women. Since it is a new field of study, teacher and learner have been thrust into a fairly egalitarian situation, especially when the learner frequently has had many "female" experiences to which the teacher may not have been personally exposed. Indeed, research often has been inspired by revelations made by women's studies teachers and students of their own experiences of schooling, mothering, sexual harassment, incest, childhood sexual abuse, lesbianism, and other subjects ignored or not deemed research worthy within the limits of patriarchal epistemology and educational praxis.

These elements in the theory and praxis of women's studies make it an excellent source for the pedagogy of critical humanism. At the New School, the issue of gender has been addressed from the feminist perspective in bands, in learning groups in most disciplines, and in the community itself.

The developing praxis of women's studies has contributed to changing the practices in more traditional disciplines at the New School, and also to the creation of other fields of interest. For some years male students have organized men's groups to share their feelings and experiences, and to analyze and deal with the masculinist ideology that has shaped their lives. Sometimes their motivation arises from the mysterious and close presence of women's studies. Men who take women's studies classes often express a need for a more authentic examination of masculinism than that supplied through the traditional patriarchal efforts at achieving a universally applicable definition of "human behavior." Over the years complementary ideology and pedagogy have developed in women's studies and in men's groups. It is only since 1985, however, that the literature on masculinism has begun to expand and to refine itself to the kind of self-consciousness necessary for serious study.

Students are interested in discussing their own sexuality both experientially and as a social construction. This interest, along with the ones outlined above, has combined in groups on sexual orientation. All of the above groups blend methodology developed in feminist consciousness-raising groups of the 1960s and 1970s with the consideration of reading materials and a critical analytic approach to the subject matter. These subjects are of enduring interest to all people, but are especially interesting to young people as they attempt to define their identities.

Over the years there have been numerous learning groups at the New School related to black studies, racism, prejudice, Native studies, political power, peace education, terrorism, and the Holocaust. These groups deal with the visceral feelings students have about these issues as well as with an analysis of the sociopolitical contexts of these subjects within the lives of the students. Naturally, many of the readings and materials used in such groups are produced by the people most affected by these issues. As women's studies, men's groups, and human sexuality groups are focused on an emancipatory model for the individual and society, so are groups devoted to the issues mentioned above. Because these subjects are so viscerally based in the students' lives, and because there is so much to analyze and learn, they lend themselves very well to a pedagogy of critical humanism that dialectically addresses the multidimensional levels of the learners' interaction with the subject matter.

There is, however, a danger of relegating the "marginalized" to a kind of liberal "lip service" education that automatically includes in all statements the rider of "gender, class, race, ethnicity, sexual orientation, and ableness" without substantively analyzing the discrete epistemological questions regarding content and pedagogy raised by each of these categories, by combinations of categories, and by their totality. Radical educators are just beginning to address the problematic issue of inclusion, which contains the implication that something is being added to or absorbed by the status quo. A radical analysis of education and these particular aspects of human life demands transformation of our ways of considering and defining those phenomena which have been excluded from academic consideration in the past.

Indispensable as sources of information for addressing each of these areas are the people who live these situations. How they view the world and how they perceive the world's view of them are essential to transforming existing fields of study and to opening new ones. These explorations must be made in tandem with an analysis of the underlying structure and political purpose of the construction of knowledge in our culture. While it is essential to contextualize this knowledge and analyze how knowledge is produced, it is also necessary to share the feelings aroused by the subject matter within the members of a particular class or learning group. Such subjects arouse immense anger, sadness, defensiveness, and guilt—among other feelings. It is important to process these feelings and to help the students find their way beyond them to understanding and further action, if such is their will.

There is no doubt that these new fields of study have had the freedom and room to initiate appropriate pedagogies of empowerment, and they have begun to provide ongoing models of educational possibility that are often very difficult to formulate and integrate into the fiefdoms of long-established disciplines.

RESISTANCE AND MOTIVATION RECONSIDERED

In Chapter 5, I criticized the limited attention Freire accords the motivation of students as well as the limitations I see in resistance theory articulated in the works of Aronowitz and Giroux. While in the best of all possible worlds, all learners would see the advantage of knowing and of critical analysis, the fact is that many students feel coerced into going to school and see little advantage either in knowledge itself or in being able to analyze the relation of their situation to the structure of power in their society.

There are numerous reasons for resistance, some of which are systemic and others of which are individual and eccentric. In some cases resistance expresses the students' honest lack of interest in a subject to which they may have been assigned without consultation. Conversely, it must be said that other students do become interested in the same subject under seemingly identical circumstances. However, it is essential to understand the psychology of strong resistance; frequently knowledge means to a student that she or he can't "go home again," and that previous explanations of reality, relationships, and expectations are thrown into question. The student may have few resources for dealing with the subsequent sense of alienation.

Resistance is almost endemic in introductory women's studies courses. A basic premise in women's studies is the power of the patriarchy and its many forms of violence against women. Many young women resist this account of their reality because it runs counter to their own agenda of having fulfilling romantic relationships with men. They do not want to see men or the male culture as an enemy, and many cherish the hope of finding a male partner who will do his share in their combined life. Any account of male behavior based on an analysis of patriarchy threatens this hope because it indicates that love cannot conquer all, that the reasons why many men, including their boyfriends, may behave in certain ways have roots far stronger and more durable than can be altered by claims of romantic love.

It does not help at this point to analyze romantic love and indicate that it may be a social construction which has different signification to women and men. One may ask why so many young women, who may have witnessed disastrous couple relationships in their families, or who are survivors of childhood sexual abuse, can be so resistant to entertaining an active analysis of their personal histories that will empower them to take charge of their lives. One reason may be that the promise held out by romantic love is immensely and immediately gratifying in a society which emphasizes instant gratification as a desirable and attainable goal. Another may be that this gives them a sense of belonging with their peers. Young women often perceive the feminist account of women's condition as demeaning, turning them into victims at a time when they want to feel powerful, attractive, and full of hope.

The latter reaction was poignantly manifested during the immediate aftermath of the massacre of fourteen women engineering students at the École Polytechnique of the Université de Montréal in December 1989. Numerous women students interviewed after the fact insisted that they were treated equally to men, and that the crime was not against women qua women, even though the murderer was heard to say he hated feminists, separated the women from the men, and killed only the women. Men and women at all levels of society insisted that this was an isolated incident, rejecting the notion that misogyny is a powerful force in our society. In this case, young women in a traditionally male profession want to carry on, fit in, and anticipate the same opportunities as their male colleagues. Perhaps they need to feel this way in the short term in order to complete very arduous and demanding courses. The notion of systemic misogyny is often resisted by men, who become guilty and defensive if they feel they are personally accused of holding such ideas. Their claims not to be misogynous often deafen them to the women's examples regarding systemic prejudice. These responses can be addressed only if the emotionally charged nature of the discussion is acknowledged and clear differentiation is made between the systemic and the personal, with an emphasis on the individual range of choice.

Here, then, is an example of real resistance that is fueled by societal values, but also by the personal needs of both males and females to feel empowered and ethically correct. Further, this resistance protects the fragility of love relationships and the hope for emotional and sexual fulfillment. Clearly, neither additional information nor ideological clarification can adequately remove such resistance in the interests of producing further knowledge.

It is, however, possible to address such resistance successfully and involve students in feminist education by helping them understand their resistance, addressing it through questions such as: How does certain information, attitudes, or material make them feel? Where do these feelings come from? Is there anything within the material that is corroborated by their own experience or that of other people they know? In what way could this information or such attitudes impel them to change their lives, and would that be dangerous or painful? What are their resources of support? Can the group organize itself to offer support? When the emotions behind resistance are examined, learners may become empowered either to take on the responsibility of dropping a subject at least in full awareness or, as is more often the case, of pursuing a subject with a strong sense of engagement.

The personal history behind resistance behavior is important in any kind of learning situation. Frequently it is essential in helping students to understand why they do not do their homework, fall behind, choose to fail, or simply drop out. The examination of the reasons behind resistance is a long process that may not bear fruit within a particular course. However, it is essential that when resistance is expressed, it is immediately addressed seriously and both individually and collectively.

The relationship between resistance behavior and student motivation is a powerful one. Quite often learners who appear to be very motivated at the outset of a course lose interest and are themselves mystified by this change. Often they are afraid of failure, or they may be afraid of the burden of success. However time-consuming it may be to establish with students the level of their motivation prior to their full involvement in course work, it is well worth the effort and time. The level of motivation should be monitored throughout a learning situation, giving participants ample opportunity to reconsider their commitments and to restructure their participation.

CRITICAL HUMANISM: A LEARNING MODEL

Humanistic and values education at their best bring people in touch with their own and others' feelings and values. The focus here is on the microcosm of the students' individual lives and relationships. Critical pedagogy, on the other hand, helps people to situate themselves socially, economically, and politically in a macrocosmic sense, as members of a local and of a world community whose power is more or less circumscribed by forces beyond their individual control. Critical pedagogy points toward systemic problems that need collective action. The approach that I have named "critical humanism" synthesizes these objectives through a dialectical process between the individual and society, powerlessness and power, the inner and outer life of the person, the interplay of the private and the public, the personal and the political, and person to person.

Neither the theorists of humanistic education nor those of critical pedagogy sufficiently address the unconscious elements in human behavior. Humanistic educators refer to the unconscious elements in learning, but they do not indicate how learners may be positively affected through the process of learning by their unconscious needs being addressed. Conversely, both Maslow and Rogers indicated peripherally that the unconscious can become an obstacle to learning. Although critical pedagogy discusses the reproduction of hegemonic forms in education, it does not really explain how this reproduction is engineered. It is difficult to explain the individual processing of a systemically determined socioeconomic reality at the same time one wishes to facilitate the empowerment of individuals and the group. Unless one is satisfied with producing a purely mechanistic and systemic account of the reproduction of knowledge resembling a natural "law," it is essential to account for the learning processes that lead to transformation and those which lead to mere reproduction of knowledge.

Having examined various models of learning, I have developed a synthesis of ideas rooted in psychoanalytic theory as well as in theories of humanistic education and critical pedagogy. These theories all relate to the ways in which one conceptualizes the learners, the teachers, and the relationships of learner to learner, and learner to teacher. There are certain consistent factors in the situation of the learner, whom I will situate within a mutually informing series of three concentric circles that contribute to the production of knowledge. At the center is the "self" with a personal and biological history, born into familial relationships and an environment that influence his or her growth in specific and particular ways. People do not always directly recall the most influential experiences in their lives; these may be stored in the unconscious, where control is nonetheless exerted over choices, fears, hopes, and a multitude of individual affective proclivities.

The second circle comprises various factors that influence the way the particular society and culture situate the learner's class, race, ethnicity, and ableness, and the social construction of sexuality and gender. The individual, with his or her specific history and personal mediation of the world, often at the mercy of unconscious and unexamined but powerful feelings, comes into contact with numerous socioeconomic and cultural definitions of his/her situation. These definitions always situate the individual within the existing power structure and are maintained by systems of rewards, punishments, and/or force that mediate both the production and the quality of knowledge.

However, beyond specific definitions and social values accorded to various factors in people's lives, individually and as a group, are the ideological rationales for those structures. These rationales form the third circle and usually are implicitly rather than explicitly acknowledged in the reproduction of knowledge.

The learner, then, lives within a complicated web composed of his or her own basic affective and physical needs and desires, the various checks to those needs imposed by the realities of his/her situation in the world, and the mediation and control of powerful and often invisible ideologies. The fourth circle is where knowledge is reproduced or produced, individually or collectively. In order to produce knowledge, the learner must interrogate both the emotional and the social constructions, as well as the ideologies that maintain them, through a multidirectioned dialectical and dialogic process. In the optimum situation involving teachers and other learners, this process is facilitated through mutual sharing, each person's internal questioning, and the collective questioning of the group.

Using the above model, I will examine how the learner is situated within four learning models. The most common one in use in postsecondary education is the "talking heads" model (Figure 1). I will also discuss models of humanistic education (Figure 2) and critical pedagogy (Figure 3), ending with a presentation of my synthesis in critical humanism (Figure 4). Each model posits a different relationship between teachers, students, and the production of knowledge. In my view, three of these models omit part of the learners' and teachers' experience; that is, only a small part of each person is available to these learning processes. In the figures, the darkened areas of the illustrations indicate which parts of the people involved are opaque to or removed from the process. It is only in the synthesis of critical humanism that the whole person is fully contextualized and transparent to all participants in the collective production of knowledge at a particular time and place.

In most conventional forms of "talking heads" education, the three inner-most concentric circles are ignored. "Objectivity" has already determined that the self (the innermost circle) has no place in the production of knowl-edge. "Ultimate truths" are supposed to transcend the realities of people's concrete experiences of class, gender, ethnicity, and race. Ideology also has not been granted an overt presence in the production of knowledge, which is supposed to be value-free. Hence, Figure 1 shows the learner barricaded within the three innermost circles, and the teacher on the outside transmit-ting or reproducing static knowledge without any acknowledgment of the real dynamics of the situation. There is no production of knowledge possi-ble in this situation; the learner is merely asked to reproduce what he or she has been told, and to use this knowledge with predetermined propriety. The outermost circle, rather than being the site of the production of knowl-edge, is the medium through which established knowledge is transmitted and reproduced in a loop that is resistant to the process of questioning which would be set into motion by the first three circles.

In humanistic education (Figure 2), the learner is all self, extracontextualized and expected to intersect and overlap freely, self to self to self, with other de-contextualized learners—including the teacher. Through pooling their feelings and often working through the medium of discipline-based subject matter, humanistic learners should produce a collective knowledge based on this proc-ess. However, the fact that important signifiers such as gender, race, class, eth-nicity, ableness, and sexual orientation, as well as the values ascribed to them, are opaque and ignored, imposes serious limits on the depth and kind of knowledge which may be produced within this model in its purest forms. Nat-urally people are often aware of some of the above-mentioned signifiers. However, when they remain unaddressed, all sorts of assumptions may re-main unchallenged and unchecked.

Critical pedagogy (Figure 3) addresses all levels of the learners' experi-ence other than their specific feelings and the personal context in which those emotions have been developed. Although it is possible for learners and teachers to share their socioeconomic situations and examine them col-lectively as signifiers of powerlessness or power, the omission of attention to the nature and origin of the participants' feelings and needs often creates a kind of resistance in the participants. The failure to validate often contra-dictory or "unacceptable" feelings in a discourse based on empowerment ef-fectively cuts the participants off from their own emotional bases. Without participants' acknowledging the affective connections they feel with the subject matter, how deeply can they connect with it? With the best of inten-tions to arrive at the truth and facilitate political action, critical pedagogy has not made the important leap to an analysis of how critical thinking is

Figure 1. "Talking Heads" Pedagogy Learning Model

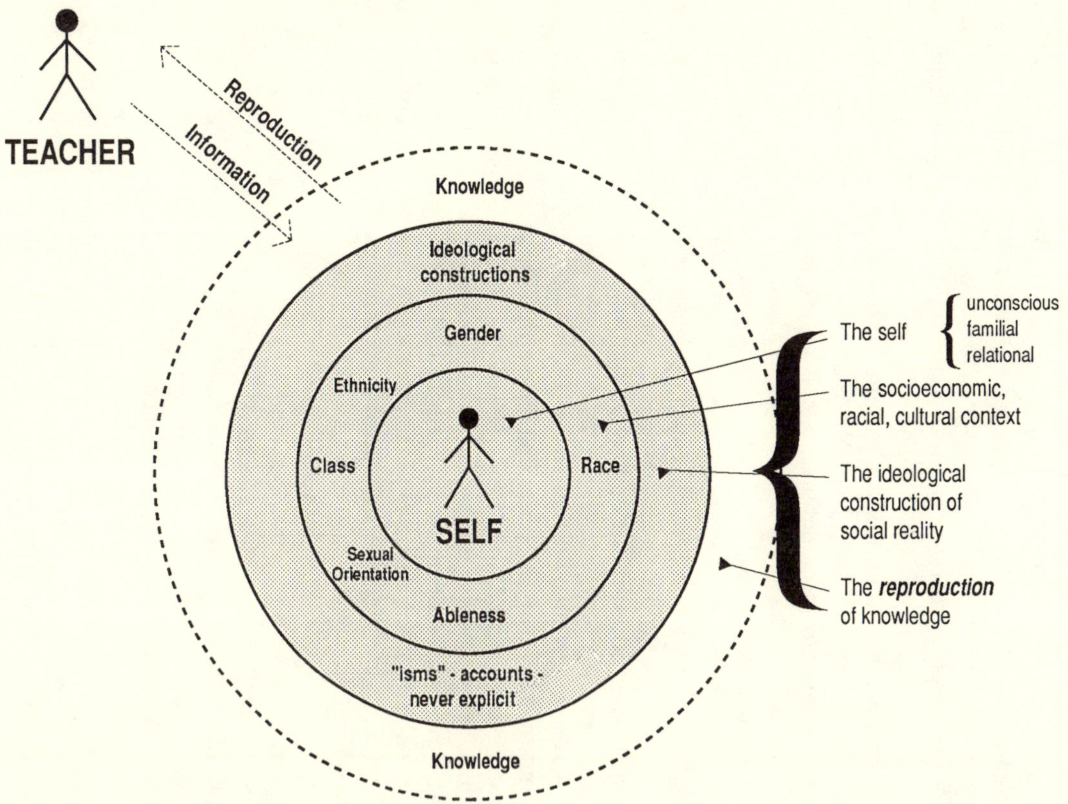

The self } unconscious familial relational

The socioeconomic, racial, cultural context

The ideological construction of social reality

The *reproduction* of knowledge

Knowledge

Ideological constructions

Gender

Race

Ethnicity

Class

SELF

Sexual Orientation

Ableness

"isms" - accounts - never explicit

Knowledge

Reproduction

Information

TEACHER

84

Figure 2. Humanistic Education Learning Model

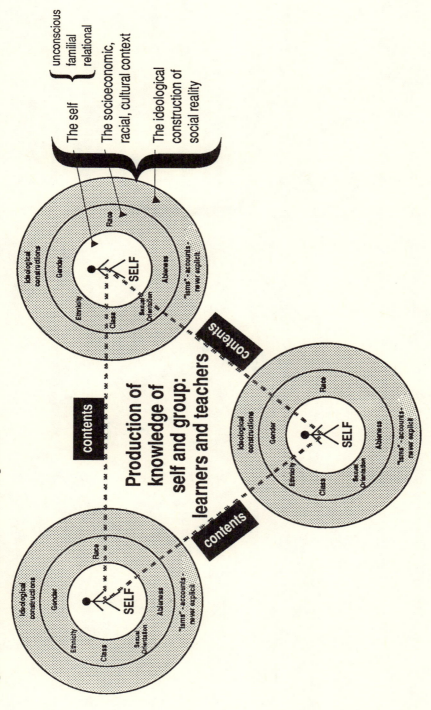

Figure 3. Critical Pedagogy Learning Model

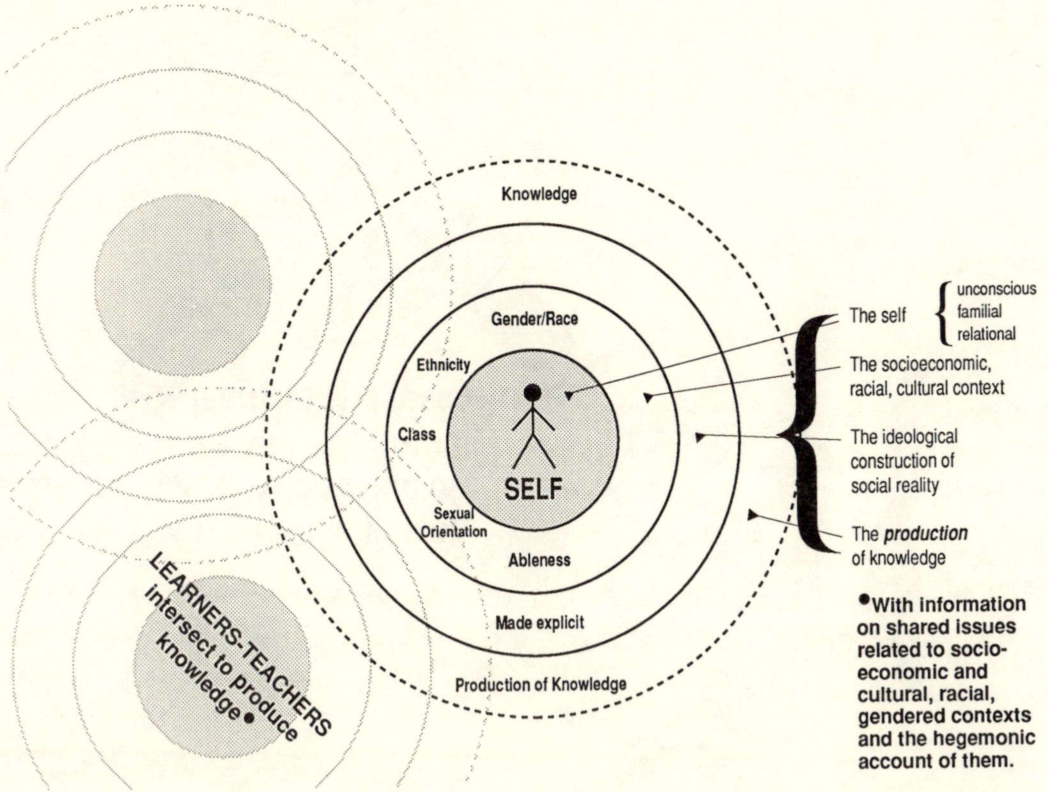

The self unconscious familial relational

The socioeconomic, racial, cultural context

The ideological construction of social reality

The *production* of knowledge

• With information on shared issues related to socio-economic and cultural, racial, gendered contexts and the hegemonic account of them.

Knowledge

Gender/Race

Ethnicity

Class

Sexual Orientation

SELF

Ableness

Made explicit

Production of Knowledge

LEARNERS-TEACHERS intersect to produce knowledge

86

Figure 4. Critical Humanism Learning Model

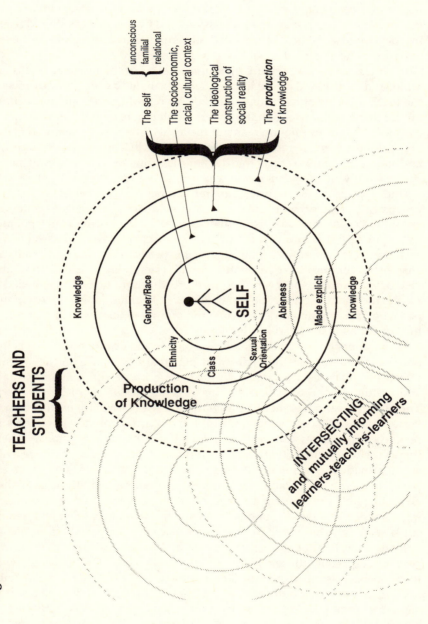

TEACHERS AND STUDENTS

unconscious
familial
relational

The self

The socioeconomic,
racial, cultural context

The ideological
construction of
social reality

The *production*
of knowledge

Knowledge

Gender/Race

Ethnicity

Class

SELF

Sexual
Orientation

Ableness

Made explicit

Knowledge

Production
of Knowledge

INTERSECTING
and mutually informing
learners-teachers-learners

internalized into the psychological landscape of each individual. The sharing of the feelings aroused by critical discourse and the acceptance of the contradiction, anger, fear, and sadness aroused by this process should result in a deepened dialectical process that adds numerous dimensions to the experience as well as to the knowledge it produces.

In critical humanism (Figure 4), multiple levels of the learners' issues are addressed and shared, according to their articulated needs. In this process, the teacher is part of each student's fourth circle of knowledge production, but it must be understood that teachers and learners intersect and dynamically inform one another on many of the levels schematized within this figure. Teachers who are receptive to this process will learn unexpected truths and should be able to recycle this dynamic learning process into both an expanded body of knowledge and a continually inventive pedagogy.[8]

Undertaking such analyses can render people very vulnerable, and groups can often provide the comforting evidence that one's experiences are shared or influenced by systemic force rather than being secret, shameful anomalies. It is also helpful to hear how others have addressed or resolved certain issues; the knowledge that is produced in such dialogue can change the composition of each individual's interior life, social context, and ideological position, and can then incite further production of knowledge for the individual and for the group. Thus, critical humanism is a dynamic pedagogy for creating an ever-widening and more subtly shaded production of individual and collective knowledge.

For teachers and learners to address one another authentically, it is important to understand the bedrock of personal experience and feeling on which personalities are formed. To be sure, each person holds important and frequently oppressive affiliations to gender, class, ethnicity, and race. The notion of empowerment holds within it the potential for each person to define his or her own situation. The application of broad stereotypes to people's experiences can be violating to them, creating resistance where there was none before. Teachers and students alike should resist the fast answers provided by generalized assumptions and check out how others experience their gender, race, class, sexual orientation, and ethnicity. Unless all participants can share in an atmosphere of acceptance where the meanings ascribed to their affiliations are viable to them, discussion will remain superficial and there is little possibility of real transformation.

Many aspects of people's lives carry a high emotional content in certain contexts, especially those which are systemically controlled by people with more socially ascribed power—like teachers. Unless learners are encouraged to express their authentic voices, they are in fact prudent to resort to stances of resistance, lack of motivation, disengagement, passivity, and/or aggression. The more opportunistic students quickly learn how to reproduce those voices which are validated within the system. It is important to provide group members with the opportunity to share information they consider central to their own lives regarding their childhoods, their family situations, their friendships and love relationships, their sexual orientations, their financial situations, their health, their aspirations, and their loyalties. One cannot demand all this information in one sitting. However, it is possible to make openings for participants to share their own particular life experiences and relate them, often with the help of their peers, to their feelings as well as to their sociopolitical situations. Making these connections removes numerous obstacles to thought and communication within a group, and provides a fund of common knowledge on which a group can build its collective and referential wisdom and support system.

While all the general questions and issues addressed by critical pedagogy are of importance in critical humanism, they must be enlarged to include questions such as: Who am I? What have been the most formative factors in my own development? Which of these are individual and which are systemic? How do I feel when I have been diminished by a person or a situation? What actions and choices can be impelled by specific feelings? By whose criteria am I making my value judgments? If they are not mine, why am I appropriating them? In whose interests am I acting, and whose "voices" are telling me what to do? What are my feelings about countering authority, and where do they come from? What part of me craves emancipation, and how does this feel?

These questions can lead to painful "reliving" and "refeeling." Great sensitivity and supportiveness are required of the educational facilitator as well as a sense of trust in the group and its collective wisdom. Great patience is also needed to help people work through the layers of their own resistance to this kind of "reexperience" and their fear of change. This kind of openness and patience is important in all group members, and a transformational teacher should be able to model it at its best. This requirement should pose no deterrent to anyone who is passionately interested in education. Rather, the transformative educator should welcome an approach based on this synthesis, which moves freely from the individual personal to the collective systemic, and back from such "factual interpretation" to the feelings it evokes. This approach offers the widest range of possibility in helping teachers and students become agents of change in their own lives and the lives of their communities.

Critical humanism starts with individual feelings, which are brought into contact with external forces that then contribute to the form those feelings take. Through the dialectical analysis of individual and collective experience, a locus of authentic discourse may be established within any group. When this is successfully carried out, members of the group find resources within themselves not only to improve their own understanding but also to contribute to others'. This in itself is an empowering experience. Only then is it possible to have meaningful intellectual discussions on how people's lives are mediated and controlled by those social definitions and institutions which serve the needs of a ruling class. When these explanations are attached to personal experiences and feelings, the ensuing insights become catalysts for change in people's attitudes, self-esteem, and courage to engage in projects for change.

The next chapters of this book will provide numerous examples of how critical humanism works in its application in various kinds of learning situations within the New School.

NOTES

1. Somer Brodrib and Micheline de Sève, *Women's Studies in Canada: A Guide to Women's Studies Programmes and Resources at the University Level* (Toronto: RFR/DRF [Ontario Institute for Studies in Education], 1987), p. 3.

2. Women's Studies College, State University of New York at Buffalo, "All-Women Classes and the Struggle for Women's Liberation," in *Learning Our Way: Essays in Feminist Education*, ed. Charlotte Bunch and Sandra Pollack (Trumansburg, NY: Crossing Press, 1983), p. 62.

3. Florence Howe, "Feminist Scholarship: The Extent of the Revolution," in *Learning Our Way: Essays in Feminist Education*, ed. Charlotte Bunch and Sandra Pollack (Trumansburg, NY: Crossing Press, 1983), pp. 101ff.

4. Frances Maher, "Classroom Pedagogy and the New Scholarship on Women," in *Gendered Subjects: The Dynamics of Feminist Teaching*, ed. Margo Culley and Catherine Portugues (London: Routledge and Kegan Paul, 1985), p. 41.

5. Margo Culley, Arlyn Diamond, Lee Edwards, Sara Lennox, and Catherine Portugues, "The Politics of Nurturance," in *Gendered Subjects: The Dynamics of Feminist Teaching*, ed. Margo Culley and Catherine Portugues (London: Routledge and Kegan Paul, 1985), p. 216.

6. For an extensive discussion of this, see Margrit Eichler, "The Relationship between Sexist, Non-sexist, Woman-Centered, and Feminist Research in the Social Sciences," in *Women and Men: Interdisciplinary Readings on Gender*, ed. Greta Hofmann Nemiroff (Toronto: Fitzhenry and Whiteside, 1986).

7. Marcia Westcott, "Women's Studies as a Strategy for Change: Between Criticism and Vision," in *Theories of Women's Studies*, ed. Gloria Bowles and Renate Duelli Klein (London: Routledge and Kegan Paul, 1983), p. 211.

8. Here I would like to acknowledge the contributions of my friend and colleague, Frances Davis, to the articulation of this learning model. Through our research and dialogues on gender-fair pedagogy and education, my original ideas have become more refined. Our dialogue of twenty-nine years is so mutually informing and so seamless that it is often impossible to sort out who said what.

PART TWO

IDEOLOGY AND PRACTICE AT THE NEW SCHOOL: A CASE STUDY

7

The Dialectical Relationship
between Ideology and Praxis

When we talk about needs, we mean something more than just the basic necessities of human survival. We also use the word to describe what a person needs in order to live to their full potential. What we need in order to survive, and what we need in order to flourish are two different things.[1]

IDEOLOGY AND PRAXIS AT THE NEW SCHOOL must be considered with the knowledge that the school exists within the context of a particular college with a particular history upon which it is dependent for every facet of its existence. The school cannot decide *not* to confer credits, or to cease existing, or to limit or increase the number of students and faculty. In fact, we must compete against other programs for resources. Many of these programs have the support of external credentializing professional associations for their career students. The college itself is dependent on the state's assessment of its needs, which must be supported by both the Ministry of Higher Education and Technology and the Treasury Board of Quebec.

The most obviously problematic aspect of our situation is our decreasing access to full-time faculty since 1982, when teacher work loads were increased throughout the college system. As a consequence our faculty became increasingly fragmented, and its members were shared with other departments in the college, often under difficult working conditions involving a great deal of travel from campus to campus across the city. These changes also meant that many gifted teachers who were instrumental in formulating the school's philosophy were affected by cutbacks and were somewhat arbitrarily replaced by people who had little sympathy with our philosophy and who, in a time of tremendous professional insecurity, were reluctant to take on new methodologies. On the other hand, because of the critiques of faculty members, we have undergone revisions and elaborations that have been very useful.

It would therefore be incorrect to assume that the ideology of the New School has simply been cobbled out of the writers, ideas, and practices described in the preceding chapters. Rather, its ideology has developed dialectically through the presence of numerous students and situations that have precipitated both discussion among and action by teachers whose contributions come from diverse belief systems: Islam, High Church Anglicanism, Roman Catholicism, Reform and Orthodox Judaism, atheism, agnosticism, personally conceived mysticism, and Rosicrucianism. There have been socialists, Trotskyites, laissez-faire capitalists, communists, anarchists, militant unionists and antiunionists, apolitical people and individualists with a clear contempt for politics or the public sphere. There have been pacifists and believers in nuclear deterrence; there have been male supremacists and feminists; there have been neo-Freudians and behaviorists, believers in social determinism and believers in absolute free will; and there has been a wide spread of class and ethnic origins.

On the whole, however, there has usually been a level of professionalism among the staff that has rendered them amenable to trying to work in concert, contributing to the development of basic structures rooted in the origins of the school. Later, I will discuss the historical development of each of the three essential sites for the praxis of the school's dialectically developing ideology: the bands, the learning groups, and the New School community itself.

It is important to relate the belief system of the school to the ideological positions described previously and to illustrate by actual examples how ideology may manifest itself through situations that arise within the school. In practice, ideology at the New School falls somewhere between the individualism of Maslow and Rogers and the collectivism of the critical theorists. Our first relationship with the student is a personal one when he or she is interviewed for acceptance into the school. We are not particularly interested in academic records except that they conform to the criteria set by the college in adherence to general CEGEP policy. We look for candidates who demonstrate an understanding of our objectives and an appetite for our methodology by a desire to grow, a willingness to try new experiences, to risk caring for others, and to contribute to a community. We do not accept people who appear to be seriously mentally ill, totally unmotivated, or addicted to drugs or alcohol. It must be said, though, that we may not find out about such proclivities until the students have been accepted. We have found that we have limited capacities to help such people and that they tend to drain attention from those learners who can enhance their lives by attending the New School. This is an important point, because frequently such people are attracted to us in the mistaken belief that we are a

Summerhillian school (although they might never have heard of that proto-type) where they will receive credentials without being forced to extend themselves beyond their current situations.

We are also reluctant to accept people whose ideological positions are rig-idly hostile to ours; too much time may be spent in fruitless argument that could be better spent working with students who are interested in exploring their own possibilities of growth. While we are willing to facilitate our stu-dents' arriving at articulation of highly variable value systems, we cannot allow them to harm others or themselves, no matter how sincere their be-liefs may be. While we encourage personal growth and personal empower-ment, we insist that these aspirations do not thrive at the expense of other people's well-being, regardless of the benefits subjectively described by learners. It is not our experience that each individual's notion of self-actual-ization leads toward the "psychological health . . . spiritual peace and social harmony" described by Maslow.[2]

Because we believe self-actualization to be the result of a dialectical rela-tionship between the inner person (complete with an individual psycholog-ical and social history) and the rigorous exigencies of a particular social, economic, and political context, we attempt to create an environment in which the students feel sufficiently safe to articulate their beliefs, needs, and feelings and to receive thoughtful feedback from each other and the facilitators. We always insist that the individual is the ultimate authority on his/her own life, even to the point of making choices we might perceive as self-denying or disempowering. The only exception to this rule of thumb is in the case where students endanger themselves before the law, endanger the well-being of the school, or are in life-threatening situations. In such cases, we intervene and often seek help for the students outside of the school.

Like Rogers, we believe that people can accept changes in their lives only when they are ready for them. We encourage students to peel away all the impositions of "other voices," of other people's expectations of and impera-tives for them, and to reach within themselves and articulate their real feel-ings and desires. While we tend to subscribe to the Blakean-Sumerhillian notion of people as basically good and tending toward health, we also rec-ognize that by the time people reach the ages of seventeen to twenty-two, they may have been very damaged by their experiences and may be only marginally receptive to risking the kind of trustingness and reaching to other people for the perceptions and feedback necessary for the informed self-confrontation that is an important stage in personal growth and empowerment. Self-actualization, personal growth, and empowerment de-mand a very difficult and lengthy process and discipline that continue throughout one's life. Sometimes people must reexperience and re-view feelings or happenings with a more objective and critical eye. Sometimes teachers at the New School must be not only bearers of painful social mem-

ories but also catalysts for the consideration of painful personal memories
that impede personal growth.

Often we must address important questions with the students, such as:
Whose interest did a particular situation serve? How did they feel about a
situation when it happened, and how do they feel now? Was it what they
wanted for themselves? What choices did they have then? Would they have
other choices now? What concrete changes can they make and, more important, do they wish to make? Often the objective view of other people can
help bring a situation into focus.

Linda was explaining in women's studies class why she could not keep up with her
homework. Some years before, her parents had divorced. Her father, a man of some
means, was providing only minimum support to her mother, Linda, and her sister,
with the result that all three women had to work hard to make ends meet. Her
mother had a low-paying job as a clerk, and Linda and her sister worked as cashiers
on Thursday and Friday nights and all day Saturday. Although the group sympa-
thized with her plight, it was pointed out that she had other free nights and Sun-
days to do her homework. But it was not so simple: the girls had to cook for their
father on Sunday through Wednesday nights. He had told them that he couldn't eat
dinners they hadn't prepared for him. Although he had not threatened his daughters, they were under the impression that if they did not feed him, he would stop
giving them financial support.

What about the nights they couldn't cook for him, someone asked. What did he
eat then? Linda didn't know; she supposed he didn't eat. "He must be very emaci-
ated," I observed, "going without dinner three days a week,"

"Not at all," Linda replied. "He's very overweight. He must weigh about 300
pounds."

Then she paused and looked stricken; she understood. Her father was getting fed
somewhere! Linda is a very intelligent young woman. Clearly the problem was not
that she couldn't figure out her father's eating habits, but that the anger, fear, and
guilt associated with her feelings about him blinded her to his manipulation. After
several further discussions on the subject in the group and between Linda and her
sister, the two young women decided to confront their father and tell him that they
could not afford both to support themselves and to feed him. Their world did not
collapse; in fact, their father undertook to feed himself and eventually decided to
give his daughters better financial support for their education.

There are many ways of approaching this situation: through a feminist
analysis of divorce and how it penalizes women and children; through analyzing the systemic factors that make the mother unskilled and poor while
Linda's father is able to command a large salary; through examining the
factors of gender socialization that make it difficult for Linda and her sister
to resist assuming the female role of nurturer. There are also numerous psychological dimensions to the situation: What is going on with the obese father that he feels he has to command Linda's attention in such a role
reversal? What needs of hers are served by this scenario? Can Linda extri-

cate herself from her parents' continuing conflicts, in which she has been consistently used as a pawn? Is it permissible to say "no" to a parent? What would be the most desirable relationship she could have with her father? How would this affect her mother? In short, given an analysis of all the factors listed above, what can Linda do to improve her situation at school and her feelings within her life situation? Over the term, all these and more issues were addressed in relation to Linda's situation with very positive and empowering results.

However, not all situations that are raised have such positive endings. The process of addressing issues is a familiar one: in dealing with presenting problems (falling behind with one's homework, in this case), students are asked to analyze the reasons for their recalcitrance. We do not proceed on the notion that people are "lazy"; we explore the situation together, trying to understand the motivation for self-destructive behavior. We then explore possible reasons and remedies for the situation. The process frequently involves great sadness, crying, and often jubilation as well. My own memory of Linda's look of amazement and delight when she discovered that her father was eating behind her back has remained an inspiration to me in the intervening years, often giving me the energy to continue to pursue lines of thought in difficult situations. Other students took part in the discussion and were able to apply parts of it to their lives. The analysis of a barrier to self-control, self-improvement, empowerment, and possible self-actualization in the life of one member of the class may become a catalyst for numerous revelations in other lives. It has the potential to be recycled many times over within the lives of all the participants.

Discussion of people's lives can lead to greater insight and sometimes to action. However, there are times when the issues raised by students fall far beyond the remedial abilities of the school or a particular group. This is especially true in cases of people whose lives have been beleaguered with poverty, familial abandonment, powerlessness, and physical and/or sexual abuse. People with such issues predominant in their lives are too focused on the lower levels of the Maslovian hierarchy of needs to exert immediate energy toward self-actualization. Although immediate remediation is rarely possible for people with very far-reaching problems, the discussion of them within the school is often very empowering for various reasons: often other people have had similar experiences and can share ways in which they have addressed them. The fact that others have had similar experiences is often empowering in that it removes from an individual a sense of personal culpability or shame. The revelation that certain situations are related to systemic oppression (poverty, family violence, and even abandonment) is often very liberating. This revelation might not resolve a particular presenting problem, but it might help direct an individual to a group, a helping agency, or even an explanation that renders the problem more manageable.

Peter has been looking out the window all afternoon, ignoring the discussion swirling around him in the room. Eventually the facilitator says to him, "Peter, you don't seem to be with us today. Is something wrong?"

Peter is silent for a moment, then says, "There is exactly five dollars between me and the street." It emerges that he has no more money, that he is being evicted from his apartment, and that he is quite paralyzed. He does not know what to do. He has no family to turn to for help. His father is long gone, and his mother is sick and lives on a small pension. He does not like to burden the group with his problems, he says.

On further discussion, it turns out that Peter has always been a "poor kid" living on the edge of a middle-class neighborhood and going to a middle-class school. He was the only kid without a bicycle in his class. He spent days making up stories about why he did not have a bicycle. What emerges is Peter's terrible shame at a poverty that is not his fault.

There is discussion of poverty, of why people are ashamed of it, and of whether they should be. The group examines the anger some members express at parents who could not or would not provide for them and the guilt provoked by this anger. Some attention is paid to the options particular parents may have in our society. Other students ask Peter if he would like a job and what he can do. Several people know of jobs and offer to accompany Peter to interviews. It is stressed that it is not for individuals to feel ashamed of their poverty, but that poverty exists to the shame of society. It is also emphasized that if people do not know of your needs, they cannot help you. Looking out the window is an ineffectual way of asking for help.

In such a situation of complex systemic oppression, it is important to develop with the group a conceptual vocabulary that addresses not only the socioeconomic factors in Peter's situation but also the feelings such situations evoke. It is only then that one can address what action Peter might like to take on a personal and/or collective basis. It is particularly important that the group develop its own tools of analysis and that the facilitator resist the interpolation of already established descriptives that may not be recognizable to the students. At the end of that term, Peter decided to get a full-time job and attend college at night. While it meant leaving the New School, it also meant that he was finally ready to take charge of his life. While we would prefer to see a society where Peter's kind of situation would be impossible, we also thought his decision to become more financially secure was a sign of growth. In this case, through the application of the principles of critical humanism, the distraction of a student became a learning experience for him and the rest of his group.

While it is important for people to become aware of introjecting others' values into their lives, there are many times when their values are culture-based; repudiating them would mean that the individual would leave a primary cultural group. While this might in some cases be a viable choice, it is a delicate situation with very serious ramifications. At the New School, we discuss ethnicity and culture and facilitate the consideration of how individuals feel about cultural imperatives within their lives and the cost of denying them. Often our students experience a double dissonance: they are children of immigrants living within a private culture different from the public one; they also give voice to values they cannot always bring into line with their reality. It is important to acknowledge that cultural values from the "old country" have worked somewhere, sometime, and should not be diminished because they comprise an honest heritage. The cost of dropping values and customs must be considered. This kind of discussion is important for the self-acceptance necessary to personal growth and empowerment. It is also instructive to people from different cultures, who can begin to appreciate the reasons behind behaviors that may look strange from a distance.

Most people in our society voice the desire to be happy. While we hope for the alleviation of pain among our students as well as the development of their capacity for happiness, unlike Neill and Leonard, we do not consider happiness or ecstasy to be the sole aim of life. It is our observation that young people want to find meaning and purpose for their lives. By the combination of humanistic and critical approaches, we work toward helping our students become skilled at accessing their feelings, which are often disconfirmed by those they love and depend upon the most. We must help them to articulate their needs, identify their strengths and resources, and define objectives for themselves, making use of their own strengths and the resources within their environment to realize these objectives.[3]

No matter how they express the necessity of establishing a life's meaning, all the writers discussed in this study acknowledge that the search for, the creation of, and the commitment to meaning constitute a long-term and ongoing process throughout one's life.

Dewey considered the development of individual power "to select and order means to carry chosen ends into operation" an essential factor in the fullest exercise of self-control, the ultimate aim of education.[4] This view is of great importance to the existential thinkers, who see the creation of meaning as the only way in which a subject can fill the existential void with meaning. "Without perception of the unique meaning of his singular existence, a person would be numbed in difficult situations. . . . Work usually represents the area in which the individual's uniqueness stands in relation to society and thus acquires meaning and value."[5]

Maslow and Rogers tend to give similar value to the notion of a "life's work" in which the "discovery of identity" is concomitant with the "discovery of vocation."[6] Maslow also identifies an almost mystical sense of wonder and awe that can inform life with meaning. To Rogers, meaning evolves from the person's discovering and expressing his/her own authenticity.

The early writers in the field of values clarification appear to believe that meaning can be achieved through learning strategies that will help people to arrive at decisions which are "personally satisfying and socially constructive."[7] It is our experience that values clarification techniques can be helpful in giving focus to student choices and student interaction. Values clarification, it seems to me, can often illuminate past choices and point the way for immediate action, but it cannot always deliver a long-term project of meaning. It is, in my view, exceptionally valuable in facilitating group organization on both formal and informal levels, taking into account individual feelings of group members as well as the tasks set before a group.

In the early days of the school, there was a Community Council to which each band had to elect a member. In this particular band, the facilitator's report that the bands had been asked to choose representatives was met by silence until Eric spoke up. "I'll represent the band," he said. The facilitator asked if this was agreeable to everyone.

"Well I don't think . . . ," began Lurlene after a pause, and then was silent.

"Do you have an objection?" the facilitator asked Lurlene. "Would you like to run, yourself?" she added.

"It isn't that." Lurlene was hesitant. "It's just that I don't think someone like Eric could represent someone like me."

"Why not?" asked Eric, somewhat defensively.

"Well, you're always talking about your car and your holidays in Europe or the Caribbean or Florida. My mother immigrated here from Grenada because we were so poor there. We can't afford to go back there for holidays. She's got no husband and five kids, and she works as a nurse's aid in a hospital. All us kids have had to work for our clothes and spending money since we were twelve. I just don't think you know what it's like, that's all."

"Yeah," contributed Aldo, "your old man's the kind of guy my old man shovels his driveway in the winter."

"You know what I think?" rejoined Eric. "I think you're all prejudiced against me. It's not my fault my father's rich. I still think I can understand your lives. You're just jealous of me."

It was clear that Eric was sincerely insulted and confused. It was not obvious that he had ever before objectively considered his situation of privilege. There was enormous tension in the room, and the task of choosing a representative had to be completed that day. Moreover, most members of the group were silent because they did not want to "take sides." The facilitator suggested that there were many criteria on which one chose representatives in a democracy. The one criterion in this band seemed to be that of equality. People did not believe they could be represented by those more privileged than they were.

But how many people really believed in absolute equality? With a piece of chalk she drew a line down the center of the floor. This line was to represent the notion of absolute equality of all people. Members of the band were to place themselves where they felt in terms of equality and explain their position to others. The facilitator took the first turn by placing herself close to the line but a bit to the right of it, explaining that she would not feel comfortable being politically represented by retarded adults.

Other people explained their positions; no one was fully on the "absolute equality" line. After all the members had explained their positions, they were asked to sit down and reflect, and then to take a position after having considered all the discussion that had transpired. Most people showed some modification of their positions. They had listened and reflected. It was clear that no one had the corner on political purity.

This exercise taught the group many things: that class differences not only exist but are important to everyone; that if a group allows a power vacuum to develop, someone will usually undertake to fill that vacuum, and the "somebody" might not be the best choice for the group; that people should speak up when they disagree; that it is important to reflect and insist on criteria for representation. The feelings behind people's positions on equality were aired, and ultimately the group came up not only with criteria but also with a representative and a model of accountability for this representative.

Naturally the situation between Eric and Lurlene had to be somewhat resolved. This does not mean that they had to become friends, but that they could recognize that their differences did not necessarily bar them from appreciating each other's positive qualities. There was a discussion of how people often globalize their dislike of one quality in a person to a total rejection of the person rather than some aspect of the person. Finally the group did an exercise called the "positive spotlight"; each member had a moment in the "spotlight," where other members of the group could give only positive feedback of the qualities they appreciated in this individual. This was effective because not only did it rebuild Eric's and Lurlene's self-esteem, but it reinforced the self-esteem of all individuals in the group and built the group itself through a shared and multidimensional activity.

This particular exercise was extremely useful because it grew out of a group issue. It brought forth not only values but also questions that could be used to clarify people's individual values and arrive at a group position. It was useful in helping the group achieve a sense of cohesion and meaning, and a way of mediating various perceptions and needs.

The critical theorists do not entertain notions of ecstasy and personal happiness. They are concerned with social and political change. Perhaps in their view it is through civic courage that individuals may find meaning in their participation in a collective dialogical learning situation which leads to social change that de facto has conferred meaning on their participation. They do not, however, allow for any idiosyncratic reasons for people to find meaning where it responds to their innermost needs, which might be rooted in very personal and/or unconscious needs more than in collectivist utopian impulses.

The concept of "voice" articulated by the critical theorists is especially useful for the self-actualization and empowerment of young people. While there are many ways related to class, gender, race, and ethnicity in which they have been silenced, they have also been silenced because they are young and not taken seriously in our society. The participatory nature of the school ensures that students find their voices. Feedback helps them to strengthen their ability to communicate clearly, and the common expecta-

tion of their feedback to others develops excellent listening and communicating skills in our students. Because of the many hours spent in primary
affiliative groups, bands, where the lives of the members comprise the curriculum, by the time students have graduated from our program, they have
spent at least 300 hours in bands listening, reflecting, responding, being responded to, and being encouraged to find and use their own unmediated
voices.

One year many students wanted to take public speaking. They were all males and
all the children of immigrants. When the teacher asked them why they wanted so
fervently to learn public speaking, their answers were "My dad is a barber, and no
one listens to him in this society." "My father's a taxi driver, and no one cares what
he thinks." "I want people to listen to me, I want some respect in this society."

While it was essential to discuss the social-political-economic factors in
their fathers' disempowerment, it was also important to address the young
men's will to power. Where did this will come from, and how did it feel?
What did it feel like to feel powerless, and what would make them feel powerful? In what situations did they feel powerless? Were there situations
where they felt powerful? What was power? Was power the ability to rule
others? Did they have any idea of why only males had expressed an interest
in this group? Was power simply to be found in voice? What was meant by
respect?

It became clear in the discussion that while these young men did acknowledge that their fathers had immigrated and contributed their labor to
the survival of their sons, these sons wanted more than survival: they
wanted to flourish. Self-actualization meant having voices that com-
manded respect; there was no guarantee, however, that these voices would
be raised with either civic courage or utopian intent. It is our intention as
educators that by covering as many facets of voice or liberation as possible,
members of the group become conscious of the scope of issues in their lives
and that this consciousness informs not only their choices but also their behavior. Most of all, by discovering and raising their voices at the New
School, they will experience response and learn that their voices can and
should make a difference where they live and breathe.

New School students are at the age when society is pressing the young to
declare themselves: What are they going to be? These questions often fill
them with panic, and frequently they simply voice clichéd ambitions that
will mollify anxious adults in their lives. By our emphasis on meaning and
the meaningfulness of their own feelings, beliefs, choices, and actions, we
attempt to facilitate the students' consideration of the uniqueness of their
contribution, their function as members of society, and their own beliefs,
values, joys, and interests as they slowly begin to formulate the terms on
which they will decide their present and future being.

NOTES

1. Michael Ignatieff, *The Needs of Strangers* (New York: Penguin Books, 1984), p. 10.

2. Abraham H. Maslow, *The Farther Reaches of Human Nature* (New York: Penguin Books, 1966), p. 363.

3. The process described here is very similar to that described by Clark Moustakas in his *Teaching as Learning* (New York: Ballantine Books, 1972), p. 73.

4. John Dewey, *Experience and Education* (London: Collier Books, 1938), pp. 35ff.

5. Viktor E. Frankl, *The Doctor and the Soul*, trans. Richard Winston and Clara Winston (New York: Random House, Vintage Books, 1973), pp. 117–18.

6. Maslow, pp. 176–77.

7. Howard Kirschenbaum, "In Support of Values Clarification," in *Innovations in Education: Reformers and Their Critics*, ed. John Martin Rich, 3rd ed. (Boston: Allyn and Bacon, 1981), p. 272.

8

Clientele, the Agenda of the State, and Pedagogy at the New School

It is because fraternity, love, belonging, dignity and respect cannot be specified as rights that we ought to specify them as needs and seek, with the blunt institutional procedures at our disposal, to make their satisfaction a routine human practice.[1]

CLIENTELE

OFTEN STUDENTS ARRIVE AT THE NEW SCHOOL with a strong sense of entitlement. They understand themselves to be entitled to something they call "my education" as in "I need my education to get ahead." It is often instructive to inquire what they mean by "ahead." The ambition is usually quite modest; just earning more than the minimum wage, having a future that promises the necessary resources for access to "state of the art" consumer goods. During their CEGEP years, most students are willing to work hard at part-time jobs in order to have those talismanic objects which they think will confer meaning on their lives and status on themselves. Increasingly over the years, we have observed that many of our students are more immediately committed to these low-paying dead-end "mall jobs" than they are to acquiring the skills they may need to realize long-term economic success, or to capitalize on opportunities for interesting work, personal growth, and social status. Learning college-level skills is sometimes difficult, requiring the ability to concentrate for lengthy periods of time and to be able to plan one's time realistically. These capacities are rarely fully developed in adolescents in our society, whose time has been planned for them and whose concentration span has been conditioned over the years to the eight–twelve minutes between television commercials. Education is seen simply as a means of getting "somewhere" beyond the work available to young part-time workers, the most vulnerable group in the labor force.

School, then, may frequently be perceived as a conduit to more satisfying commodities. While education is seen as entitlement, so is consumerism, a notion continually supported by the media to which young people are addicted. It is my impression that the desire to have increased access to "things," coupled with a reluctance to defer gratification in order to ensure future success and achievement, is partially caused by the emotional vacuums and states of alienation in which many young people seem to live.

It is important to review the Maslovian hierarchy of needs based on the satisfaction of physiological needs (food, water, sleep, physical comfort); of safety needs (stability, order, freedom from violence, disease, and disorder); of needs for "belongingness and love" (friendship, giving and receiving affection); and of self-esteem needs (recognition, respect from others, self-respect)—all of which must be satisfied in order to strive for self-actualization.[2] Maslow developed these theories primarily in the post–World War II period when there was great nostalgia in North America for a fantasized version of the family life that had been interrupted by the war. People had short and sentimental memories, often overlooking the havoc created in family unity and life by the depression of the 1930s. Customarily many of the physical and belonging-love needs were expected to be provided for children by the nuclear and extended family, by the neighborhood, and by the cultural and/or religious community. Because of the prevailing ideology of the time, Maslow had every reason to imagine the possibility of a clear, orderly, and sequential development of human potential.

Later, in *Religions, Values, and Peak Experiences* (1964), Maslow expressed an understanding that society had fallen into a "chaos of relativism" that could be called "valuelessness."[3] The period since Maslow's death in 1970 has brought even greater social change. Currently, one out of three children in the United States is a child of divorce. It is predicted that by the year 2000, one out of every two children in the United States will be in this position. While the statistics are not available for Canada, they usually follow the same trends as those of the nation to the south. This means that by the year 2000, half of the population will have undergone the trauma of family bifurcation; this should clearly have a strong effect on people's expectations of human institutions and relationships. A fifteen-year study of the effect of divorce on families conducted by Judith Wallerstein in California indicates that adolescence is a period of particularly grave risk for children in divorced families—the single most important cause they identify of enduring pain and anomie in their lives. They have been found to be left with an enduring feeling of both physical and emotional abandonment, and to continue feeling the effects of family breakdown ten to fifteen years after a separation or divorce, especially if they have witnessed family violence. In the longer run, these children appear to experience real anxiety about their own

ability to create families; this of course affects their attitude to possible positive results produced by the deferment of immediate gratification.

In the United States, children from divorced families account for an inordinately high proportion of children in mental-health treatment and in special education, of children referred by teachers to school psychologists, and
an estimated 60 percent of child patients in clinical treatment and 80 to 100
percent of adolescents in mental hospitals.[4] Parents frequently do not get
their lives on track after divorce and suffer a diminished capacity to provide
guidance and those child-rearing functions necessary to ensure the psychological health of their families. In many cases it is the child who is expected
to provide psychological support for a distressed parent.

In addition, children who remain with their mothers often experience a
serious drop in the family's standard of living that is accompanied by regular observation of a lasting discrepancy between their parents' standards of
living.[5] By no means do most children of divorce benefit from resources ex-
ceeding the minimum child support awarded by courts. In Canada, 75 percent of the child support awarded to mothers and children by courts is not
paid by fathers. Frequently children become pawns in power games between parents years after they have stopped talking to each other or have
even formed relationships with new mates.

The subjects of Wallerstein's study were economically stable, white, middle-class, educated Californians. Before divorce, the families did not have
the problems of poverty and general resourcelessness that exacerbate the
emotional problems of *all* children of divorce. Increasing numbers of our
students are from single-parent families and often have very tenuous ties
with one or both of their parents. Some of them have no contact with their
biological parents and call themselves "system kids," having been ware-
housed by social welfare agencies in foster or group homes. Even in intact
middle-class families, young people frequently are expected to provide for
their personal needs except for room and board. This means they must pay
school fees and expenses, travel expenses, and lunch, clothing, and recrea-
tional expenses themselves. Since they are not eligible for financial aid,
they must find jobs.

Many families have lived unrooted lives far from relatives, and in many
cases family stability has been permanently disrupted not only by divorce,
separation, or death but also by one or both parents' drug or alcohol abuse
or mental illness. Often young people are especially undermined by uncomfortable and ill-defined situations in blended families or disastrous ser-
ial marriages of one or both parents, and they are sometimes subject to
family-related and more public forms of sexual abuse. Statistics tell us that
one in four Canadian women will be raped at some point in her life, and
that one in five Canadian women has been a victim of childhood sexual
abuse. Many boys also are victims of family violence, or at the very least of
wounding relationships with their fathers.

Many students work to support themselves away from families or the remains of families who have the means to support them at home. Frequently their physical or psychological survival is dependent on their being removed from a pathological family situation. It is very difficult to persuade people in such situations to consider the long-range possibility that the acquisition of knowledge will improve their lives. This is especially difficult with students who have histories of poor academic performance, because frequently as children they simply could not concentrate on schoolwork. Every aspect of their lives was mediated by problems at home.

We think of belonging as permanence, yet all our homes are transient. Who still lives in the house of their childhood? . . . We think of belonging as rootedness in a small familiar place, yet home for most of us is the convulsive arteries of a great city. Our belonging is no longer to something fixed, known and familiar, but to an electric and heartless creature eternally in motion. . . . Perhaps above all we think of belonging as the end of yearning itself, as a state of rest and reconciliation with ourselves beyond the need itself.[6]

Like all young people, our students hope that somehow it will all work out in their lives. They frequently take a passive spectator role in their own lives and seem to feel powerless to effect change. Many of them love futuristic fantasy and science fiction, and yet the future seems to hold within it the promise of further alienation. It is almost impossible in this situation to set down strong roots of belongingness. Indeed, we are frequently alarmed by young people who have the ability to connect with anyone within seconds of meeting (they are experts at being moved around) but panic at the thought of closeness, of continuity, of striving.

For many young people, the pervasive presence of drugs provides an illusion of belonging, of solidarity, of meaning, and of freedom. Drugs promise an ersatz but instantly achievable sense of self-actualization and affiliation. Relationships with dealers and other users are fraught with meanings and loyalties. While most of our students are not consumers of "heavy" drugs, some of them are sufficiently regular users of marijuana and hashish for their habit to interfere with their ability to do college-level cognitive work. It is also clear that there is no young person in our urban landscape who is not fully acquainted with the language of drugs and more capable of gaining access to them than his/her teachers. By direct contact or by peer contacts to whom they may remain very loyal, increasing numbers of young people are implicated in the general violence and criminalization of our society.

Students of college age are experiencing enormous physiological, emotional, and social changes in their lives. Their bodies are still undergoing internal changes that may result in a radical change of appearance. Very often, leaving high school means parting from good friends, or at least from a context in which they occupy a unique place. Sometimes coming to college is the first time they have been consistently absent from their neighborhood on a day-to-day basis. All these factors can destabilize their sense of well-being and self-esteem. Thrown into the crucible of a large urban college, they often have difficulties maintaining a strong sense of identity. If they do not have a stable base of security in their lives, their need for self-esteem makes them vulnerable to the illusion of self-esteem provided by drugs, alcohol, and casual sex.

They also are vulnerable to an adolescent culture that markets "image" and "life-style" rather than any substantive sense of accomplishment or identity. "Image" is attainable through the possession of magical objects manufactured with the intention of creating a temporary sense of well-being. Their precarious self-esteem is in constant danger of sudden invalidation by cleverly orchestrated changes of style that will force the young consumers to struggle to recapture that ephemeral sense of well-being through buying their way into the next market-researched image. Because of their lack of long-term goals, many young people from fifteen to twenty-four years of age possess a large disposable cash income attractive to manufacturers who undertake programs of lucrative image-vending designed to maintain a constant distance between the young people's low self-esteem and idealized new versions of themselves that will keep them buying, keep them working at exploitative dead-end jobs, and keep them deferring serious education. They become increasingly deskilled for the kind of concentration required for academic work.

Frequently education is meaningful to our students only as a means of getting into a higher income bracket in order to buy more. They have been appropriated by the notion of "self-esteem through possessions." The "farther reaches of human nature" posited by Maslow become transposed into the substitution of consumerism for human solidarity. Maslow's notion of self-actualization is reachable through a slow and organic process based on individual safety and belongingness. Without extensive discussion of the emotions hidden within our students, self-actualization may very quickly become transposed into a glitzy mirage of illusory safety and well-being that is not unlike the instant nirvana promised by drug experiences or sexual orgasm.

> Being human is an accomplishment like playing an instrument. It takes practice. . . . It is a skill we can forget. A little noise can make us forget the notes. The best of us is historical; the best of us is fragile. Being human is a second nature which history taught us, and which terror and deprivation can batter us into forgetting.[7]

While many of our students are not children of divorce, sexually violated or physically abused, or continually involved in alcohol, drugs, or casual sex, most of them nonetheless have difficulty understanding the value of education-in-itself. All schools have the mission (whether they recognize it or not!) of piercing the prevalent notion of education-as-entitlement-to-esteem-through-possessions and somehow celebrating the value of knowledge and of understanding the universe.

While it is possible and desirable at this juncture to undertake with the students a project of critical pedagogy regarding the source of their values and whose interests are met by them, it is our experience that it takes much more than intellectual argumentation to convince people to give up comforting fantasies which have been created to compensate for the absence in their lives of the real human entitlements: comfort, safety, community, respect, love, self-esteem, and the ability to form independent judgments based on an unmediated understanding of their personal interests and needs. Such change may devolve only from reexperiencing in full awareness the lacks they are trying to fill. Critical humanism brings to bear on their lives the critical pedagogy described earlier, as well as a pedagogy of the emotions that connects them to the innermost roots of value and behavior within themselves.

THE AGENDA OF THE STATE

At the New School we have developed a pedagogy that is designed to address the students' deepest feelings and the experiences and realities within which they are rooted. This holistic pedagogy has as its objective addressing the students' emotional lives through individual and group work in the bands and in the learning groups, where all learning should evolve "from self to subject," from the students' innermost needs to the pursuit of learning about a subject that will illuminate their understanding.

Our survival, and the survival of this last alternative program in the college system, depend on our ability to flourish within a political context that negates the very values on which we are based. It is ironic that many of our concerns are overtly shared by those bodies which determine state policy on education. A report on the failure and/or dropout rate in the CEGEPs acknowledges that only 59 percent of all students entering college receive a diploma.[8] The report attempts to explain the reasons for the low success rate of a very costly educational system in various ways, the first of which is through characterizing the student and his/her values:

Today's student must situate himself in a society that has undergone a shock to values which in the past were considered fundamental. Spiritual values, in the widest sense of the term, are no longer surrounded by the same aura of prestige as before, and this change is reflected in the students' attitudes to school. If the youngster who goes to college today is a citizen in a society strongly based on consumerism and on utilitarianism, he also has his own personal values. . . .

On the other hand, the needs and expectations of today's student are conditioned by an economic situation which is in a state of constant evolution. The diploma for which he is working is no longer, as before, a passport which will offer him the guarantee of obtaining full-time, stable, interesting, and well paid employment at the end of his studies.

In this context, we must not be surprised that for the student, at the threshold of adult life, studies are not always his only or his principal interest. His life is composed alternately of studies, leisure, paid work and other occupations which contribute, each in its way, to fulfilling his different individual needs but also to fulfilling his role as a consumer.[9]

Beneath the pompous generalizations of this profile, one can very clearly see the complicity of the state and the business community. Consumerism has become a nationally defined "need." There is no effort to analyze what "needs" are defined by the students and whose interests are served by them. For this reason, it is unlikely that the Quebec educational establishment will launch a systemic effort to provide the students with an argument for the values inherent in simply knowing more about the world, its past, and how it functions, and learning to pose critical radical questions regarding the status quo. It is precisely because the values are dictated by the combined manipulations of government and industry in a free-market economy that consumerism is emphasized concomitantly with training for jobs at the college level. The utmost cynicism is to be found in the caveat that no one is guaranteed a full-time, stable, and interesting job upon graduation.

The report also identifies seven important reasons why students fail and/or drop out of school: their past school experience; the shock of passage from secondary school to CEGEP; the fragmented organization of studies at the CEGEP level; the motivation and academic aspirations of the students; the economic situation of the students and their employment; the teachers; and the milieu of the colleges.[10] While these reasons for student dropout and failure are all recognizable, it is nonetheless suprising that the report makes no mention of the general social disorganization in which many young people live. Drugs are not mentioned at all. The report does, however, mention the fact that increasing numbers of students work between twenty and thirty-five hours per week, which greatly affects their ability to perform well within the college system. It does not investigate why the young are working so much, or how many of them are working for the basic necessities of survival and how many for the disposable income they need to feel self-esteem.

I suspect that a substantial number of students, who are working more hours than they need to survive or even to have some disposable income, are simply placing their bets on several horses. As Canadians they feel entitled to a good standard of living and lives as charmed as those beamed to them on television. In the long run, they want the insurance policy of "their education" (which even the government claims bears no promise of financial reward). Since they are unable to defer gratification sufficiently to try to "make it" in any substantive way, they must labor to acquire ephemeral instant reinforcers of a desirable "image" and "life-style."

While governments will certainly continue to undertake studies of students, it is very difficult for them to arrive at remedial solutions without incurring greater expense. This is a highly undesirable result for governments, which are trying to trim their expenses in order to reduce (or not increase) enormous deficits. Perhaps asking the state to address the real issues that render so many of the students incompetent, and thus impoverish current and future generations, is somewhat like asking the wolf to baby-sit Red Riding Hood. When it deems such action necessary, the state can always cobble together a revisionist notion of the legitimate priorities of college students that can miraculously validate the changing priorities of the state itself.

THE PEDAGOGICAL RESPONSE OF THE NEW SCHOOL

I think the New School has made me more open-minded . . . that those are values and they're within me and those have been recognized and they surfaced here. I remember the first time I was here, the first thing I thought . . . was, "My God, I'm in business for myself!" That's what the feeling was. Like coming from the working world, I always felt that I was in business for someone else, and it was true. I felt so good thinking that I was coming to school. It was, "Yeah, I'm in business for myself." . . . It's like here you have to make more effort . . . to spend yourself, just to spend your own talents and your own energy. It's a great feeling.[11]

At the New School I learned that each person, each individual, was very important and worthy of special attention and care, because that's basically the kind of care we got at the New School.[12]

It's really giving you the occasion, probably for the first time in your life, to consider your identity in the real world, in the world away from your family, and the New School requires that you consider who you are honestly. You can't do less because people in your band get to know you so well that . . . you'd have to be honest. You don't have a choice but to admit to certain things, and so it's difficult, it's really difficult to explain, but I think that it has a lot to do with providing a safe environment in which to look at aspects of yourself. Then you form relationships as a way of testing . . . those aspects. . . . I guess what I'm saying is that perhaps the relationships are as lasting as they are because of that foundation of honesty, of candidness, of being exposed.[13]

It's expected and anticipated that you will look beyond yourself and look to other people, take responsibility for the growth of others as well as your own growth, as it's expected others will do that for you. You can't leave without taking it with you, and I think it's certainly something that affects every part of your life in a very fundamental way as you go on—be it work, be it daily relationships or encounters, be it school. I think it really is a tool and a training that stays with you.[14]

I really think I'm taking a strong awareness of people and the earth [from the school]. I've developed a compassion for the people and the earth as a whole and I've learned a lot about . . . [those subjects] here, and I always plan to have those strong feelings and will always try to do what I can for peace and solidarity.[15]

As these quotations indicate, students are often initially surprised to see that they are expected to be responsible and accountable for and to themselves and others in the community. The school also communicates to them an expectation that self-disclosure in a safe and accepting environment is an important means of arriving at self-knowledge, personal growth, and authentic relationships with other people. Students soon hear that there is a dialectical relationship between personal growth, the growth of others, and the creation of community. Finally, students are exposed to the fact that they can make a difference wherever they are, and that humans have a responsibility to the living and those still to live, that our stewardship of the present is important. It is our contention that by helping the students to build the skills necessary for living authentic lives determined by their own values and beliefs in peaceful community with others, we will help them to create, find, and maintain meaning in their lives and make commensurate contributions to the society.

One of the abiding clichés of liberalism, and one held by mainstream educational ideology, is the tenet that if one wants something enough, one will get it. Naturally the logical end of this train of thought is that those who do not "succeed" in our society are emotionally lazy and have succumbed complacently to their oppression. "Underprivileged" students bombarded with this doctrine cannot develop very high self-esteem with such explanations of their situation. Indeed, in a society that invalidates their environment, their "cultural capital," and often their race, ethnicity, and gender, they get a message that they and theirs simply have not tried hard enough. I have noticed that they are often shocked when I ask them who they think works harder, the director general of our college or the cleaners.

Doctrines of "mind over matter" are morally irresponsible in a world where "matter" threatens us continually with annihilation far beyond our power to contain it by feats of personal and individual will. We do not encourage the students to imaginary power or self-esteem based on chimera; rather, by a pedagogy developed (and still developing) over seventeen years and continually refined to meet their changing needs, we work with the students to develop individually and collectively those tools they will need to liberate themselves from low self-esteem and social values that work against their individual and collective interests.

It must be said that the age of New School students lends itself to openness, to change, and to a desire to explore. Finishing high school is always a time of reflection and choice for young people. Will they continue in school? What do they wish to become? Do they want to work? To what extent can they risk making choices that will alienate or disappoint their parents? Should they move away from home . . . travel . . . live with a mate? Indeed, it would be amazing if no change were to happen between the ages of seventeen and twenty-two, the average age range of our students. It is important at this juncture in the development of young people to intervene with ideas and experiences that will broaden their world beyond the narrow confines of the consumerism which has dominated their lives since they saw their first television advertisement.

The students who enter the New School often come from a situation of disenchantment with the regular high school or college programs. They will say they "do not want to be treated as a number," or that they feel "lost" and disconfirmed in the regular academy. One transfer student said about his experience at the New School:

I got a certain amount of confidence because I was validated as a person, whereas I hadn't been in other structures. New School helped me to find the balance, to realize that no, I'm not the one with all the answers, but at the same time there's certainly value in what I have to say, and I can trust my perceptions about things.[16]

Clearly, in order to provide a realistic arena for such explorations and feedback, schools must give considerable space to students. Where active learning is valued, students must speak, argue, listen, discuss whatever interests them. They must also be encouraged to reflect on the reactions they elicit, to respond, and sometimes to effect changes beneficial to them. While the bands are the essential locus for such concerns, in practice we do not differentiate between "academic" subjects and personal growth. The self may be academically addressed, and the academic subjects pursued by the students must proceed from their articulated affective needs. It must also be emphasized that the students' membership in a recognizable small community is accorded great importance in our pedagogy as a locus of learning, personal growth, and political consciousness-raising.

It is generally viewed as a privilege to be in a position to facilitate growth at such a key moment in the life of a young person. Certainly many of our graduates have identified their time at the New School as the beginning of a new era in their lives:

It marked a watershed in my life. It gave me an awful lot of confidence, it let me learn a lot about myself. . . . I think of the New School as being one of the highlights of my life up to now, and I believe the skills I learned there and the types of things I spent my time doing still figure very much in my life . . . ten years later.[17]

I consider my adulthood to have started when I was at the New School, and some of the relationships that are most significant to me now began . . . at the New School.[18]

One of the things I would like to say is that often I think of my past in terms of different phases and different periods and the current period. What I would consider the modern times of my life or the contemporary times of my life seem to lengthen and lengthen because I always think of it [sic] as starting at the New School. The modern era for me started at the New School.[19]

NOTES

1. Michael Ignatieff, *The Needs of Strangers* (New York: Penguin Books, 1984), p. 13.

2. Abraham Maslow, *Towards a Psychology of Being*, 2d ed. (New York: Van Nostrand Reinhold, 1968).

3. Abraham H. Maslow, *Religions, Values, and Peak Experiences* (New York: Viking Press, 1972), p. 75.

4. Judith S. Wallerstein, "Children after Divorce: Wounds That Don't Heal," *New York Times Magazine*, January 22, 1989, pp. 41–42. Adapted from Judith S. Wallerstein, *Second Chances: Men, Women, and Children a Decade after Divorce* (New York: Ticknor and Fields, 1989).

5. Wallerstein, p. 20.

6. Ignatieff, p. 140.

7. Ibid., pp. 141–42.

8. Conseil des Collèges, *La réussite, les échecs et les abandons au collégial: L'état et les besoins de l'enseignement collégial. Rapport 1987–1988* (Québec: Gouvernement de Québec, 1988).

9. Ibid., p. 10. Translated by the author.

10. Ibid., p. 21.

11. Patrick, interview, 1985.

12. Ilona, interview, 1984.

13. Suzanne, interview, 1984.

14. Susan H., interview, 1984.

15. Rachel, interview, 1984.

16. Daniel, interview, 1984.

17. Martin, interview, 1984.

18. Suzanne, interview, 1984.

19. Ilona, interview, 1984.

9

The Primary Affiliative Group as Locus of Learning: The Bands

If you could picture about fifteen people coming into a room and sitting down and talking to one another. Getting to know one another very slowly—it's not something that happens automatically. And you find out general things about people, you find out where they're coming from, what their past is and what they're doing with themselves now. And slowly you get to understand different things about people's personalities and you create friendships. You don't always create friendships. Sometimes you realize that you don't necessarily get along with certain people. But that's okay, too, because you start to work at that. Because you develop a certain trust, you can sense when somebody's having a problem, when somebody's not feeling too good. . . . You confront them, . . . you ask, and you realize that the problems people have are very similar to the ones you have and that there aren't that many different feelings. That most people feel quite the same things but maybe in different circumstances in their lives. . . . So I come as an individual and . . . the differences in my perception are accepted at the same time.[1]

We learn human interaction, and I think that's very, very special nowadays in the society we live in, because of the very inhuman way that people go about things. The very superficial way we interact, like the fast food society, and I find we really slow down. We look at what's essential, and . . . we disclose about our lives, about ourselves and what we feel, and it's very rewarding to know that other people are interested and the interest comes out.[2]

A band is a group of New School students who meet twice a week for a few hours, who sit down to get to know each other as people and aren't afraid to be themselves with each other, and are presented with the opportunity to be free and to be relaxed, and to say "This is me" and have other people accept that for what it is and not try to change and judge them. It's a place to talk and to discuss whatever you feel needs discussing.[3]

A band is my favorite group. It's just a place where I can be with people whom I haven't especially known before and I get to learn about them and what they've gone through; and even if they dress differently and they look differently, and they may act differently, somehow there's always a common ground and you're always able to have a lot of understanding for that person. . . . I've . . . learned how not to be so judgmental, to have an open mind and to be just a lot more accepting.[4]

BANDS ARE GENERALLY CONSIDERED THE BACKBONE of the New School, the place where the most intense personal growth can be facilitated. Although there have been numerous modalities of bands, numerous ways of forming them, and several *crises de conscience* on the nature and function of the bands throughout the history of the school, they have nonetheless been the locus of some of the most meaningful insights, communication, and growth at the New School.

The purpose of the bands has remained fairly constant, although there have been many experiments with their structure and content. They are compulsory primary affiliative groups of ten to sixteen people, usually formed for the duration of a term and for one credit per student. Their curriculum is to address those issues and concerns which are most crucial to each band's membership. In most cases, each band has a facilitator who is a faculty member or a resource person brought into the school to facilitate a band. Students choose their bands by a process of "band shopping" in which they usually interview all the facilitators and choose their band on the basis of the facilitator and of the other students they think are gravitating toward a particular band.

The facilitator usually is important at the beginning of a Band for setting the tone of the group, and should become decreasingly important as other members of the band develop the skills and confidence necessary to become facilitators themselves. While some band members may have shared other bands or groups within the school, or know one another from experiences outside of the school, bands usually begin with a group of individuals who are all slightly wary of one another. By the end of the term, the band should have sculpted itself into a unique group with its own norms and expectations in which each member is essential.

There are basic skills we want to emphasize in the bands: expressing one's feelings honestly and taking the risk of being genuine with other people, even if it means asserting one's dissidence from a majority; learning to listen carefully to others, to be sensitive to the feelings underlying what other people are saying, and to be responsive to others in a consequent and honest manner; remembering what has happened and developing the skill of connecting "information," such as people's feelings, stories, and experiences, throughout the term in order to get a clear picture of the other members and to mirror back to people how their patterns of behavior appear; being open to understanding the cultural, ethnic, and social values within our society without passing judgment on them; learning to solicit and accept constructive criticism as well as affection, compliments, and support; learning how to celebrate other people's good news and to express compassion for their bad news; learning how to confront and deal with disagreement; learning how to question the status quo in a nonconfrontational but firm way, when necessary; learning how to consider the group's needs as well as one's own and to make ethical and just judgments; learning how to improvise, how to "make do," how to organize events for the group; and learning how to be reliable, punctual, and fully present, and how to maintain the confidentiality of the group.

This is a demanding set of skills, many of which most adults in our society have not acquired. It is our conviction that those people who do manage to acquire these important skills will fare well in the most important parts of their lives: their relationships with other people and the benefits positive relationships bring to people's lives in both the public and the private spheres. The feedback of many students and teachers has indicated that the skills learned in bands are central to people's experience in the school and are usually considered "portable" when they leave.

FROM BANDS OF HUMANISTIC EDUCATION TO BANDS OF CRITICAL HUMANISM

In the first year of the school, bands were composed of thirty students and the equivalent of two full-time teachers each. In practice this usually turned out to be one full-time teacher and two half-time teachers. Bands were supposed to accomplish all of the behavioral goals indicated above; all academic work was also to be done within the bands. Teachers were placed in bands according to their disciplines, and students tended to choose bands on the basis of their academic interests. Neither students nor faculty found this a good arrangement, claiming that when it came down to subject matter, academic interests often vied with the need of the group to talk of its functioning and the feelings of its members, as well as issues in their lives. They attributed equal importance to academic pursuits, addressing people's personal issues, and the development of a viable group, but they felt that these objectives could not be met in so large a group, or in a group that had so much to accomplish at once. For this reason, after that first year bands were reduced to fifteen students and one facilitator, and they focused on individual growth and group skills.

Faculty would offer academic groups related to their disciplines and interests, which would be arrived at through the students' relating themselves to appropriate subject matter. These changes radically increased the students' academic choices.

Another matter addressed was that of "curriculum-of-self," a component of the original model that was close to the heart of the founder. This was initially a highly contentious subject in the school, for despite long discussion, no one could really agree on the nature of the self. The development of "curriculum-of-self" led to the refining of the pedagogy within both bands and learning groups. True to some of the doctrines of humanistic education formulated at Esalen in California and the University of Massachusetts, each student in the school was to undertake a compulsory self-related project that was called "curriculum-of-self." The approach to "curriculum-of-self" favored by the founder was essentially programmatic and usually demanded only a few sessions for each group. There were specific exercises, many of which had been developed by people connected with the institutions mentioned above; the response to them was highly variable.

Some students did not want to take part in any programmatic exercises. Some bands and band facilitators claimed that through the normal course of a band's life, all of its members addressed themselves, and that the band itself was a curriculum-of-self that did not need to set aside special time for such exercises. Other modalities for curriculum-of-self were then developed: journal writing and sharing; small curriculum-of-self groups within the band who met privately and kept the band informed of their progress; individuals undertaking specific projects to explore themselves, such as self-portraits, creative writing, and musical composition.

Eventually it became accepted in the community that since the bands addressed the "self" in each member, it was not necessary to have "curriculum-of-self" outside the bands or even to identify it as a separate entity in the pedagogy of the school. Rather, it was thought to be one end of a continuum that stretched from self-study through the study of more objective matters that responded to personally felt needs. "Curriculum-of-self," as a term, disappeared from the New School parlance in 1975–1976, to be replaced by the term "self-study."

An in-depth questionnaire completed by 102 of 140 students and 8 of 13 staff members in 1977 indicated that self-study was considered a focal point of the school, and that those students who had self-study sessions were the most enthusiastic about them:

In my experience self-study is not a program per se, yet it hangs about this school and lurks in every corner. It has spilled over into my life outside the school. Its value is inestimable to me. I feel as if some of the staff have really encouraged me to get down to the real nitty-gritty, and I'm immensely satisfied that in my case, at least, it does not exist as an exclusively band function.[5]

The school, however, did not have the resources to offer this option to each person, and therefore the use of peers through bands and small self-study groups was essential.[6]

Self-study became increasingly integrated into the bands, and various kinds of learning groups with an obvious self-study component were becoming almost institutionalized because their subject matter was sure to appeal to the affective needs of the students: sexuality groups, men's groups, and women's groups as well as creative arts groups in theater and self-portraiture.

Below are descriptions of bands that indicate how much self-study had become integrated into band practice:

The Band experience is a reminder to me, twice a week, that the most valuable and meaningful knowledge that one can achieve is not knowledge of some external subject matter, but knowledge of our own internal subject matter. This bi-weekly experience puts all other academic endeavours into proper perspective, a perspective which says that a vast accumulation of information and know-how is not sufficient to make an individual into a fully capable and developed participant of the world. It is only when all this is accompanied by an understanding of the self, and the relevance to the self of this information and know-how, that a student has had a true education and becomes whole. [Whole: being in healthy or sound condition; free from defect or damage; well, intact; having all its proper parts or elements.]

Bands are a place to learn about human beings. A Band is a group of people with the sole aim of learning more about themselves and others. In an atmosphere of confidentiality, respect and honesty, individuals share matters of vital importance with each other, and through the feedback of fourteen others, achieve a clearer image of themselves. Skills of leadership, listening, responding, understanding and support are developed and serve to enhance all interactions and relationships in and outside of the Band.[7]

Most important, Bands are responsible for making a student feel that he or she is attending a school which caters to all his or her needs, intellectual and emotional, where one feels that he is being seen as a whole person, treated that way and where, consequently, one comes out feeling whole.[8]

A student who had transferred to the New School from another CEGEP wrote these observations:

I can remember quite clearly the kind of words of encouragement given to me by teachers and graduates of the CEGEP system during those times of boredom and deflation: "Stick with it, kid, it's only two years"; "Look, everyone's gotta go through this crap before university, so relax and make the best of it"; "Hey, what would you be doing if not going to school, working in a warehouse? Finish the damn thing! My God, it's free!" I found the year and a half very long and the re-signed atmosphere spewed from the walls quite contagiously.

This student claims that it is the band which makes all the difference in the New School. The characteristics he values in the band are that it is a forum where people may be "heard and accepted as individuals." It is also an excellent support system:

What are the traditional systems of support offered the early adult? Where can a young person go to ask questions, seek help and advice, share joy and achieve-ment? Where can we go when we feel the need for someone to help carry us, even if for just a short while? Families have in many cases been reduced to vague entities, often struggling to find the meaning of their own existence. In such a transitory pe-riod of life as ours, the risk of parental subjectivity looms so great in response to the growing need to express individuality and self-affirmation.[9]

He rejects "any form of professional help" as placing a stigma on the stu-dent: "We are too young and optimistic to want to consider ourselves fail-ures." Rather, he values the peer objectivity of the band. "Issues are accepted as the property of everyone. One of the key words in band vocab-ulary is 'empathy.' We try to sense what each person is willing to share with objectivity and attentiveness. Band is always willing to walk with us." Fi-nally he finds band a discovery where we "find reflections of ourselves . . . that are perceived individually and speak personally to each band member. . . . The New School is giving me an education with an added dimension . . . me."[10]

In 1983–1984, numerous teachers were disturbed by the increasing self-centeredness they noticed among the students. With the hindsight of 1989 one can perhaps claim that the much-vaunted "spirit of selfishness of the 1980s" had hit its stride even with the New School. A faculty member de-scribed it thus:

There was a distinct lack of goodwill and openness which we have counted on in the past. Students seem to hold the "personal" in lower estimation and have incred-ible difficulty in reaching levels of trust. This is part, it seems, of the general conser-vative and fearful ethos of the times . . . and of a need for safety. The band, especially, shows a lack of school orientation. People do not adequately understand or accept the basic project of the programme, I feel . . . but comprehension and ex-perience are not sufficient for this desire to overcome fear of intensity and engagement.[11]

Other faculty members shared this vision of the increasing discrepancy between the school's values and those of the students. To counter an atmo-sphere of growing individualism, one year all bands were required to do community-based projects within the school or the larger community. The projects had to be shared in some way with the entire New School community. Some of the band projects included a graffiti board within the school, focusing on freedom of speech; a community newspaper; a study and children's book on sexual assault; a collective writing project that was supposed to be a novel but became a "document of process"; facilitating a community afternoon of workshops on sexuality with films, guest speakers, and student and faculty participation; a term book, a portrait of the school with contributions from the bands and members of the community at large; a project on peace and disarmament that culminated in an exhibit; a videotaped play written, directed, and acted by band members; exploring their own feelings, researching the Maison de Père project for male vagabonds in Montreal, and then creating and producing a dramatic production on the subject for the community.

The response to this model was mixed; while there have been community projects for the homeless, recycling projects, antiapartheid projects, and projects directed to other worthy causes, this particular mode was not to be repeated. Since 1987, the school has had increasing cutbacks of support personnel; this has forced us to turn to our only remaining resource, the students, to help with the tasks of maintenance, office work, telephone answering, organizing events, recruitment and interviewing of prospective students, and managing the school resource room. While many of the students conscientiously do their bit for the school, there is some resentment that these jobs are allocated through the bands. To the students, the bands are the armature on which our pedagogy is built.

When the bands are their most effective in addressing the students' heartfelt concerns is precisely when the students become jealous guardians of the individual focus within the bands. They do not want the introjection of any information or demands beyond the limits of this interpersonal sharing. Since the school is committed to a pedagogy of personal growth through both introspection and collective action, we are continually seesawing between models meant to stimulate one side or the other of this dyad. There is dialectical and reflexive planning each term as we try for that ephemeral moment of equilibrium that is as rare as it is valuable.

The most devastating matters in bands are violations of the basic band contract of confidentiality. In several cases where a member has broken the confidentiality, he or she has been asked to leave the school. Such events always have a long-term deleterious effect, seriously undermining people's trust in the pedagogy as well as in each other. The issue of confidentiality is a serious one that has become increasingly problematic in the past few years. There is a temptation to speculate on why this is; it occurs to me that the value of one's word of honor is decreasingly respected in our society. Politicians guilty of perjury and conflict of interest get by unscathed and sometimes are reelected. The notion of keeping one's word is not strongly entrenched in the minds of people to whom significant adults frequently have not kept their word. So while students agree wholeheartedly to honor confidentiality, it is sometimes difficult for them to carry this through. While the number of times such a breach is revealed is almost negligible, considering the amount of time spent in bands and learning groups, it is still unacceptable. It is difficult but worth attempting to swim against a public trend that enshrines gossip in a multimillion-dollar communications industry that spans magazines such as *People*, the very popular yellow press, and numerous talk shows on television.

Because the bands are not always effective with students who have serious personality problems, we often refer them to appropriate counselors in the community. It is not possible to force them to go, and some people decide they do not want to. While they may impose too much on the patience and time of a band, they often benefit from honest feedback on their behavior rather than being trapped by unchecked assumptions regarding others' attitudes toward them. While we have seen some extraordinary behavioral changes in some young people, it usually takes much more than the feedback provided by peers to effect changes in people with very complex problems.

An overwhelming percentage of our students, faculty, and graduates still consider the bands to be the mainstay of the school, necessary both to the encouragement of personal growth and to the critical pedagogy of the school, in which issues relating to our social context and personal lives need a wide arena for the often charged discussion of personally relevant issues.

BAND PROCESSES

Band Shopping

Each band is assigned its space (which is also used as a classroom), a room comfortable for approximately fifteen people. The rooms are carpeted, and have easy chairs and cushions; they look somewhat like small student lounges except that over the years, the band that occupies a space is likely to decorate it. Times are allocated for band shopping, and students circulate, spending time with the facilitators who interest them and seeing which other students may be gravitating toward banding with a particular facilitator. The interviews usually involve an ever-changing group of young people who want to discuss what they would like to see in a band and to hear the facilitator's views. After approximately two days of band shopping, there is a finalizing process where people go to the band of their first choice. If a band is oversubscribed, it must reduce its size. Sometimes students with strong second choices volunteer to negotiate into their second-choice bands to ease the pressure. If the band is still too large, usually an arbitrary means of reducing its size (like drawing lots) is used. Eventually the students redistribute themselves into the bands that still have places. The doors close, and negotiating and contracting begin.

Band Negotiating and Contracting

Band contracting is a serious business. It is important to establish people's reasons for having chosen a particular band. This gives an immediate indication of the climate of the group. It is often wise to find out if people know one another from other contexts, so that incipient conflicts may be addressed by the group. Bands usually establish their behavioral norms from the outset regarding punctuality, attendance, eating in band, listening and talking, smoking breaks, and attendance at band events such as suppers and outings. Often they will set up the evaluation process for the band grades at the end. They may establish what issues are the most pressing to discuss and include them in a written contract, signed by everyone and photocopied so that each member has the contract for further reference.

Various exercises are useful in focusing the band on its objectives. Following is a list of concerns I elicited from a band when I asked each member to list the five central issues in his/her life at the moment. The lists then underwent a refining exercise: members were asked to put a P beside anything too personal to bring up with the group, and to write the name of someone with whom they might be comfortable discussing their Ps, as a reminder to reflect on important issues; they were asked to write a B beside anything that could be discussed in band; they were then asked to underline their most pressing issues and to put an S beside those they felt like sharing that day.

The original inventory of individual concerns was very long. A tour of the room elicited these B and S concerns: attitudes/sexual relationships; self-assertion; family and independence; phobias and fears; future education and/or job; friendship; boyfriend/girlfriend; expressing feelings; creativity; time management; health; personality change; school; success; action/challenge; spirituality; money; indecision; work habits; isolation; authenticity; social class. We discussed themes that ran through the list and developed a shorter list of those issues most frequently cited: family and social class; friends/isolation; self-assertion/expression of feelings; sexuality; future success; and, equally, independence, time management/work habits, creativity, spirituality, phobias and fears. This list still looked unmanageable, and so we finally agreed on this prioritized list of concerns: family, self-assertion, friends/isolation, sexuality, future/success. The band contract looked like this:

BAND CONTRACT

1. Punctuality expected. If late or absent, phoning in is compulsory.

2. Attendance compulsory.
3. Confidentiality expected.
4. Cigarette limit—one at a time. [For the past eight years there has been no smoking in Bands]
5. Five-minute break per band.
6. Self-study will be done by spotlighting people for them to receive feedback and then respond.
7. Tidiness (clean your mess after band meetings).
8. Focus on what's going on: i.e., eye contact, no reading, writing, or drawing during band.
9. Active participation.
10. Ongoing evaluation of our processes.
11. Issues for self-study in band:
    a. Family/social class
    b. Self-assertion/feelings/personality change
    c. Friends/isolation
    d. Sexuality
    e. Future/success.
12. The band is for one credit for each member.

Members' signatures and telephone numbers.

There is a midterm evaluation of the process for all groups within the school, at which time contracts can be renegotiated. At any time, however, any member can ask for an evaluation of the group's progress. Sometimes groups get out of focus and need the contract to bring them back on track. At other times they find their new focus more important and renegotiate the contract.

Band Processes

It is often useful to make an "inventory of concerns" later in the term to see if concerns have changed or if new ones have arisen. A band came up with this enormous list in its seventh week: choosing the right program in university; improving my music skills; increase job participation; future as an actress; time management; survival of the school; hate and war; the nature of my participation in the school; nature of the individual . . . what makes an individual; concern to get to university; fear of being a dummy; getting my father off my back about school; fear I won't be able to finish CEGEP; summer job; trying to get through CEGEP; going to university; writing skills; finding true love and happiness; finding a good situation in life; it's the last semester, leaving the school; relationships and reasons for them; work I do now and how it relates to my life's work; family; the fears that incapacitate me; university; what is my future in writing; relationships; family; career/future; becoming an accomplished musician; knowing myself better; summer job and getting through red tape for it; women's rights;

helping friend and sister through problems like divorce and battered women, helping them to see themselves as people.

This list was typed and given to each member to reflect upon over the weekend. The next week we reduced it to four prioritized themes: the future, the family, fears, relationships. We then divided our remaining time accordingly to discuss these topics in the students' lives.

Some bands ask students to write personal contracts with their own objectives in them, share them with the band, and perhaps contract to do some self-study on an issue that is not shared by others in the band, and to discuss this issue with the band from time to time.

The bands have various exercises and ways of getting to know one another that I will discuss below. It is important to emphasize that ultimately the bands are focused on the here and now. For this reason, the best laid plans or agendas can be overturned by a crisis in someone's life. It is important to be judicious in meeting the needs of that individual while maintaining a focus on the needs of the group.

Name Sharing. This exercise is useful for any group. Members are asked to think of some important aspect of themselves or their lives the group should know. They then introduce themselves. For example, "My name is Anne Smith, and I'm nervous about starting my first band." A second person may say, "My name is Paul Jones, and I'm crazy over playing my guitar in a group." The band will then review the names in reverse order: "Paul's crazy about his guitar, and Anne's nervous about her first band." With each introduction, another name and concern are added. By the time each person has introduced himself/herself, people know a bit about one another and have had all sorts of low-risk interaction, to the point of sharing nonverbally the boredom of repetition or the amusement at some people's introduction.

The Personal Profile. Some bands ask members to prepare profiles either in writing or orally to present to the band regarding themselves, their lives, and their aspirations. After each profile is presented, there is usually time for members to ask clarifying questions and to give feedback. While this exercise often reveals important facets of the members' lives, it is very lengthy and can absorb a large amount of the band's time. Here is an excerpt from a student profile:

I'm glad I'm here to do this profile. One of the only reasons to leave high school was to get to the New School, and considering it was the only school to which I had applied, I'm glad I'm here.

My interest and what talents I think I have lie in the creative arts. I have written poetry and plays on my own, and would like to do the same here along with Women's Studies, Children's Literature, Psychology, the Occult and the Surreal.

I find I am open about myself. I am more emotional than rational. I like to be and work alone as a rule. Lately I have been more of a slow learner. I hope it's just a phase. I am a spur of the moment person. I love new surroundings and clothes. Occasionally I need a push, otherwise I tend to get lazy. I hear people getting angry at me without telling me why. . . . Meeting new people now, in the way of really learning about them, scares me because during the past year I've been sheltered, staying in my own community and talking to the same people. I feel as if I've forgotten how to relate. The Band is important to me because even though I may feel frightened, I'll be among people learning over again how to relate, which I find as an absolute essential in life. This particular Band, I feel, holds most of my interests, and I feel good about the people. I hope the best will be brought out in me and others and that the others will feel good about me as well.[12]

In many ways this profile is typical in that it leaves out many of this young woman's most pressing concerns. After she presented it, people asked about her family. Her parents were divorced, she explained. She adored her father but lived with her mother, with whom she continually fought but whom she felt she had to protect from depression. Throughout the discussion it became clear that her desire to "relate" and her difficulty with her peers were tied to the difficulties she experienced, torn between her parents, and by her own ambivalence toward them. Band members learn to listen not only to what is said but also to what is left out.

The Paper Bag Exercise. Here members are asked each to bring in a bag with at least three items that are significant indicators of who they are, and to share them with the band. This can be shorter than the profiles and is favored by some groups.

Numerous other self-identifying exercises are useful; however, bands often can slow down or develop all sorts of avoiding behaviors when there are important issues or conflicts to confront. In such cases it is often helpful to suggest exercises that will unite people in the group, or that will bring out areas of discord with a view to reconciling members.

Garbage and Flowers or Clearing the Air. This is often a good exercise for beginning a band session. A tour is made of the members, each of whom must share a prevailing feeling about and toward the band, or about his/her life in general. It can be very positive (flowers) or negative (garbage). This gives a quick and accurate sense of the mood of the band, and it often brings important issues in members' lives to the forefront. It also may provide an opportunity for people to articulate and settle conflicts.

The "I Wonder" Exercise. In this exercise different members are "spotlighted," and people are asked to suggest aspects of the individual they would like to know better. This gives all members individual feedback on how they are perceived and whether they have disclosed as much of themselves as they think. Anyone can "pass" on such exercises and is not obliged to answer all the "I wonders." It is also possible to use this exercise for members to express "I wonders" about themselves, thus helping to get the band agenda on track. Here are some of the latter type of "I wonder's" from a band:

I wonder to what extent as a band facilitator it is appropriate for me to disclose my personal feelings about members to them.

I wonder about myself and whether I'm going to stay at the New School next year or not.

I wonder if I'm really as objective as I'd like to be.

I wonder if I will be able, as an individual, to meet the seemingly infinite demands that my family is making on me at this time, as far as leaving Canada and going to another part of the world with them.

I wonder what Gary is thinking now.

Clearly there is enough material in these few quotations to absorb some of the band attention for elaboration and response.

A Band Sociogram. This can be done in several ways. Usually a large piece of paper or cardboard is put on the wall, and members write on it to indicate their relationships to one another. They may put their names where they please and then draw lines to each other, writing on the lines what they consider their connections to be.

Members may want to ascertain how members gauge their "belong-ingness" within the band. In this exercise the "heart of the band" is drawn in the middle of the paper. Each person is asked to indicate where he or she stands in relation to the heart of the band, and why. In both cases, the band usually has a very colorful and full diagram that shows the complexity of people's interconnections and connections to the group. There is usually a great deal of positive information on the paper; this is encouraging to the group and consolidates people's commitment to it.

Closeness Exercise. Here a person is asked to sit with his/her eyes covered in the middle of the floor. People then arrange themselves on the floor in relation to how close they feel to the person. They then explain the reasons for where they have located themselves. This is often valuable in knitting a group together, but it should be used only diagnostically, when there is little closeness in the group, or as a reinforcement when a group has sculpted it-self into a recognizable entity.

Positive Spotlight. This is useful when there has been a great deal of negativity in a group. Each member is "spotlighted" while other members each express some positive opinion or feeling they have about the person. This often gives people an opportunity to acknowledge something helpful the person has done, sometimes inadvertently, and it always is useful in en-couraging and knitting a group.

Gift Spotlight. This exercise is useful when someone has shared a really important and sad experience with the group and has expressed his/her sadness. The person is spotlighted and everyone is asked to "give" the person something verbally, perhaps only to express what they wish they *could* give the person, to counteract or help the person cope with his/her feelings of sadness. It is often very useful as an exercise of closure for a band that has dealt with very upsetting matters.

There are numerous possible exercises, and they must always emerge from the articulated needs of the band. Sometimes the need is for physical activity, relaxation, or contact. Sometimes an exercise emerges from a discussion. Sometimes a student is able to contribute an exercise. Often matters are simply dealt with by discussion and interchange. It is of prime importance, however, always to evaluate the efficacy of an exercise after it has been used, giving the band a chance to judge its own processes.

Though band outings are not exercises in the same sense as those described above, they are often very useful in knitting the band together. Members also learn other aspects of one another when they are removed from the school context. Often individual band members invite the group to a potluck at their homes, giving everyone the chance to share with a more private part of the person. Other outings may involve sports, bowling, theater, concerts, films, clubs, museums, restaurants, lectures, hikes and walks, or a visit to someone's country house.

People often wonder how real crises are handled in the bands. It is very important for the facilitators to know their limits and to refer members in serious crisis to professionals within or outside the college. The New School maintains a list of experts and institutions for such referrals. On the other hand, the group itself often has the requisite common sense and expertise to bring to bear on an issue. It is part of the school's philosophy to demystify helping relationships and to facilitate for each member of the community the possibility of both offering and receiving help from others who have had similar experiences or who have particular insights or resources for them.

George, a very avid athlete, had already shocked some band members by sharing with them that he was a homosexual. There had been discussions about homosexuality, people's attitudes toward it, and speculation on the reason for people's making that choice. One day George was very upset and told the band that some years before, he had had a cancerous growth removed from his leg. The doctors now believed he had a tumor in his testicle. If there were a tumor, they might have to remove one testicle. Everyone in the band was concerned, even those who had the greatest reservations about his homosexuality. The students organized themselves to accompany George to the hospital for his tests and other appointments. In the end it turned out that he had a cyst which required no operation. The celebration in the band was extremely moving; members had been tremendously impressed by George's quiet courage during this monthlong ordeal. At the end of term, the most "macho" and homophobic male in the band told George that his courage was the true courage (as opposed to bullying) to which all men should aspire.

When the students help and support one another, an atmosphere of real trust forms, and they never forget the experience. A true bonding takes place and moves the band into dimensions of trust and sharing that are extremely touching and that create for the members models of exemplary behavior for future reference.

Another concern is closure. Often students who have problems to discuss will wait until the time to end the band is only a few moments away. It is important to judge whether the matter can wait until the next band; if the student feels it to be pressing, the facilitator may suggest extending the band or, if that is not possible due to people's other commitments, that some people volunteer to stay behind and work through the difficulty with the person. If the person feels an in-depth discussion can wait, the band frequently will contract with that person to be prepared to open the next meeting with discussion of this particular issue. In the normal course of events, however, it is important to start gearing down about ten to fifteen minutes before closure, ensuring that people have said what they wanted to that day, evaluating the process, and perhaps suggesting an agenda for the next meeting. It is essential, however, that closure is clear and that nothing which has been said or decided cannot be reviewed in the future.

EVALUATION

Eventually bands must evaluate the students and the facilitator. There are many modes of doing this. Sometimes bands suggest an average performance, against which each student's work is judged, that covers certain of the behavioral objectives listed in the contract. In other cases, the bands evaluate each member on the basis of his/her self-evaluation, the feedback of the group, and the objectives the particular student started out with. Students usually suggest their own marks, which are raised or lowered by the band as a whole. In most cases there is little argument with the marks; students most frequently underrate their performance and have to be reminded of their triumphs and successes within the group. Usually members have developed the capacity to remember each person's participation and present the person a well-considered overview of it. The process of evaluation is always considered more important than the grade. It is a real stocktaking for people to see if they have been true to themselves and to the commitments they have made within a group. Here is part of a written self-evaluation:

If I were to pinpoint a definite behaviour change (no matter how minimal), that would be my sensitivity to people and partial acceptance of their uniqueness. I must stress, however, that old habits and vices are difficult to shed, so I still find myself slipping back into the "mask," but now at least I am aware of my goal. Awareness is more than half the step to change.

Since the band facilitator is not the sole arbiter of evaluation and grading, he or she is fairly likely to get an honest evaluation from the students. These evaluations are very important in improving the facilitators' skills and in encouraging further development. The students are able to show significant affection even when they are very critical. Here are some examples of student evaluations of me:

I think you are a very strong, responsible person. You keep your own sadness to yourself and are always ready to meet people's legitimate needs. I find your judgements sometimes too quick and final, but so often accurate that they are usually not too resented. You are extremely perceptive and your methods are extremely valuable to many people . . . whether they recognize the value or not.

I chose this particular evaluation because it touches on the ambivalence that my speedy judgments may evoke in people. It is always important for me to keep aware of the fact that I must slow down and sometimes prevent myself from frightening people by revealing my perceptions too precipitately. It is a fault I have tried to improve since the first evaluation I received, and I hope I have improved somewhat; but since this quickness and exuberance of expression are positively reinforced in many other circumstances, I need constant reminding within the New School that it is not always appropriate in bands.

Greta, you have really been an important force in my life. I admire your quick mind and your intelligence. You take people seriously, and I appreciate that. I feel that I can talk about myself to you and that you will care. I only wish that I would talk to you more. I guess I fear entering your office when I see you in there. It's a big step entering the den of sanctity.

This particular evaluation was important because I often forget how completely unreachable I can appear when I am concentrating on work. My office must become accessible, but I also want students to respect my need for solitude in order to do my work. Since I have received several such evaluations over the years, I now try to make it clearer to students that if I'm not immediately available, I will arrange for another time.

Greta, although your main focus seems to be far removed from mine, I was very pleased to discover that you had taken the time and energy to attempt something outside of your normal activities, that is, those listening exercises for turning off internal dialogue [which he brought to the Band]. . . . That was an attempt at cultivating another real and great part of you.

This student was very interested in religious experiences, which inspire a certain amount of skepticism in me. His evaluation makes me realize how important it is to the students that I stay open and try to understand their values and beliefs. I have to be prepared to suspend my disbelief and try something new. It is clear that this particular student was especially pleased to be giving me something of value from his own life. The need for the students to give to the facilitators and for the facilitators to accept what they are given with open hearts is an essential factor in building trust for a positive learning situation.

WHAT DO PEOPLE GET OUT OF BANDS?

There are as many benefits from bands as there are people reporting on them. Often the benefits perceived in the short term are very different from those perceived in the long term. However, there are themes that arise frequently in students' accounts of the benefits they realized through the band experience.

One of the prime factors that makes bands effective is that all expression of emotion, values, or ideas is accepted and that there is tacit support for the person. This can encourage people to risk expressing their authentic values and tastes, and to experience the instructive feedback within the group without fearing rejection:

Band is really the sort of synthesis point that . . . brings all the different things that have come up in all . . . parts of your life and interrelates them, and you come out of it as a whole person. . . . It's freedom to speak, freedom to confront people, freedom to cry, freedom to laugh, freedom to discuss any issue and have the fact that you're feeling something . . . is valid enough reason for the whole group of people to discuss it with you. And the obvious, the manifest caring involved. And the wonderful feeling of support and solidarity and people that are often in the same position or have similar positions to your own.[13]

The feedback in the bands is essential in helping young people at a crucial time of change in their lives decide how they want to behave:

Being able to share the way you're feeling and get an opportunity to exercise some of your own skills in communicating and . . . seeing people's response to you and see[ing] how you respond to other people, to different situations. You learn a lot about yourself as well as other people.[14]

Another important aspect of the bands is that they break down people's

prejudices about one another. Students certainly learn how faulty their perceptions might be and how much communality there is in the human
experience:

The feeling of closeness, of having to take seriously people one wouldn't necessarily associate with on one's own. We were, some of us, thrown together in the bands.
You know, people who wouldn't socialize together or were from very different
backgrounds, and I learned to take their concerns more seriously. Normally I would
just write them off. I would just type people, they're that type or this type or whatever, and I think that's not the type I'm interested in, and that would be that. And I
found that there were things of value and worth in all sorts, all types.[15]

It is often within bands that people's cultural differences become the
clearest. When an issue emerges that highlights cultural differences and
mutual misunderstandings, the bands are presented with an excellent opportunity to explore members' differences and also their communality:

Althea was the most beloved person in the band. She was an exceptionally beauti-
ful and charming young Trinidadian woman with a delightful sense of humor. Indeed, during band negotiations, it became clear that many people had entered the
band to be with her. She came to band one day in a terrible state. It turned out that a
cousin of hers, one her age with whom she had been brought up, had been shot
dead the day before in San Fernando, when he was bringing the cash payroll from
the bank to his employer. She began to cry; she had reserved a ticket home for the
next morning, and would be gone for three weeks so that she could attend the fu-
neral and be of comfort to the family.
  The band received this information in a stupefied silence. The facilitator expressed her condolences and asked if there was anything the band or the school
could do to help. There was nothing. More silence. The young woman, who was
the only black person in the band, looked around the room, burst into tears, and
ran out. She was followed by another member. The facilitator asked the band if they
had any idea why Althea had left. After another prolonged silence, a member said,
"I guess we weren't very supportive of her." The facilitator agreed, and wondered
aloud why this was, since everyone seemed so fond of her.
  What emerged in the discussion was that no one knew what you say when someone dies. They had been embarrassed. At this point, Althea returned. She wondered why no one had spoken to her. The embarrassment was explained to her, and
she was quite shocked. She was a member of the Church of God, where everyone
knew exactly how to behave in a death. The rest of the band was devoted to discussing people's attitudes to death. It turned out that everyone in the band had experienced the death of a person or a pet they had loved. In most cases the loss had
been ignored in conversation. How did that feel? It felt terrible and lonely. This was
followed by discussion on what people would have liked to hear, which culminated
in a round-the-room exercise of "When . . . died, I wish . . . had said . . . to me." Finally everyone expressed feelings to Althea, who, understanding the reasons for
people's silence, was able to accept their condolences.

In this situation the students reviewed their own feelings about death and about how the bereaved should be treated. They also were able to re-dress their original silence toward Althea. Finally, behavior-at-death was demystified, and they left the meeting confident that in the future they would know what to do. It is a sobering comment on the socialization of children in our society that these skills must be learned in school.

The band experience is also central in building the self-esteem necessary for personal growth and self-actualization. The hours spent in interchange are very confirming because people see that others share their experiences, and they also see that their perceptions can be of help to others. The experi-ence of speaking up and confronting others improves people's confidence in their communication skills:

I learned what self-esteem was and I worked on it a lot with the help of others in the band. . . . I learned how to be my own boss and to change. I'm the only person in the world who has power to change or form change in my life. . . . I'll take that out-side with me, and I do take it outside with me now. I find that I learned self-empowerment . . . I suppose that is the right term.[16]

Numerous people have reported that the bands were instrumental in helping them with highly diverse future work. It is abundantly clear that those students who went into the helping professions were deeply influ-enced by their experience at the New School:

I'm sure that my experience as a student in band was probably the first occasion of paying attention to group dynamics or becoming aware of myself in a group, my ef-fect on a group, my presence in a group. . . . I think that I was at that time develop-ing skills which I've later had to use as a social worker: being able to read people and evoke repsonses, gather information, pay attention to what is not said as well as what is said, help people to communicate with each other.[17]

Another graduate worked in a mission for indigent men in Toronto. She describes her experience in this way:

I found it interesting, especially at the mission, because it's run unbelievably like a real bureaucracy with management having no association with the men . . . it's run at that kind of level, hierarchical, and I found myself in boardrooms and meetings with department heads and supervisors, and I found my ability . . . was . . . refined at the New School to . . . see the truth in what someone's saying and to be able to pinpoint it and look . . . them straight in the face and say, "What are you talking about?" I think I learned that at the New School . . . not to take what everyone says literally and to look behind what they're saying, and I really appreciated that tool.[18]

Because the New School is based on the possibility of achieving a truly just society where people do care for and about one another, it is not coincidental that graduates take from the band experience, and the entire school experience, the notion that they have the necessary skills to re-create aspects of the school in other circumstances:

I learned . . . the way I want life to go, the way I want life to be like, and I want to be able to share with people and get close to other people and accept other people, and I want to form close relationships with as many people as I can. After all, you know, I am sharing this life with them. The thing that I realized was that it's not so much the New School is the only place that is this way, it's not just a feeling, but to me it's the way life should be. That everybody should be that way. People should care about, watch and listen to each other. It's seeing what I wanted in a place and knowing that I want to continue to do this with other people . . . taking what I believe life should be with me and having my own type of New School, my own type of band throughout my life.[19]

We have no way of preparing people for every eventuality they will meet in their lives. However, we do know that most people experience periods of depression and doubt in which they need support and insight. Many of the values and techniques learned through band can be helpful to people in future times of crisis as well as in the future workplace. Bands help prepare people to find ways of coping with many of the contingencies that arise in the course of a lifetime.

ARE BANDS PORTABLE?

Having imported bands to other contexts and seen other people use band techniques elsewhere, I have concluded that they can be made portable under certain circumstances: The members and the facilitator must be convinced of the value of the group, must want to participate and be committed to their contract; there must be no foreseeably dangerous long-term consequences to the members for participating in the group; and the objectives of the members and of the group as a whole must be clearly defined.

From 1974 to 1979, I introduced the band concept into a large (100–125 students) women's studies course at a Montreal university. So many deeply personal feelings were touched by the lectures, and most students had no way of venting their feelings in a large amphitheater. I introduced the option of a primary affiliative group, which I called an open-agenda conference group, that I would facilitate. It was purely voluntary, but once people had made their commitment to the group, they were expected to show up regularly. Twelve women volunteered to meet every week for two or three hours. We honored an open curriculum; although the texts and subject matter of the course were regularly touched upon, the content was essentially the lives of those women qua women. At the end of the year we compared the group members' grades with those of the rest of the class. The women in this group took the first three places in the course, and no one had a grade under B+. The average grade was about 84 percent, compared with 73 percent for the entire class, including the members of the conference group.

This suggested that a strong affective investment in a course could be correlated with a high level of cognitive attainment. So successful was this pilot group that for the next five years, when I was still teaching the course, there was sufficient interest for three conference groups per year, all of them facilitated by former students of the course who had been in conference groups. Not only did these groups provide a locus for the discussion of people's feelings and their insights into ideas, but they also became training groups for feminist action.

It would seem to me that home rooms in high school could become bands. Perhaps if students felt more powerful, more implicated in one another's lives, this would break down the cliquishness of adolescents and motivate them to come to school, if only to find out what happened next in someone's life. It is precisely in adolescence that young people's self-esteem is most vulnerable to undermining by external events in their lives as well as by their changing bodies and value systems, and their need for seemingly endless peer company. By being taken seriously and by having their perceptions addressed and confirmed, they would take themselves more seriously. By intentionally forming a small community, they would break down isolation and anomie, and also learn how to live collectively those values so important for global survival. A band of adolescents in high school would be an excellent antidote to the individualistic and violent information communicated to them through the media.

Some critics might here interject that bands would cut into important "academic" time. I would counter this argument by the claim that the time devoted to bands increases students' motivation to learn and to acquire academic and social skills, as well as their sense of responsibility to themselves and others. Because of the rigorous demands of bands, students increase their concentration span. Rather than wasting time, bands would be an investment in an experience whose quality can positively affect student attitudes to learning.

Another site where I had the occasion to develop primary affiliative groups was a large national conference I helped plan in 1984. Four hundred women gathered in Toronto to discuss "Educating Women in the Eighties." The planners were aware that one of the values of conferences is that they help people to network with others of like interests. Since our participants would be staying in various hotels and university dormitories, it was unlikely that they would have much occasion to meet outside of the conference workshops and meetings.

We decided to form primary affiliative groups, each with a mix of women from throughout the country. The groups met each morning for an hour before other activities started; they were facilitated by women who were known to have facilitative skills. On the whole they were a success, rating in the top three items of the participants' conference evaluations under the rubric of "best things about the conference." In my opinion it was a good way to facilitate networking and would be useful in other conference situations.

Bandlike groups could theoretically be useful in situations where people must work closely at a high level of stress. They are especially valuable in breaking down the isolation of people who work on a one-to-one basis in the helping professions, and need both lateral support and personal renewal. Well handled, such groups may become an excellent antidote to the epidemic of burnout that is widely seen in the helping professions.

There is no reason why a bandlike structure could not be introduced into any kind of workplace or the volunteer sector as a means of creating community, confirming people's experiences, perceptions, and contributions, and making the workplace more productive as well as more stimulating for the workers. This suggestion is made in full knowledge that in most workplaces management does its best to block anything which would provide a means for the employees to organize and empower themselves to effect change. Most work sites are still run on the principle of overt and/or concealed threat to people's economic and personal security. While it has been indicated that burnout and poor morale in the average workplace bring on expensive wastes of time and energy, many employers still seem to believe in the stick rather than the carrot, in social control rather than freedom, assuming that the workers are out to cheat them. These beliefs can become self-fulfilling expectations.

Significantly, in an atmosphere of extremely low trust most employers who provide such services at all offer employee aid plans that operate on an individual basis, shrouded in secrecy. Many people's problems are systemic; when the malaise of workers is addressed on an individualistic basis, the workers frequently blame themselves for their problems. Such treatment often is as useful as an aspirin is as a cancer cure. For a short period in the late 1960s Abraham Maslow and other humanistic psychologists were in demand by large businesses for group facilitation. Maslow was interested in addressing the workplace as a source for individual self-actualization. He criticized the basic premises of classic economic theory as inadequate for human motivation. He was optimistic that the work he was doing could transform the workplace into a site which stressed the "higher human" needs of self-actualization and a "love for the highest values."[20]

The concept of bands under critical humanism always bears within it the dialectical model of mutually informing personal growth and personal and collective empowerment. It is not possible to participate in a band without contemplating change. Therefore, bands are portable, they are workable only in environments where the values mentioned here are operant. People will not be open in an atmosphere of coercion and/or social control, and they are right not to be. If employers are willing to pay the price of low motivation, morale, and productivity in order to retain a nonfunctional, coercive power, then they are indeed getting what they have paid for, and presumably there is no need for change. If, on the other hand, unions, professional organizations, individual workers, and management are interested in improving all facets of the workplace, bandlike groups can provide a viable way of transforming the workplace.

Bands, however, could never take the place of the political organization necessary for the fair redistribution of power and resources in society. What they will do is to provide people with a forum to discuss their feelings and the sources of those feelings in their personal lives as well as within the public sphere of the workplace. Sharing of feelings breaks down individual isolation and validates people's perceptions. Through this process, they should be able to establish the mutual support and understanding necessary for the formulation of a praxis for change. Since the essential question members would have to address relates to their own interests, it is unlikely that members of a properly constituted and facilitated primary affiliative group (or band) would merely become accomplices in the development of only those qualities which would make them more efficient grist for the mill.

NOTES

1. Lianne, interview, 1984.
2. Mona, interview, 1984.
3. Carole, interview, 1984.
4. Deborah S., interview, 1984.
5. Lianne, interview, 1984.
6. The New School Evaluation Questionnaire—May 1977, presented in *New School Annual Report: 1976–77*, Appendix. Responses were anonymous.
7. André, *New School Annual Report: 1983–84*, p. 8.
8. Michael, *New School Annual Report: 1978–79*, p. 8.
9. André, *New School Annual Report: 1978–79*, p. 9.
10. Ibid., pp. 10–12.
11. Jerry Wadsworth, faculty member, *New School Annual Report: 1982–83*, p. 16.
12. Maria, band profile, 1974.
13. Peter, interview, 1984.
14. Michael, interview, 1984.
15. Ilona, interview, 1984.
16. Mona, interview, 1984.
17. Suzanne, interview, 1984.
18. Eileen, interview, 1984.
19. Lianne, interview, 1984.
20. Abraham Maslow, *The Farther Reaches of Human Nature* (London: Penguin Books, 1966), p. 277.

10
Formal Curriculum: The Learning Groups

CURRICULUM VIABILITY

WHILE THE BANDS FORM AN ESSENTIAL ARMATURE for the praxis of our educational philosophy, the pedagogy developed in the academic learning groups is equally important. It is inaccurate to separate bands and learning groups into discrete categories, because in both cases we attempt to offer holistic education, addressing the students' multiple needs. Very often the contents of a band meeting could be described as a combination of psychology, anthropology, and sociology, while frequently the learning groups become sites for self-revelations leading directly to the students' personal growth.

Curriculum viability in the context of the New School means that at least three necessary conditions must be met. The first is that the pedagogical practices of learning groups must conform with the following processes: choice by self-to-subject; negotiation; contracting; ongoing evaluation; peer evaluation; and self-evaluation. The second is that a diversified curriculum must be developed each term in order to meet the widest range of interests and needs expressed by the students. As in the bands, all subject matter of the learning groups evolves from the intersection of the students' articulated needs and the resources available to them. Third, we must "harmonize" with norms established by the state, which accords credits to our students.

Our pedagogy is based on the contention that the students' motivation to learn is of primary importance in their intellectual and emotional development. While it has been demonstrable for centuries that people can learn numerous facts and methods that do not really interest them, they generally do so under two forms of coercion. The first is brute force, a threat-based methodology in which some sort of overt or subtle punishment or withholding of privilege lies in store for those who are not willing to undergo the rigors of learning; the second is a situation in which matters learned are not in themselves of primary importance to the learner but are essential as a means of attaining other desirable skills, status, or money. I will call this "secondary motivation." One thinks here of all the medical doctors who have disliked certain required courses in medical school but who worked hard at them, either because these courses were necessary cognitive stepping-stones to more desirable advanced knowledge or because their successful completion enabled medical students to become doctors.

At the New School coercion is not ideologically acceptable; it must be said, however, that sometimes some students do work under some sort of subtle coercion: They may want to mollify a parent; they may think they need "their education" to "get somewhere"; they may be reacting to the social control of a group after having committed themselves to a contract, and thus feel obliged to follow through on their commitments. However, the worst punishment they are likely to suffer in a learning group is either the anger of their peers, if they do not respect the contract, or a failing grade.

Some students at the New School may initially experience secondary motivation as they approach their studies. They are willing to undergo a certain educational experience (CEGEP) in order to be able to move into a desired position or field. However, all of our students are obliged to attend information meetings before applying to the school, and so they know that the school is different from other CEGEP programs. Hence, even if they see CEGEP as a stepping-stone to university (or to the kind of material entitlement discussed previously), they come to the New School fully aware that they will be addressed holistically and expected to contribute to the school in ways not required elsewhere. We assume that they start with a large fund of interest and goodwill toward our educational philosophy and practices, even if it is only in the spirit of the school's being the best of all available "evils."

While the bands deal with students' emotional, social, political, economic, spiritual, and creative lives in an unmediated fashion, learning groups are based on the students' self-articulated learning needs and address the complexity of their lives with and through disciplines or subjects mutually agreed upon. Many students have "skills needs." They may have great difficulty with reading, with oral and written expression, with critical thinking, or with analyzing and arriving at syntheses of diverse ideas and facts. While elsewhere these needs may be met through particular programs or course content directed toward skills acquisition, at the New School we begin with the students' feelings and attempt to draw out their motivations to improve their skills. All too often, young people know that they have to improve "their writing," for instance, in order to proceed to "their education" at university, but they have no real impetus within themselves to seek this form of expression. This is especially evident when they imagine the skill being applied to the writing of term papers on subjects that appear to be arbitrarily selected and that they may find exquisitely boring. This is not to say that mainstream academic research is looked upon with disdain, but simply that the cultural gap between many students and the academy is so great that many of the practices of the academy present themselves to the students as bewildering tasks to be stoically and uncomprehendingly carried out in the interest of a distant credentialization.

The underlying principle of academic work at the New School is that everything must be explicit: Why are we choosing to do what we are doing? What is the most appropriate area of interest we can find to meet the needs we have expressed? What are the most appropriate tasks for us, given our individual and group needs? With what would we like to emerge from this pursuit? For those students who have addressed these questions and found a subject or discipline appropriate to meeting their needs, there is yet a further question to pose in order to assess their skills/learning needs: What are the epistemological "givens" or methodological necessities imposed by this subject, why are they imposed, and do I want to learn them? For example, a learner whose French is very poor but who intends to remain in Quebec as a full and comfortable participant in the society must accept the fact that second-language learning always involves some memorization, the use of dictionaries, reading, and writing.

When considering the need for a highly diverse curriculum, it is important to emphasize that we are limited by very restricted staffing formulas which make it virtually impossible to introduce new disciplines in the New School. We cannot offer a sufficiently varied curriculum to satisfy the needs of students if we rely entirely on the resources allocated through the college's staffing projections. Currently our offerings and staffing are officially based on the following disciplines: English, the humanities, psychology, sociology, art, ceramics, cinema, theater, and music. In order to vary our curriculum, we interpret the disciplines we offer in the broadest way possible and supplement the learning groups offered by the faculty with groups given by volunteers from the community beyond the New School, by maximizing the resources within Dawson, by numerous graduates, by students who have shown particular success in various fields, by developing outreach projects, and—where possible—by attracting the services of interns in university counseling or adult education programs. While these are all excellent strategies for expanding the school's resources, their supervision is extremely labor-intensive. Currently we have instituted, through the college's continuing education program, a diploma course in critical humanism to train our nonfaculty teachers. The following represent our educational resources beyond the regular teaching corps.

Community Resources. People from the greater community of Montreal have shown an interest in contributing their skills to the school in numerous ways: for several years we have been able to attract t'ai chi, physical fitness, and jazz ballet teachers to the school; there have been poetry writing workshops and creative writing groups that have published small journals; a group of students who were devoted Christians wanted to further their knowledge of Christianity. We were able to obtain the participation of a Ph.D. candidate at McGill's Faculty of Divinity to facilitate the latter group. The Women's Centre of Montreal trained a group of New School women and their women's studies teacher as volunteers in numerous facets of its community services. Many musicians have contributed their skills in guitar, choir, percussion, and composition.

Sometimes the school has been able to connect with other groups and draw in resource people to coordinate work within the school and some external project. We have also benefited enormously from the work of performing arts professionals in the city: clown workshops and intermittent direction workshops by visiting directors in Montreal theaters; a very exciting class in contact improvisation given by a local dancer; several plays have been directed by young professional actors over the years. There have been numerous volunteer art teachers, young artists, and art education graduates who wanted to get teaching experience. On one occasion, the mother of one of our students, a nursing administrator who works in a palliative care unit in a Montreal hospital, offered an excellent learning group on death and dying. We have even been able to have the services of an anarchist scholar and publisher to meet the needs of one of our students interested in anarchist thought.

Resources within Dawson. In this case we rely on the goodwill of our colleagues in other services. On two occasions we have been able to attract the participation of members of Student Services. One counselor was cofacilitator of a men's group and later led some groups on love and human relationships. Another member of that department gave excellent learning groups on community organization and facilitation for three consecutive years. Many members of the college's support staff have been finishing graduate degrees. We have been fortunate to have the services of two technicians who would like to try their hand at teaching. One has given groups on "the tao of physics," and the other has offered groups on a wide range of topics related to religious studies.

Since its beginning, staff and faculty at the New School have enjoyed the same power in the school community but not, unfortunately, the same salaries. For this reason, when I refer to New School staff, I am referring to all workers in the school. "Administrative assistants" refers only to clerical staff, and "teachers" or "faculty" refers exclusively to the teaching staff. When we had full-time administrative assistants, we encouraged them to participate in the school, join bands and learn how to facilitate them, and contribute any specialized knowledge they might have. Over the years they have facilitated bands, directed plays, and taught photography, folk dancing, women's studies, creative writing, term paper writing, jazz ballet, science fiction, and office practices. With the loss of the New School's two clerical positions, however, a resource has been closed to us. The fact that clerical workers contributed to bands and participated in all staff meetings meant that they felt very committed to the school. Their contribution was immeasurable.

Graduates. Increasingly our graduates have been called upon to make contributions to the school's curriculum. As the rate of staff turnover increases, we need to ensure having enough experienced people to cofacilitate bands with new faculty. On several occasions we have called upon graduates with great success. Graduates have directed plays and taught drawing, painting, ceramics, music, photography, and cinema. Graduates who are in advanced studies have returned to teach anthropology, religion, philosophy, history, English, and psychology. Increasingly we are appealing to our graduates to return and give something back to the school. On the whole we find them quite receptive and excited to "be back."

Student-Led Groups. Students within the school who think they have the expertise to lead learning groups must find a faculty member to sponsor them and ensure that the quality of work is appropriate for the school. This is a grave responsibility and an excellent learning opportunity for students. In order to be eligible for such a task (which earns a credit), a student must have completed one term in the school with good marks and must have attained some sort of credibility. Over the years numerous groups have been facilitated by students, beginning with the group in the second year of the school that helped facilitate the curriculum of affect, as it was called at the time. Students have taught t'ai chi and jazz ballet, directed plays, taught art and assisted the ceramics teacher, and taught performance art, instrumental music, introductory photography/darkroom, women's studies, poetry workshops, journalism through creating a school paper or magazine, and science fiction and fantasy. Their role modeling is empowering to all the students, and on the whole the quality of their work is responsible.

Outreach Projects. Another curriculum possibility lies in encouraging students to do outreach work on projects they themselves devise, or that already exist. From the very beginning of the school, there was a strong commitment to outreach work in the community. Some students interested in continuing a first-term group on children's literature were able to organize an excellent weekly seminar with the chief librarian of the local children's library on this subject. In this case, the organization of the group and the group's processes was undertaken by two student resource people; the content was supplied by the librarian, who had been given a clear indication of the students' needs.

There have been many excellent outreach learning groups: a project in which a New School group worked on educational theory and as animators in a program at an inner-city elementary school; students formed a group of tutors for students who were having difficulty in high school—some of them tutored in basic skills while others worked on drama and filmmaking projects with the students; some students worked at a tutoring center in conjunction with a developmental psychology learning group; in conjunction with a religion course at Dawson and one at the New School, some students worked in a project helping to meet the needs of elderly citizens in the downtown area of the city. In the fall of 1987, the first year of my research for this book on the New School, I facilitated a learning group on this project. The students did all the interviews of former New School faculty for this project, and their trips in the community were very meaningful to them, although this was a very modified outreach approach. In her survey on the development of "academics" at the New School, one student observed that the number and frequency of student outreach commitments trailed off seriously after the 1983 strike.

It seems that over the years, it is more often that an outside resource person must come to us: as students, we go out into the community much less than we used to. The increasing reluctance of New Schoolers to "reach out" into the world around us and find learning opportunities there is echoed in the facilitators' observations that a greater proportion of students than ever before appear to be lazy, unmotivated or just not very involved in their learning groups. New Schoolers also appear to have increasing difficulty attending outside events that relate to, or are even required for, a learning group. I'm not sure of the reasons for this, but one factor is probably the growing number of students who have part-time jobs that occupy much of their free time.[1]

Outreach activities take a great deal of supervision in order to be creditworthy. The resource person within the school cannot simply send the students out to "do something" and then record an arbitrary mark. If the student is working with an external supervisor, the supervisor must be informed of the school's philosophy and methodology. The resource person must ensure that the school's pedagogy is being supported and that the methods of ongoing and final evaluation are consistent with the school's ways. Usually the sponsor of the project must make onsite visits. Because of all these variables, an outreach activity can be even more labor-intensive than an ordinary learning group. With the increase in faculty work load and in the students' commitment to part-time jobs, there is less energy available for displacement from the college and the supervision of outreach projects.

While it is important to offer the largest possible choice of learning groups to the students, it is also of primary importance that the pedagogy within the learning groups be consistent with the New School's philosophy and methodology. Our efforts to maintain a high level of critical humanism and a concomitant praxis within the learning groups have meant a continual struggle against the tides at work in the politics of higher education in Quebec. While to some extent the tides we have tried to overcome have to do with an increasingly individualistic zeitgeist informing the values of our students and staff, the structure in which we work has forced us into increasingly labor-intensive adjustments in order to maintain a viable system of accountability within the New School that conforms to the criteria of a system with which it has little of essence in common.

THE FORMATION AND PEDAGOGY OF THE LEARNING GROUPS

Over time, a New School methodology has developed for organizing learning groups, formulating their content and methodology, and evaluating the group processes and the students' and facilitators' participation and performance within the groups. While I will describe this method as fully as possible below, it must be remembered that we try not to exert any coercion whatsoever upon the faculty regarding this methodology. Experienced students are likely to ensure that the methodology used in their learning groups is consistent with the school's regular practices and ideology, but there have been some instances where teachers have either ignored these pressures or have refused to comply with the students' demands. In a school where the content and methodology of all learning groups must evolve from the intersection of the students' and the facilitators' interests and needs, any use of coercion is untenable. There have also been cases where very well-intentioned teachers simply could not get the hang of remaining loyal to their subject matter and métier while having the flexibility to allow the students power in determining the structure, content, and processes of the groups.

Learning groups are formed in the first week of a term. By the time the students arrive, the faculty for that term has had workshops in which facilitating skills have been discussed and objectives have been set for the term. Frequently the setting of objectives is in reaction to interests or crises that arose in the preceding term. If, for example, there has been large-scale poverty identified among the students, it might be important to give attention to life and work skills; if there have been racist, sexist, or homophobic incidents, there may be a need for groups on prejudice; if students seem not to understand the basic philosophy of the school, there may be a need to examine the tenets of humanistic education. Often in the winter term, teachers are aware of students who may want to pursue on a more advanced level a study undertaken in the first term. All these possibilities are discussed with the understanding that the faculty's assessment of the situation may not be the same as the students', and that the students may not accord the same priority to the same issues even if they do recognize them. It has been our experience that even when students do not pursue learning groups on issues identified as important by faculty, discussion on these issues may still percolate through the school on an informal basis, or in bands or community meetings.

FORMING THE NEW SCHOOL ACADEMIC PROGRAM

Academic Shopping. When the students arrive, there is always a period of orientation to acquaint them with the school's philosophy, pedagogy, and objectives for that term. The faculty and all learning group resource people and/or facilitators have written profiles of themselves that are distributed to the students. The profiles say something about the kind of people the facilitators are, what their basic areas of interest are, and how they like to see learning groups develop. Under no circumstances should the profiles include course descriptions or outlines. At the most, they should simply allude to areas of study. Here is an example of a faculty profile:

Back for a second consecutive year at the New School. Now it's that time for profiles, to try to put down on paper what my concerns are and how that might affect what will be the learning groups under the title of "Psychology." So here goes.

First, I'm interested in learning how to parent an adult. My son is 18 and that is requiring changes in our relationship. This has led to a lot of thinking about what our expectations are of our parents: what do we want them to do, who do we want them to be. I have to look at this both as being in the parent role and being in the child role. So perhaps some of you might be interested in looking at your own mother/daughter, father/daughter, mother/son, father/son relationships. This would be in the context of your own growth toward adulthood and autonomy.

I'm also the resident science buff and computer buff (not hacker, buff. This means I'm more interested than knowledgeable!) With respect to psychology this means that a learning group on the brain and its functioning is always an option. With respect to the computer part, depending on what access we have to a computer, we might do a methodology course in which we could use computers to construct and analyze interview data.

As you can tell, I'm desperately awaiting *your* ideas for developing learning groups.[2]

As it turned out, in this case two groups formed: one on adult/child relationships and one on the brain. Here is the teacher's account of them:

I think both of them worked well, although as normal with the "developing curriculum" set up, there are things that I would do differently "next time." What amazed me the most was the interest of so many students in a science-based course—The Brain, and I may offer it again if demanded. The Parent . . . course was good but needed much more development, mainly in terms of what readings are appropriate and a more structured and varied way of having the students write what they had learned. Also the drop-out rate was higher as it touched on some very "dangerous" emotional material. I enjoyed them both—but as I said, there is the frustration of "knowing I could do better next time."[3]

When the students have read the profiles, they spend several days shopping for academic groups. The facilitators are available for this process, in which they are interviewed by students, singly or in groups, who question the facilitators' interests and describe their own. Experienced faculty will be open to exploring the students' interests and motivations with them. In the course of this process, the facilitators take notes on the people who have expressed interest and what those interests are. The schedule has not yet been released because we do not want students to choose their groups on the basis of scheduling and planning "on" and "off" days. Students are advised to choose more than the six groups they will need for a regular course load. Since time conflicts may force students to make choices, they are advised to keep other possibilities in reserve.

Negotiating/Finalizing. After the shopping has finished, the facilitators must decide which groups they are going to facilitate. Usually this is done by examining their own interests and training along with the interests expressed by the majority of students. They will then post the names of the groups they are giving and when they will take place. Students are given times to come together to finalize the negotiations for the learning groups by participating in the initial contracting process for the subject matter of the group. If this appeals to them, they will make a commitment to that learning group. Sometimes a configuration of interests will result in a learning group with a fairly broad description that will enable members to pursue multiple possibilities:

Relationships: Winter, 1982. At the outset of the term, several students approached me about giving groups on the family, on friendship and on romantic love . . . all subjects which they knew interest me. Since it was impossible to give a separate group on each of these topics, I suggested a compromise: there would be a group on relationships, and people within that group would formulate the curriculum. At our first session, I asked people to "brain-storm." Here are the issues that they found important: 1) Love: They were interested in "falling in love," the importance of love relationships, women and love and men and love, women's role in relationships, infatuation versus love, is the Harlequin Romantic vision true? long distance romance, physical affection vs. sexuality, finding the perfect partner, reciprocity . . . is it essential? Romantic love vs. "real love," must love deteriorate to dependency? love and power, monogamy, and long-term love relationships. 2) The Family: our relationships within the family; how does the family perceive us and how does that affect our own future relationships? 3) Friendship: does physical affection ruin a friendship? "Platonic" vs. sexual relationships, reciprocity, power, selfishness. 4) Saying Goodbye: How do we terminate love relationships and friendships and separate from our families?

This was a big order. We finally constructed the following syllabus which we adhered to very closely ... with weekly commentary in the students' journals and class discussion:

A. The Family
   1. inter-relationships within the family;
   2. the family as teacher and perceiver of the individual;
   3. the family's effect on one's future relationships;
   4. "saying goodbye"—detaching oneself from the family: what to take and what to leave.
      Readings: Virginia Satir, *Conjoint Family Therapy*, and various articles.
B. What Is the Function of Love? Do We Need It to Live?
   Here we read Plato's *Symposium*, had a guest lecturer to comment on it, and discussed it at length.
C. Romantic Love
   1. Its history and function
      Readings: Capellanus, *The Art of Courtly Love*; Denis de Rougement, *Love in the Western World* (excerpts); and poetry from the fourteenth through the twentieth centuries.
   2. The infatuation "hype" vs. "real love"
      Here we talked and intended to read a love comic or a Harlequin Romance but never got around to it because everyone already knew the "hype" very well.
   3. The Long Haul
      The importance of love, reciprocity, monogamy, and dependence vs. independence and polygamy. Readings: Karen Horney, "Distrust between the Sexes," from *Feminine Psychology*.
   4. Putting the puzzle together
      Why relationships? Where do they take us? What else is important in life? Readings: Constantine Safilios-Rothschild, *Love, Sex and Sex Roles* (excerpts).[4]

Contracting. Once the students and facilitator have negotiated the general contents of the learning group, they negotiate other aspects of the group, such as expected tasks and behavioral expectations. They also discuss the evaluation process that will be used for determining students' final grades. Eventually they arrive at a written group contract that everyone signs. The following passage describes the process undergone in contracting the relationship group and some of its outcomes:

Aside from their weekly journal entries, which were all immediately commented upon by me, the students had to do a long final essay, integrating all the readings with their own experiences. These, for the most part, were excellent. As well, they formed small "relationship" groups within the learning group. They were all formed arbitrarily and their task was to form relationships within the sub-groups and monitor their progress in the journals. Of the four groups [of four] so formed, one disbanded due to lack of interest, another disbanded due to lack of interest and anger at this lack, another met successfully informally but could never manage to meet formally (an interesting comment on the need for casualness in the students' lives), and one was highly successful. This latter was composed of the three most reticent members of the learning group, two women and one man. They had wonderful outings and exchanges, dinners at each other's homes, movies, etc. They claimed that having to meet helped them overcome their natural shyness.

The students were gripped by the class. We shared some inter-personal crises with some of the students, and that also was demonstrative of relationships and what they can mean. With one exception, they all finished the course with good work; the rate of absenteeism was less than 5%.[5]

The learning group contract should be reasonably specific and should be signed by all students and the facilitator, with copies made available to everyone. Frequently members of the group append their telephone numbers so that people can contact each other to discuss the work.

The contracting process is a very important one in the school. It is essential that all members of a group "buy into" the contract. The facilitator must make sure that all students understand and state their own motivations for the group. If this is not established at the outset, students may later claim they did not realize what the group entailed, that they were less interested than they thought, or that they had simply gone the route of least resistance in following the other students. The following excerpt is from a student who has not made a close enough connection with the material in two learning groups and has been unable to complete her work. She would now like to complete her work, and she describes how she has become remotivated. It would appear that the sources of her new motivation are unrelated to the subject matter per se. However, they certainly are related to her regaining her self-esteem, which she emphasizes as a necessity for her learning.

I haven't been doing the work in Children's Literature or Creative Writing. I didn't feel like I was doing it for myself but because you asked us to. It was becoming too distant from me. I really want to do the work now.

There's something I want to tell you. I just realized there might be a connection . . . on Thursday night both you and Ron really gave me a really good feeling. I was feeling really tremendous and I went to Rosemere with this feeling. I'm tutoring one person there, but what happened was I ended up helping out three people. Michael asked me after if I wouldn't mind working with all three in a spontaneous way. I felt really terrific. I felt it was important to give some feedback to me . . . especially positive.[6]

While the contracting process may be very time-consuming, it is central to the success of the group and worth the investment of time. It is central not only in specifying the motivations and interests of the students and facilitator for pursuing the content but also in helping the group to form its own identity.

Personal Contracts. In some learning groups, students are expected to write personal contracts explaining their particular motivations for the group and what they as individuals hope to achieve. These are shared with the group, consulted if students want to renegotiate their contracts, and used in the process of final evaluation. They are especially useful in providing an occasion for students to reflect on those feelings which provide motivation for the group and for linking individuals to the subject matter. Often the students' personal contracts will mention their fears and anxieties as well as the interest they have, as is the case in this contract for a learning group entitled "Memoir Writing."

I took this course essentially to refresh and improve my writing skills. The past couple of terms I've immersed myself in the visual arts, and though that has been very fruitful, especially in affirming my ability as an artist, I feel the need to revive my interest in structured writing.

I've never taken a course specific to writing before. I hope that it can give me a clearer idea of how literature is created as well as . . . practice in writing more efficiently and effectively. I should like to examine how to write factual yet creative prose and also to develop my own voice.

Finally, the subject of the course, my memoirs, excites me yet scares the Hell out of me. I think at the end of the course I will have encountered a number of personal obstacles and skeletons and I intend to overcome them. I believe that the most one can write about is what one has experienced, and it excites me a lot to take a look at and create from my past.

I hope this sufficiently outlines my goals (and my apprehensions) about this group, and I can hardly wait to get started.

In order to demonstrate the variety of needs and the way in which they may be brought together, I have chosen to focus on contracts and a renegotiation in a women's studies group. Here are examples from two personal contracts for a women's studies group that focused on the conceptual history of women:

The reasons why I wish to take Women's Studies are many. The most obvious is because I am a woman and a feminist. I feel it is necessary to study in this area because of the manner in which women have been regarded in the past, and the way women are thought of now. I think it is important to me personally because I have just been married and need assurances that my identity isn't being snuffed out the way my name was. I am interested in the thoughts and writings of contemporary women, as well as . . . women in history. I would like to study how women were viewed in history, to see how those thoughts have evolved today. I am particularly interested in reading the works of Sylvia Plath.

In the above example, the student clearly is concerned primarily with her own identity as a woman. She wants to situate herself historically. She has already read Sylvia Plath and is aware that this gifted young writer committed suicide, leaving a husband and two small children. Perhaps she is worried about being "snuffed out" like Sylvia Plath. All these issues were explored when she read her profile to the class. As it turned out in this group, she was the only person interested in doing an in-depth study of Sylvia Plath. She was able to satisfy this need by writing a paper on her and sharing her work with the group.

From an early age, I have had mixed emotions about being female. On many occasions I had actions and reactions toward prejudice which stated that I had accepted my given role, one of passivity and inferiority, and ought to consider myself fortunate when permitted to join in a game of hockey. Even then, it was only after I had paid each of the boys a long-saved and precious quarter from my allowance that they let me in.

It seems that each time I begin a job I am not a "new employee," "fellow worker," or even "friend," but simply the "new chick" to be tested and flirted with. In addition to the fact that I "can't do" this or that kind of job, I must cope with the harassment from the men and competition from the women. As determined as I am not to get involved, I must admit that the whole situation distresses me.

I find male neighbors who used to call me [a nickname] and . . . carry me on their shoulders suddenly giving me the once-over at my parents' parties.

These are various situations that are ever-occurring. I know that I am placed in defined roles and that people react [in] certain ways to me. The conceptual history of women should help me to understand why, as well as assisting me not to be as bitter.

This contract carries with it two important concerns that may be shared within the group: the first is the young woman's dealing with her sexual identity—the way people are reacting to her now that she is grown up. The second is the theme of justice and equality in the public sphere (sports or the workplace). That particular learning group covered, among other subjects, the historical and current treatment of woman as the sexual temptress, as the mate, as the creative artist, and as the worker. There is something very liberating in understanding the historical contingencies that have led to one's personal sense or fear of oppression. Both young women indicated that this was an important factor in their choice of the learning group. Both of them also expressed the need for help in knowing how to react and how to stand up for themselves and be autonomous people.

Here the teacher was shopped for a women's studies group. She and the students then negotiated for its general content and considered a preliminary contract. Then each student wrote a personal contract indicating how she related to the generally designated subject matter. From the process of sharing the personal contracts and recalling the larger outline of our interest, a more detailed group contract was drawn up.

Renegotiation. All learning groups undergo an evaluation of their progress and functioning halfway through the term. The group reconsiders its original objectives and decides if it wants to make any changes. Often, in groups with personal contracts, students will indicate that they would like to renegotiate their contracts. New interests or personal experiences and insights have changed their direction, as was the case with another student in the same women's studies group whose contracts were quoted above:

Owing to my situation at the moment, I would like to negotiate some changes in the focus of my work. . . . I have found the work so far quite interesting, but it lacks a personal identification which I feel I need right now . . . to maintain my involvement.

Over the past year, my relationship with my family, particularly my mother, has been going through changes as I have begun to assert my physical and emotional independence in establishing an identity apart from my family. My frequent absence from home, my questioning of their values and opinions, and the transferral of emotional support from my family to my friends and myself; all of these changes in our traditional pattern have created confusion and strangeness in our relationship.

I have begun to work on a character sketch of my mother which I am finding very difficult: the real person, my mother, who has a past that extends beyond my beginnings, who sometimes sits up late at night and thinks and feels and remembers is a person I have never known or considered. She will always be my mother, just as I will always be her daughter, but as I move into adulthood, our relationship must expand and maintain itself through love, not dependence. I feel that through writing about my mother, I can begin to clarify my feelings towards her . . . and the recent dynamics of our relationship.

Another change going on inside myself which has preoccupied me a lot lately is the facing and admitting to my sexuality, something I have attempted to deny for most of my life. Recent experiences and discoveries have forced me to face the fact that I am a woman and have led me to want to explore my sexual values and mores. I have been writing fairly prolifically on the topic, and I have started to write poetry again, which I would like to work on with you.

Recent exposure to very different, traditional attitudes towards women has provided a contrast to my middle-class Protestant values and my so-called "liberal upbringing." The people I work with are of various ethnic groups, most are immigrants, and their beliefs are rigid and outdated in the context of contemporary North-American society. Their treatment of me and our relationship is something I have never experienced before, and this too has broadened my awareness of myself as a woman and what it means to be female.

So basically what I am saying is that I would like to explore my own womanhood directly, taking an affective focus. I would like to continue reading and doing a cognitive exploration also, but I'd like to deal with material more directly pertinent to myself.

While it is clear that all three contracts have many themes in common, the focus of each student is somewhat different, depending on her preoccupations at the time. It is also likely that the preoccupations shared by the majority will become the group's focal points. These young women between the ages of seventeen and twenty-one all have strong emotional needs to clarify their situation qua women. Sexuality and autonomy are clear themes. The mother-daughter relationship is related to both of the above. The workplace is also important. The teacher must find ways of tying the subject matter together and must be dedicated to helping the group investigate the feelings surrounding subject matter. This requires well-honed facilitative skills as well as a very broad and deep grasp of the subject matter and its literature. More often than not, the facilitator can find readings whose level and content touch many of the concerns of the group.

Evaluation. It was the initial belief within the school and has always been its practice that students take a significant role in the evaluation of their own performance, that of their peers, and that of the facilitators. While there are always occasions when some students are more interested in getting their marks and/or their credits than in the process of evaluation, on the whole the majority of evaluations are conducted in an appropriate way and the people who participate in the process learn a great deal about themselves and others.

Frequent criteria of evaluation, outlined within the group contract, are attendance, punctuality, participation in the group, written work, progress from the point of departure, and any extra work done for the learning group. In most cases, students are asked to write self-evaluations or to arrive at the evaluation prepared to present them orally. Sometimes they are asked to write evaluations of the other group members as well. Students present their own evaluations and then receive feedback from the group, and eventually a grade is negotiated. The process always includes an evaluation of the group itself, its functioning, and its honoring of its original objectives. This is an important facet of critical humanism, in which the interaction of individual and group holds a fundamental value within the process.

The questions to be asked are the following: Did the group work together as a group or simply as a collection of individuals? Did the group acknowledge and meet the needs of the individuals who compose it? Did individuals within the group all recognize the importance of maintaining the group's integrity and infrastructure of mutual support and critique as central to its success? Sometimes members of a learning group arrive at a group mark and then scrutinize individuals in relation to the established norm. This usually works well, unless there are exceptional cases of students at either end of the spectrum who feel they are being cheated. In the case of exceptionally gifted students, whose capacities have developed above the group norm, it is possible to ensure that their contributions to the group are congruent with their level of comprehension. Here is part of an evaluation by an exceptional student in a learning group on holocausts:

> I think that my two main contributions to the class were the influences I had on our intergroup relations and as a kind of second animator, helping to bring up the level of intellectual disscussion. [*sic*]. I felt (quite happily) that I was sometimes a sounding board for your [the facilitator's] ideas, and you for mine. I was, however, at time[s] worried that some of the other . . . members might be bored or even resentful of this principally two-way relationship. Yet, as a whole, I think it helped the class. . . . One of the things that I like best about the New School is the fact that many classes can adjust to the level that each . . . member[s] can deal with. This is to me part of the true meaning of "self-to-subject," and I think that in this group we have seen this principle actualized to its full potential.

His views are corroborated somewhat by two other students:

> We covered the work, but we also became more involved with each other. A lot of time was spent on human feelings, ours, and I feel that was also a great part of the course.

> I feel good about having taken this course and I found that it triggered a search to redefine my own principles. We were a strong group with a lot of fabulous ideas to contribute to the learning process. Had I not felt so strongly about my denial of Jewishness, perhaps I would have been more vocal about what I experienced at [a Jewish religious school].

Another important aspect of evaluation is peer evaluation. While sometimes it is delivered orally, it is often delivered in writing. This gives each student something to carry away for reflection; it also allows for the evaluation feedback to be made in a time of reflection away from the dynamics of the group rather than in reaction to those dynamics. Here are one student's evaluations of other students in a creative writing group where the criteria for evaluation were the students' work and their contributions to one another through written critiques of submitted works:

> *Ruth:* I was a bit disappointed with Ruth's writing. I felt that she wasn't aiming as high as she could, especially in her story about Emma. I felt that some of her oversimplification was an effort to keep the story short and to remain uninvolved with her characters. However, she seemed to put more effort into her poetry, which she likes better. Her comments were very positive but not very critical, and her impact on the class was cryptic. However, I felt that she progressed over the semester.

> *Phil:* Phil was also pretty regular with his work. There was a glaring difference, however, between his last-minute and his well thought out work. Needless to say, I much preferred the stuff that had been pondered over. In class his participation was good. He held up his side when it came to discussing readings.[7]

It is clear that the performance and commitment of all the class members is essential to the well-being of the group. Often discussion about a particular individual's lack of productivity or blocks to learning are important for the whole group: "I also think that the time spent on discussing certain students' problems with writing wasn't wasted, at least with me."[8] One of the most important factors in our emphasis on group discussion and group work is that it breaks down systemic and personal barriers:

I have learned that a lot of different people have the same experiences as myself. It is strange listening to people read their work and being able to relate to it.

I have also learned how some of the work can be used practically. For example the piece on politics [they were asked to write on what politics meant to them] and the discussion in class helped me to understand how politics works in the New School.

I think one thing that will stay with me is the sharing of common experiences, even though I was convinced that I had my own . . . [and] . . . nobody could have the same.[9]

While one might argue that only poor and mediocre students "need" group support to excel, very able students are also very positively reinforced by the group environment:

I have enjoyed our creative writing sessions very much this term. More than this, I have gained from them. I now find it not only easier to criticize others' works, but also to take criticism myself; as I grow more secure with my skills, I will also become less defensive about them.

I got a lot out of watching people creak that tiny bit out of the coffin we all keep ourselves locked in. I got a lot out of seeing people's writing skills improve. There is definitely something to be said for working in a group.

I think our group was very successful; the improvement in our writing has been evidence of that. But what I'd also like to believe is that we've learned something besides, and that maybe our appreciation of each other has deepened as well.

Eventually, students must be individually evaluated by themselves, their peers, and the facilitator. There are numerous ways of initiating this aspect of the evaluation process. Sometimes it is useful to use exercises like "on the one hand . . . on the other hand." In this exercise each member of the group writes on one side of a sheet of paper (or an index card) what they liked best about the student's performance in that particular learning group. On the other side, each member of the class is asked to write one criticism. This can be varied, particularly in art classes, where there is a product visible to all. Here, members may write something they like about the person on one side of a card and a critique of the work under consideration on the other side of the card. The point here is to help people learn how to accept and contain criticism. So often people globalize critiques, thinking that their total being is under criticism and being rejected, when in fact what is being discussed is only one facet of their lives.

Sometimes the facilitator will reserve part of the grade for the quality of the student's written work, which in many cases has not been seen in its entirety by the group. In this case it is important to emphasize that the group must trust the facilitator's judgment and integrity. Progress is very important to our pedagogy. However, it is often difficult to arrive at equally fair and just assessments of both the talented student who is able to produce high-quality work with little effort and the student whose quality of finished product is inferior but who has invested enormous energy and effort and has improved considerably over the term. By having to tackle these issues, students are impelled into fascinating and consciousness-raising discussions about the nature of evaluation itself, its efficacy, and its purpose. While evaluations in the New School usually result in students' receiving credits, their more important long-range contribution to students is in their process, in the intensity and openness with which individual students and entire groups assess their own processes and give and receive feedback.

It [evaluation] teaches you how to evaluate yourself fairly which you've never had the opportunity to do before, and then you can't avoid looking at what you've done more honestly because people don't let you. You can't say, "I did this," when you didn't. So it gives you a sense of really taking a good look at yourself and measuring what you've done, and it also allows you to do that for other people. This give[s] you a better idea of what it's like for a teacher or facilitator to have to mark and what really goes into it, the considerations you have to make. So I think it teaches you about a whole new angle of education that you should know about because it's very pertinent to you.

If sometimes the students initially imagine that being party to the evaluation process will bring them better grades than the regular teacher-evaluator system, they soon become very clear about the educational value of the evaluation processes in the school—especially as a source of empowerment. Here are the remarks of a graduate:

I think one of the important things about the New School is that people here felt that they could have an influence, that they as individuals and collectively with other people could make an impact on their learning process. Well certainly that's what we felt at the New School, but I think we also took that with us when we left and felt that we could affect other areas of our life and other people, and I think that's very important.[10]

Some subject matter lends itself especially well to a kind of self-to-subject evaluation. In the following extract from a self-evaluation in a learning group on reading and writing memoirs, one student refers back to her contract, where she said she wanted to deal with her feelings about her parents' current divorce proceedings:

My first reason for taking this class was that I felt that I had to stop running away as I was, to look back and see where I was at. I think I achieved that and I even started to walk again towards my future.

I realized a lot of things about myself, and especially about my solitude and my relationship with my parents. I haven't written the paper on the separation of my parents, though. I didn't feel I was able to deal with it in an honest way, so I preferred not to do it.

Significantly, this student shows her ambivalence about dealing with her feelings in the concluding paragraph of her self-evaluation:

I will continue writing about myself. I realized that writing about a situation helps me see it more objectively when I read it after. That is what will stay with me because I know I let my passion take over too often, less often now than I did in the past, but still too often.

The assurance that a learning group is just a beginning in the development of a new interest is common in written and spoken self-evaluations. In an excerpt from another memoirs group four years later, a student expresses more or less the same feelings:

I do not feel that the end of term and of class signifies the end of my memoirs, but a beginning. Writing my memoirs will become a continuing process that I will learn from for as long as I keep faithful to the practice.

While cynics might imagine that students misrepresent themselves in the evaluation process in order to get higher grades, this is rarely the case. For one reason, if a reliable norm of honesty has been established in the learning group, their peers will confront dishonesty. Naturally, the functioning of evaluation sessions is always informed by the entire school environment and atmosphere, especially since the students frequently share or have shared various bands and learning groups. This is why it is so important to maintain an atmosphere of trust, accountability, and personal honesty within the entire New School community: the whole is not only greater than, but also influences, the well-being of all its parts. Here is a student's assessment of his participation in a creative writing group:

I try as hard as I can when I do write, but sometimes it just doesn't come out. I have found myself working on my writing more than I have in the past. This may be because I have had to write more than I ever did before. I am trying to keep up a journal . . . the need to write on a daily basis.

If any of the . . . criteria is [*sic*] lacking, it is in my effort. I am still battling with myself to write on a daily basis . . . I still find myself doing other things when I could be writing. Effort is where I must keep working hard.

And another student's self-evaluation in a memoirs course a decade later:

As far as my own contributions are concerned, I feel that I have given as much as I could in this class, considering the size. . . . I did go through a disruptive stage during this semester, but I feel that I kept my disruptive behaviour outside of this class, aside from my extensive laughing.

In the latter case, it was up to the class to decide whether the disruptive behavior of this student was problematic. In the end they judged that while it had been difficult in the beginning, both he and the class had eventually adjusted to a norm of acceptable behavior which seemed to work for all concerned. While this was taken into account in his evaluation, it was not considered the most important factor in his case.

In their written evaluations, students will often critique the structure of the group, the quality of the readings, and the teacher's participation. Their views are always worth considering, as are these of the holocausts course of 1985:

Frankl's book, *Man's Search for Meaning*, should not have been used to start us off. The de Beauvoir would be a great replacement because the "otherness" theory is useful in understanding men's nature. Once people can see what would prompt a fellow human being to destroy "the other," the specific instances where this took place throughout history can be better examined. Keep the course moving in chronological order rather than jumping back and forth. Your idea about reaching back to Biblical times sounds terrific. My only problem with it would be that you already "squoze" so much into such a short few months' period, I am afraid of an overload of information.

Sometimes the teacher's pedagogy and choices are critiqued:

I found Greta to be highly motivating and the choice of readings to be excellent. I felt, however, that there was too much time and emphasis on plot for me in this [creative writing] course. I know that it was important for the group, but I didn't feel that it did anything for the quality of my stories, since my seemingly overriding problem is verbosity. However, I found the comments on my work to be excellent. I much prefer short comments that straighten out one point at a time to long, explicit, nit-picking critiques.

Sometimes an evaluation of a facilitator really is a demand for further dialogue, for a resolution not found within the group for various reasons. In this evaluation from a group on existentialist drama, a student seemed to have been classified by himself, his peers, and the facilitator as a "cynic." Even after the group is over, he still wants to find a bridge for more open communication between himself and the facilitator:

I realize that you and I are quite different. The first indicator is the direction each of us tends to take with relation to the written word. You are the poetry man and I'm the prose man, huh? . . . But our respective leanings do represent, I think, very different sets of values and underline two distinctly different approaches to life. I am cautious, lazy, at times immovable. I stress comfort and use this outward slovenly appearance as a protection when I am not comfortable in a situation. I have a deplorable lack of initiative and expect much more from other people than I am usually willing to give, in return, of myself. I suppose I miss out on much in life from this approach. . . . I know very little about you, Pat, but feel you are an intense man who brings a great depth of feeling to both The New School and outside situations. I know I would like to become more outwardly intitiative [sic] with my life and more receptive of other people. I think, though, that differences in our respective viewpoints would remain. And I guess we used, both of us, the differences as a cause for not taking each other as seriously as we might have. Or for not getting to know each other a little better. I didn't take the initiative to talk to you and you gave me looks and made jokes about my "cynical" approach to the things we were doing. I laughed in the beginning as well. The role seemed fine. But did we/do we need the crutches?

Students in many groups often like to speculate in their evaluations on how they will use what they have learned in the group later in life. Students in women's studies always entertain such speculations because of the way the material has an impact on their inner lives:

I stated once in a group that I felt that women could never be happy in our society; what I was of course expressing was my own loneliness and unhappiness as a woman. I realize now that I had a very big chip on my shoulder about being a woman, that I was desperately trying to prove the obvious. I also realized that I would never be happy, content, or even comfortable with a part of myself if I had to defend it so rigidly; I *can* be happy as a person. I had created an image of myself as feminist, strong and "liberated"—an image I could not live up to, that I see now is unrealistic, in terms I was using, to assume I could live up to.

Sometimes the material in women's studies forces students better to understand their families and their own positions within their families:

When I negotiated into this group, I spoke a lot about my family and the influence they have over me. There is a lot of preaching but not practicing done in my house. . . . Women's Studies didn't create any miracles for dealing with my parents and my brothers and sisters. If anything, it has made me more distant from my family. I don't think this is wrong. I think this is growing up. I'm trying not to feel guilty about disagreeing with them anymore. I'm trying to understand them. This is where Women's Studies has helped. My parents were also brainwashed; even more than I. So no wonder hints of chauvinism show up in their liberal attitudes.

While very few males choose women's studies, those who do certainly indicate a change of understanding, and often a desire to change their behavior:

I think my views on women's issues haven't so much changed as they have been educated. When I enter a discussion on women's issues now, I am much more aware of the subject and the seriousness of it. . . . What Women's Studies did for me primarily was to awaken my emotions to a subject that I had only slightly pondered before. . . . I believe that I haven't done enough, perhaps because I do not want to be called a feminist, but in the future I will demonstrate my feelings on many of these issues.

Sometimes the last evaluation students write enables them to sum up their entire New School experience in a valedictory way. It is often touching to read these evaluations, most of which exceed the demands of the group by far, and to understand that the students are situating themselves here at a point of reference to which they may return with pleasure later in their lives. It is often, as it must have been in this case, most heartening to the facilitator to witness this kind of synthesis of an experience.

As always, I realize that only the thinnest of lines separates exactness of language and reason from a self-induced alienation from people and events around me. I will continue to push myself for a better use of my language. This is, on my final evaluation in The New School, the thought I wish to leave others with. Again, thanks to people for this group 'cause I enjoyed it and 'cause it provoked me enough to write this. For which I am grateful.

NOTES

1. Kathy Presner, "The Development of New School Academics: 1974–1987," unpublished paper (Montreal: Dawson College, November 1987), pp. 2–3.

2. Susan Caldwell, *New School Annual Report: 1988–89*, p. 14.

3. Ibid., p. 25.

4. Greta Nemiroff, *New School Annual Report: 1981–82*, pp. 41–42.

5. Ibid., pp. 42–44.

6. Note from a student in November 1974, asking to renegotiate her work in two learning groups.

7. These remarks come from an evaluation of a learning group in 1984. The names of the people involved have been changed.

8. Ibid.

9. This evaluation is from a memoirs class in which this particular girl was the only member of a visible minority, a common experience of hers. It is clear that she was finally able to see some communality between her and people from other ethnic and racial backgrounds.

10. Olga, interview, 1984.

11
The Struggle for Community

Words like fraternity, belonging and community are so soaked with nostalgia and utopianism that they are nearly useless as guides to the real possibilities of civic solidarity, and our language stumbles behind like an over burdened porter with a mountain of old cases.[1]

THE FACULTY AND THE COMMUNITY

THE CONCEPT OF COMMUNITY or a particular kind of "civic solidarity" was integral to the New School's original mandate and remains even more important now in our increasingly alienated society. The ambition to form a close community has never died, but it is increasingly difficult to realize in a constant sense. At best, we have been able to sustain an environment rich with the possibility of moments of community.

One way in which we have tried to ensure a good quality of community building in the school has been through faculty/staff development—involving faculty, external resource people, and full-time administrative support staff when we had such luxuries.

The original model of the New School proposed an ongoing program of staff development, and since 1975, there have been many different approaches. The most common one is group discussion of problems within the school and sometimes within people's personal lives. Staff members are usually ready to support one another in adversity. At their best, the staff workshops have provided staff with the occasion to express their feelings about the school, each other, and themselves in this context. Mutual support is always helpful in building a good community.

The staff workshops tied together many threads which had been left hanging. They reiterated our need for mutual support throughout the constant stress during the term. Almost all of us expressed the desire for an opportunity to share our joy, our distress, our success, and our quandaries in midstream. Hopefully we can provide this opportunity in the terms ahead.[2]

At its best, intrafaculty support is a very positive factor at the New School, and even when staff find the meetings a bit of a burden in their busy lives, they also look to them for morale boosting:

I think the striking difference [from participation in regular college departments] is the tremendous support system you get from your colleagues; although they're very hard on you when you make a mistake, also they're there to support you with those mistakes and to point the way. You can really be yourself with them also. You're not alone . . . here I'm part of something, I'm an important part of something; when I'm not here, I know I'm missed, and when I'm here, I know my contributions are valuable. I feel part of something that's going on, and you feel that support and that belief in you. They trust you.[3]

While the school has certainly had numerous problems that result both directly and indirectly from the larger systemic changes around us, it continues to provide a great deal of satisfaction to those teachers receptive to what it has to offer. One area that has provided great satisfaction over the years has been team teaching, although opportunities for this are fewer with the increasing fragmentation of faculty availability.

One of the things that I've done within the last eight or nine years is . . . a lot of team teaching. I think I'm the professional on the staff for team teaching. Almost every year I've had an opportunity to teach a course with someone else and that's always quite exciting. It's not only exciting, it's also a bit of a relief. You don't feel all the burden on yourself.[4]

Although there is much support among the staff to make the New School community work, teachers also derive much energy from their work with the students:

I think of times when things can suddenly turn around. For example, when you come in and either students aren't prepared or things aren't going according to the set pattern. You can turn it around into something very exciting and suddenly you get a different kind of feedback from students. . . . One time there was a workshop last term and I was feeling very low. Very overworked and extremely pressured, I sat down in the theater and said, "This is going to be a misery-loves-company session." I talked about the things that were upsetting me and the problems and pressures that I was experiencing. We then went all the way around the group. From that sharing there emerged no solutions but a very strong growing together just by the fact that we could stop and say what was uppermost on our minds. In fact, it made the work that we did for the rest of the term much more of a team effort, much stronger.[5]

Some teachers, however, have been less receptive to experiencing this kind of closeness with students:

In my regular college courses I get involved with students whom I choose to be involved with. It's a more personal kind of relationship based on some kind of personal connection. . . . I much prefer it here [in the regular stream] . . . I don't feel obligated to have a personal relationship with everybody, and people don't expect it here. . . . For me that's more comfortable because I'm not a particularly outgoing person.[6]

On the whole, those teachers who have found the close contact intolerable have been in the minority, and they have managed to relocate themselves. Some teachers find it difficult to adjust to having their authority challenged by students. Maslow expressed a similar sentiment when he faced such challenges in his seminar on experiential approaches to education at Brandeis University in the 1960s:

I think of the contrast with my own way of learning at their age. I got whatever I could out of all my teachers, bad and good, even if only a little. [Here] I feel ineffective, not well used, not using my full power. It's as if I took a job in a chewing-gum factory. . . . What am I being paid for? Listening to them? This is a job in which I cannot grow, or enjoy myself . . . I'm doing therapeutic work, not teaching psychology.[7]

Maslow left teaching soon afterward. It is ironic that the man who was to become for many the guru of alternative education and humanistic psychology was himself incapable of meeting a personal challenge to his authority.

New School teachers cannot achieve the same satisfaction as they might in mainstream teaching, where teachers control the subject matter and how it is to be presented. This often determines the nature of questions asked and discussed in class. Even with the most recalcitrant of classes, in a room thick with boredom, teachers can thus deliver a lecture that they believe to be well prepared and well delivered—and so it may be. There is no formal mechanism of feedback to inform teachers if they are doing well or badly, and frequently teachers are buoyed up by sincere or insincere responses of interest on the part of a very small percent of their students. Teachers in this situation have more control over maintaining a high level of self-esteem. After all, if they have been fulfilling their self-defined commitments to the students, students who fail or do poorly are to blame for not having taken advantage of the situation. In the New School it is impossible for teachers to avoid engaging with all their students. While they certainly may lecture from time to time, most contracts assume the importance of student partici- pation. Thus, a teacher's sense of well-being and self-esteem is based on how the students perform or succeed in what they undertake to do.

Appreciating the possibilities of this system can appear risky to those teachers who over time have established an "official story" about their teaching and the unreceptivity of the students. Other teachers, disillu- sioned with teaching, frequently have taken their hearts out of it in a move of self-preservation. They may resent being put in a position to risk disap- pointment in themselves as well as in others. However, there is no doubt that those teachers who like this kind of education both contribute to and receive immeasurably from the community. The same closeness and con- frontation disliked by some faculty may be prized by others:

In the New School . . . I think about the students I'm in contact with . . . and that's the big thing I like, the priority of humans over subjects, over books. . . . You jump in, you volunteer, you have a sense of willingness. The commitment you make to the opportunity at the New School, for instance, comes at the time when you start to realize that it is not an organization or a school that is separate from you; you don't refer to it as "them," you refer to it as "us."[8]

Since about 1983, it has become increasingly difficult to attract students to community participation. Scheduling conflicts prevent staff from attend- ing all New School events, and fewer students are available to the commu- nity because of part-time work.

The amorphous community. . . . The community seems to me to be that "element that is precisely that which is greater than the sum of its parts." To some extent our battered principles . . . our diminishing resources, our increased fatigue, our age (ever-increasing while the students continue to enjoy youth) . . . these problems weigh on us, on our place. I have often felt that the "community" of The New School is a low priority for a vast majority of its members. Even some of the basic principles of Humanistic Psychology . . . one thinks of Maslow's hierarchy of val- ues, for instance . . . are frequently at odds with the kind of participation and politi- cal consciousness needed to keep the community alive. . . . I feel frustrated. We need a boost at the level of community, and I have no idea where that can come from. . . . The students need this critical education in politics, and perhaps we must be more conscious of our role as facilitators and role-models in the community context.[9]

One of our administrative assistants suggested this reason for our difficulty in achieving real community:

In my opinion, the school offers the guidelines or structure for Humanistic Educa- tion, but the values never quite get imbued into the community. Is it due to lack of time, lack of resources, lack of trust in the system? Perhaps students today don't want to take a self-directed approach to learning, but want more direction from facilitators.[10]

It is daunting to realize how very important staff morale is to the maintenance of the kind of New School community that we envisage. Our experience has taught us the following:

1. External factors to the program have an enormous effect on our possibility of achieving community. As resources for education dwindle, so does our chance of ensuring community.
2. Staff bonding and satisfaction are necessary conditions for a thriving community.
3. Mere survival is not enough in the long run; programs based on our ideology and pedagogy need room to thrive.

THE STUDENTS AND COMMUNITY

You don't always create friendships. Sometimes you realize that you don't necessarily get along with certain people. But that's okay, too, because you start to work at that. Because you develop a certain trust, you can sense when somebody's having a problem, when somebody's not feeling too good, and you confront them and you ask, and you realize that the problems people have are very similar to the ones you have, and that there aren't that many different feelings. That most people feel quite the same things but maybe in different circumstances in their lives. . . . So I come as an individual and . . . the differences in my perception are accepted at the same time.[11]

Students often have difficulty relating to the notion of community. The issue of power has always been important in the school. In the first years some students expressed the concern that faculty, having too much power already, should not have the right to tenure, but should leave after a year. They also complained that some teachers were not sufficiently accessible and tended to separate their private lives from their teaching. The staff responded that since student complaints often arose in community meetings, students were able to exert a great deal of influence and power in an environment where they were the clear majority. Students responded that although they liked working with the faculty on a one-to-one-basis, they found them daunting as a group. They bitterly resented the fact that teachers had staff meetings without them:

In some groups that I was in, the staff member pretended to be just another member of the group; in fact it was obvious, if anyone watched the group, that they weren't just other members of the group. The paycheck separates them, the fact that if there was some sort of a split, people automatically looked to the staff member.[12]

On the other hand, numerous students reported a feeling of empowerment in their experience within the community:

We were 140 students, and we were the ones that made a lot of the decisions about how we wanted things to go during that year that we were together. Being part of a community, a small community like that, where people are listening to what you have to say . . . people are willing to base their decisions on what you have to say . . . I guess one of the things that I really learned was how to be effective in a group.[13]

The school's original structure of governance by a formally constituted community council never flourished after its first year. Some students claimed that it smacked too much of high school elitism. As a result of various meetings, the governance of the school was undertaken by the most interested—those who attended community meetings. Since it was difficult to get everyone to feel ownership of decisions they had not made, sometimes decisions of the "interested" would lead to friction in the community. These situations, although difficult, have always been very educative to those uninterested members: inevitably they understand their own stake in the school. While some students have great passion about issues discussed in meetings, others are quite indifferent. Sometimes meetings are chaired by staff and sometimes by students.

It has become virtually impossible to get the entire community together at once. There are many other commitments vying for people's time and attention (e.g., jobs and other teaching), and the notion of sharing a community is becoming increasingly opaque to the students. The word itself has become cheapened by its euphemistic use in describing competitive groups as communities: the investment community, the science community, the defense community. Governance does not necessarily imply community. While on the whole students have been rather capricious regarding formal governance, they have always been interested in wielding some power. This is one of the things that attracts them to the school, even if it is only initially defined as "doing what you want to do." When they arrive, they soon figure out the following: Do what you want, as long as you don't harm anyone or impinge on the rights of others. You must also determine an act's appropriateness for you.

Regardless of the rate of their participation in formal governance, many graduates express a strong sense of belonging at the New School. This sense of affiliation may not be a sufficient condition for a sense of community, but it is a necessary one:

It was very much like a large family. It was a very exciting place, a very intense place. I was always one of the first to arrive in the morning and one of the last to leave because it was . . . one felt so much at home there. . . . It was very exciting. You were never exactly certain what was going to occur on any given day; there were a lot of dynamic people there, a lot of people from very different backgrounds.[14]

Very often the sense of belonging becomes connected to a sense of empowerment:

I've learned a lot of group skills and group dynamics, and I've learned how to speak and how to express myself. I had a very quiet voice, and I had a very hard time speaking when I first came to the school. People joke about that now when they listen to me speak, and they say: "Remember, remember first term when she came in here?" And they make comments about my voice. . . . I'm going to miss the closeness with people, and I realize that it's going to be a lot harder in a different setting to get the relationships that I almost take for granted here.[15]

An important aspect of the students' participating in a community where they feel comfortable is their growing conviction that they should be able to make such community happen wherever they are:

The thing that I'll miss the most about the New School is the friendly atmosphere, the community sense. When you get here, you feel as if you belong, that it's kind of a home away from home. And although I might miss it, I know that I can probably establish it in other places, too.[16]

One strong indicator of well-being in the community has been the students' bonding with faculty. A frequently expressed response regarding the teachers in the 1984 interviews was that the teachers believed in and wanted to be at the school, and cared about the students. It is very clear that those characteristics, coupled with an egalitarian pedagogy, were essential in creating sufficient trust to connect students to the community:

Well, I can say that I liked most of them as people, which I can't really say about a lot of other professors that I've had . . . they certainly worked very long hours. They put in a tremendous amount of effort. I mean, they went above and beyond the call of duty because they really felt it was worthwhile. . . . I mean, they were really part of the whole experience, they weren't really removed . . . they were very idealistic.[17]

The New School staff: . . . the main thing that I think about them . . . is that they're very approachable and they're experts in their fields. When you get to speak to them, you can tell they know what they're talking about, which is great, but at the same time they impart it in a very equal way. It's not this idea of they know it and I don't, and I really appreciate that. They've become friends, which is nice.[18]

Students often arrive at the school feeling apart from the community and unsure of what a community really is. This student very graphically described the process of moving into the community:

It's something that personally I had to get used to because I think when I first came in here, it was obvious that it [the community] exists. . . . But you also have to feel powerful enough to go get a piece of that community and include yourself. . . . I think at first, if you're not used to doing that, it seems that the community exists and you exist out of it. But if you learn just to take your own space and jump into it . . . there is a space for you. You just need to go and get it. It's there![19]

In our individualistic society, the more difficult aspect of our ideology to experience is the move from a relationship of self-differentiation to one of community: from "I" to "we." One year in the course of a community meeting it emerged that many of the students were hungry and had no money for food. Then and there a soup kitchen was organized.

The first thing that comes to mind is our kitchen committee and the fact that we make meals for the community; and the fact that people donate money and . . . food and . . . time to make things like this work, because I think that's a perfect example of what makes this place so special. What goes on here is a real feeling of giving and wanting to give and getting a real satisfaction in doing that and helping other people and sharing.[20]

In discussing our community, one of our teachers used to say, "The real New School community is out there." What she meant was that our graduates form a complex network outside of the school in Montreal and in other places in the country.

I think what was most positive for me was the sense of community, the sense of motivation that people had in coming here, in learning, the sense of caring and interest that people had in each other. . . . I felt often that we were one community, one whole. Many of us have kept in touch after the New School, and I think that's an indication of the level of the sense of community that we had.[21]

Most of the interviews quoted in this chapter took place in 1984 with graduates and students currently in the school. It is interesting to examine the positive nature of their recollections and attitudes in light of the fact that from 1981 on, there have been numerous references in each of our annual reports to the changing ethos among our students and consequently in the school. Increasing numbers of CEGEP students are survivors of family violence, social violence, rape and childhood sexual abuse, and poverty. These factors turn them to heavy dependence on drugs and alcohol and to an addiction to acquiring material objects. Their use of drugs and the need for money often give them access to and create a dependence on a criminal

element in our society. Their general unhappiness has turned them away
from school in crucial years and toward strong peer bonding of short duration. Consequently they are deskilled and have great difficulty in concentrating on reskilling themselves. With their preoccupations with survival
and materialism, as well as their low tolerance for deferred gratification,
school is only of tertiary interest to many of them.

Each time we think we have seen the ultimate destructive experience in a
student's life, we later find out we haven't. Our common ground seems to
be shrinking when students, many of whom do not think they matter much
to anyone, treat their surroundings—their own community—as if it and
they did not matter. We use our pedagogy and whatever skills we have to
help the students recognize their own potential as individuals and their obligations to each other, the school community, and society in general. While
our community might not meet our original expectations, there are many
times when the community has managed to transcend itself and reach that
ephemeral oneness.

It is our experience that sadness can often draw our community together.
Graduations are often very sad times for students who have loved the
school. They are sad to cede it to others and also somewhat apprehensive of
the coldness of the "great out there."

The saying good-bye of the graduates was one of the high points of the term—the
whyfore of all our striving. So many students—"good" ones, "not so good" ones—
articulated with great sensitivity the turnaround they had experienced in being at
the New School. Their capacity for living is forever renewed, they said.[22]

Sometimes the community becomes very close over sad events, such as
the occasions when two very much appreciated graduates of the school
died. In both cases staff and students together organized memorial ceremo-
nies for them. Here is a response to a "saying good-bye" session and a memorial ceremony by our drama teacher:

Another high moment was a gathering together of all members of the community,
past and present, whose lives had been touched by a former student. He had died
very tragically in the early spring. Derek's spirit was almost tangible in the midst of
so many people recalling, reminiscing, paying tribute. One of the times the New
School really works, I found myself saying. It was a most healing way of dealing
with his death.[23]

It would be seriously problematic, however, if we were able to rely on
tragedy only to define our parameters as a community. This is not so. We
have many rituals of celebration that draw us together: orientation rituals
and events; potluck lunches (often strange and wonderful mélanges); graduations where each graduate is given appreciative words by faculty who

have worked with him/her; annual "saying good-bye" workshops for those who are leaving; visitors' nights; drama and music productions; exhibitions; coffee houses organized by the students; and the reunions we have had with our graduates. All these not only help us to experience the uniqueness of our community but also give those of us in "active duty" the incentive to continue struggling for our common cause in community.

Initially, some people find the word "community" provocative and feel coerced into self-government or indiscriminate giving. One student wrote in an essay, "I don't like having my rights pushed down my throat." However, even people who experience such irritation participate in those glowing moments when the community really works; perhaps it is important to realize that a sense of community is not an end but an epiphenomenon, a result of many factors working together.

A common theme in interviews with graduates is the positive effect their sense of belonging to a community had on their success at the school:

I remember most positively, I guess, the feeling of belonging that I had when I came here. Feeling there was a place for me when I came through the doors off the bus from Chateauguay, feeling that there was a place for me. I could go and get myself a coffee and plunk down in somebody's space, in a classroom, and sit down and feel at home, knowing that there was something for me and a real purpose to my being there. Not that I was just there to sit and take notes and get up and leave.[24]

Many of our graduates have identified the sense of community and their experience in interpersonal and group communication as one of the most important aspects of the school when they were there:

I think the communications skills that I learned here, the basic social skills which I take for granted, but which I'm learning are very, very important when you're out there working with people, you have to know how to communicate . . . especially in the field I'm in . . . nursing. Communication skills are extremely important when you're dealing with the emotional and physical health, well-being of the patient. Also communication between health team members is extremely important. You have to communicate information accurately and you have to get along with people in the work situation.[25]

Another aspect of community life that seemed helpful to graduates was the imperative toward mutual understanding and problem-solving in the creation of a community:

I used to think that my attitude was the only attitude, the only opinion. You get more open-minded because you realize that there's [sic] just so many viewpoints about one thing that you have to open your eyes, open your ears, open your heart a little bit, and listen to other people.[26]

This capacity has been applied by many of our graduates who travel or work in international services later in their lives:

I went to Malaysia with Canada World Youth . . . which is a youth exchange program with Canadian youth and Malaysian youth. . . . Just going, having come from the New School and being able to meet people from all over, going to Malaysia and being surrounded by a foreign culture is very shocking and can be very hard. My New School experience helped me to be more open. I don't think I would be the person I am if it weren't for the New School. . . . I see possibilities and ways that it's possible to do things differently. You don't have to do things the way they've been done before. And I think the New School taught me that.[27]

The two years the students spend in the New School is a very short time; this often makes staff anxious about their ability to absorb and assimilate our values in such a compressed period of time. Ideally our ideology and praxis must lead from the feeling of self to the empathy with many and thence to action. This growth has happened for many of us—faculty, staff, students, hangers-on—who took the risk of the unknown and gave the New School a chance. I do not think any of us can help but draw on this experience when we attempt to change the status quo:

The New School gave me the opportunity to reflect inside and to realize that you really have to know yourself if you want to create change. It has to come from your own actions. . . . I've learned that you've got to take the initiative and you've got to take that first step and realize that if you want to go out and make some kind of change in this big bad world, you've got to look at yourself and see how you're relating to people. You realize after you've reexamined this that those kind [sic] of changes really mean something.[28]

NOTES

1. Michael Ignatieff, *The Needs of Strangers* (New York: Penguin Books, 1986), pp. 137–38.
2. Margo Ford-Johansen, *New School Annual Report: 1981–82*, p. 80.
3. Vivianne Silver, interview, 1984.
4. Patrick Powers, interview, 1984.
5. Margo Ford-Johansen, interview, 1984.
6. Shirleen Schermerhorn, interview, 1987.
7. Abraham A. Maslow, *Journal 2 1972*, quoted in Edward Hoffman, *The Right to Be Human* (Los Angeles: Jeremy P. Tarcher, 1988), p. 313.
8. Patrick Powers, interview, 1984.
9. Patrick Powers, *New School Annual Report: 1984–85*, p. 49.
10. Deborah Gaudet, *New School Annual Report: 1984–85*, p. 53.
11. Lianne, interview, 1984.
12. Daniel, interview, 1984.
13. Bridget, interview, 1984.

14. Martin, interview, 1984.
15. Carole, interview, 1984.
16. Michael, interview, 1984.
17. Violet, interview, 1984.
18. Jonathan, interview, 1984.
19. Ibid.
20. Carole, interview, 1984.
21. Olga, interview, 1984.
22. Margo Ford-Johansen, *New School Annual Report: 1981–82,* pp. 65–66.
23. Ibid.
24. Angela, interview, 1984.
25. Olga, interview, 1984.
26. Karla, interview, 1984.
27. Ursula, interview, 1984.
28. Bridget, interview, 1984.

12
Conclusion: Critical Humanism and the Transformation of Education

CREATING CHANGE IN SCHOOLS

THIS BOOK HAS OUTLINED in some detail the roots, context, and development of the educational philosophy of critical humanism. It has also illustrated how this philosophy has been developed dialectically at the New School of Dawson College in Montreal.

When I am asked if I think critical humanism is really beneficial for all students, I always respond that it can be of use only to students who are receptive to both its ideological basis and its praxis. However, it claims a lower percentage of casualties than many other educational philosophies that demotivate learners, whether those philosophies belong to that vast domain of hidden curriculum or to an openly articulated educational position.

If critical humanism is to work, authenticity must be encouraged in all participants within the process. This means that both learners and teachers who find their learning environments to be inappropriate contexts for themselves should be encouraged and supported by their peers to search for a more comfortable educational berth. While not everyone is either comfortable with or interested in the preoccupations of critical humanism, its inherent respect for individuals' expertise regarding their own lives should guarantee that all learners will respond to its challenge with honest reflection and that they receive support in this process.

Because this philosophy runs against strong socioeconomic currents, critical humanism swims against a powerful tide in current North American society. This is especially clear in hard economic times, when people view credentials as their only hope for upward mobility or the maintenance of a privileged status quo. For some reason, they associate a punitive and boring educational environment with the acquisition of "superior" credentials. Humanistic and supportive environments are viewed with suspicion, as not preparing people for the Darwinian battles of tooth and claw in the "great out there." Although these hard economic times militate against a total revamping of existing educational institutions, it is nonetheless desirable for those interested in critical humanism to consider creating centers based entirely on this educational philosophy. Because of the gigantic task of reeducation inherent in critical humanism, one can best give integrity to this philosophical position in an environment holistically dedicated to it rather than through piecemeal arrangements in courses here and workshops there.

This having been said, it is difficult to imagine adequately available resources for the creation of an educational setting like the New School in these times of retrenchment and decreasing support for educational innovation. So, while a holistic institutional structure is highly desirable, it may be more realistic to find ways of creating pockets of critical humanism in existing institutions. In postsecondary institutions this can be achieved through clusters, programs, or cross-listings of clusters of courses offered by like-minded people. The same principle can be applied in high schools, since secondary education is almost universally in crisis. School boards may consider developing schools based on critical humanism as one of the options with which to try to convince adolescents to stay in school. In elementary schools, principles of critical humanism can certainly be introduced by teachers, most advantageously in those schools where much of the teaching is still done by one teacher. It is wise to team up with others for such enterprises because it is important to maintain a dialectical relationship with other educators in order to test one's ideas.

Since the pedagogy of critical humanism is labor-intensive, it is often particularly difficult to maintain innovative programming among educators who already have punishing work loads. For some people, the trade-off of time versus more meaningful implication is worth it; for others, it may become part of a burnout problem rather than its solution. It is most important to be assured of some faculty continuity in an educational alternative; otherwise, its philosophy will become diluted and its purpose vague and unresponsive to any clientele.

Certainly critical humanism could be a unifying factor in career programs in high schools and community colleges, and in professional programs in universities. Critical humanism is an educational philosophy through which many teaching strategies have been successfully developed. There is no reason why it cannot be adapted very successfully to a critical approach to science and technology. Such an approach, which situates these enterprises in their sociopolitical reality, would be a beneficial addition to the vacuous and often extracontextual way in which science and technology are taught, as if they represented an absolute reality and truth. As well, attention to the affective life of the learner in these disciplines is helpful in stressful rote-learning situations encountered in medical and other professional schools. Most learners experience doubts, lack of confidence, the need for skill upgrading in some area, and occasional bouts of low motivation. It is difficult to imagine a person who would not benefit from this kind of education and from the community of learners inherent in this kind of learning.

While the most probable locus for an entire school founded on critical humanism currently appears to be the private sector, it is somewhat contradictory to advocate critical humanism in any context of privilege and intentional homogeneity. In the North American context, critical humanism should be an especially useful approach at all levels of education for a socially, economically, and culturally diversified society undergoing extensive demographic change. Rather than reproducing divisions that already exist within the society, critical humanism is able to elicit creative solutions to help society transform itself from its brutal forms of racism, economic and social stratification, sexism, homophobia, and ethnocentricity to a society based on mutual understanding and respect where opportunity is shared equally and all members of the society contribute to the formulation of its future shape.

Critical humanism is an education of empowerment. Its efforts at reconstruction are not meant to remain within the field of speculation, but to become part of each person's agenda of possibility. It is most effective and exciting when it is initiated within a heterogeneous population with a stake in social transformation, the creation of community, and the discovery of their own unobstructed voices.

SO YOU WANT TO START AN "ALTERNATIVE"? SOME CAUTIONARY REMARKS

It is my hope that this book will encourage educators in both formal and informal settings to make radical changes, not only in the small corners where they work but also in entire institutions or organizations. While my examples are drawn almost exclusively from my experience as an educator in an alternative program within an atypical community college system, it is my opinion that general principles of critical humanism can form a viable philosophical basis from which to elaborate pedagogies appropriate to numerous actual situations: high schools, colleges, universities, labor education, unions, management training, government training programs, career training, technical training, community-based educational initiatives, and as many more settings as there are ideas for them. These cautionary remarks are directed to those who wish to broaden the scope of educational experience to include the kind of personal and contextual considerations raised through critical humanism.

Many academic institutions evaluate their efficacy through those results which evolve from quantifiable analysis. Often they are committed to assessing the viability of their management of resources with reference to quantifiable academic criteria. Can one realistically initiate alternative programs within academic institutions managed strictly on actuarial models? There is a demonstrable need for alternative education when students in postsecondary institutions (where they are not retained by legal fiat) drop out at an alarming rate. Alternative programs can attract new clientele to institutions and help retain an existing but alienated group of students.

There are several strategic steps for successfully introducing alternatives within a mainstream structure.

A Critical Mass of Participants in the Founding Process. Ideally the founding group should be representative of a wide range of departments and services: academic, administrative, and support. It is wise to involve some people with high institutional credibility either as active workers or as supporters who can be called in for the critical moves. Where possible, involve newcomers to the college: those rare younger staff members who have both energy and excellent insight into the experiences of the students. Sometimes it is worthwhile to have two tiers of participation: active participants and "friends of" who are interested and supportive, and will speak on your behalf, but who have little time for direct participation. It is indispensable to have good relationships with unions or employee organizations.

Without a high level of trust within the founding group, there is little chance of growth or survival. It is therefore wise to begin with some staff development or group formation work before entering the final stage of program proposal. These important questions must be addressed: What is the group's common stock of shared values? What are the members' individual differences and bottom lines? Can they accept these differences and work together? How much time and energy is each person ready to invest in such a project? What do people have on their plates, emotionally and professionally? What assumptions should group members check out with one another? What are the members' hopes for the group, and their concerns? What is the group's inventory of skills? What skills are needed? Should the group invite the participation of people whose skills are needed? Should specific training be made available to the group? When these questions have been addressed, you will have begun the process of formulating your ideological base.

Ideological Base. You must agree upon and write down your ideological commitments as an alternative. Since the alternative will be part of a larger institution or system, you will eventually have to "translate" your ideology into language consistent with the prevailing norms. This does not mean altering your values, but simply presenting them in a way that will get them accepted. You should not compromise your basic ideology. It is important to keep sight of your ideological base in order to resist institutionalization and to examine and reinvent yourselves. Your clientele and membership will change, and you will have to elaborate and expand your ideology to accommodate the rapid rate of social change. You cannot afford to lose touch with what you consider unalterably right and irreversibly wrong as educational philosophy. Your vision must remain bright before your eyes.

Praxis. It is important initially to agree on praxis, on how things will be done in accordance with your ideology. The group will have to decide its tolerance for diversity. Resist the ease of providing bureaucratic rationales for decisions having an impact on praxis. True, often the external institution that supports you will force you into accommodating its bureaucracy. When survival depends on this, you will have to cooperate or dissolve. However, always start with the understanding that you must not do violence to yourselves or to your ways of doing things. The accommodation should only be bureaucratic: finding a way of giving the providers what they want (usually a "translation" of your praxis into their language) without losing touch with your own ideology and its appropriate manifestation in praxis.

Praxis should not become institutionalized. Always reexamine what everyone is doing. Discuss it with all members of your educational community. Ask them: Are we living our beliefs? If not, which ones are we betraying, and how should we get back on track? An alternative has to be an open enough community for any individual or group to come before the entire group and say, "I'm having trouble, help me." The combined wisdom of the group is always helpful in clarifying issues and finding solutions.

Staff Development. In alternative programs, new staff members need enormous support in unlearning the values and practices of their own educational formation and experience. This is best done when staff gets together on a regular and authentic basis. Never regard personal interchange or disclosure as a waste of time; it is only through taking good care of oneself and one another that a helpful esprit de corps can develop. You will need this group spirit for many reasons. First, so that you can maintain the dialogue necessary to the building of community consistent with your ideology; second, because you will need a great deal of energy to provide what you idealistically have described as your mandate. You will need the opportunity to share your experiences, frustrations, failures, and successes with others in your immediate environment. Such interchange can give you more energy and support your hope to continue. The third reason is that it is important for one's sense of affiliation and well-being to have honest relationships with colleagues. The fourth is that if you are embedded in a larger institution, you can count on your colleagues in other parts of the institution to snipe at you over resources and "privileges" (true or imagined), and you will need strong solidarity for your survival.

The best staff development programs require a communal agreement to address personal as well as professional issues on an ongoing basis. It is important to insist on this, because the pressures of the students and of day-to-day operations often make us forget our obligations to ourselves and our colleagues. There must be room for honest disagreement within the group and for time devoted to resolution where possible. Because there is often so little external validation for staff within alternatives, it is important to give great energy to acknowledging those situations which call for celebration.

Importance of Attitude. In order to ensure the survival of funded alternatives within regularly structured institutions, educators must be willing to live in contradiction, accepting that they will have to exist in a situation of simultaneous translation where their most sincerely held ideas may appear compromised when "adapted" to conform to institutional norms. They must accept the fact that outsiders often will attempt to "explain" them to themselves in terms revealing profound misconceptions. They can maintain tranquillity in the face of such misinterpretation through keeping a strong hold on their own ideological and pedagogical positions.

Since they will be so focused on survival, they will often be struck by the unfairness inherent in the distribution of resources in their institutions and the injustice of their being continually asked to justify themselves while other programs with less heart are never put to such tests. On the other hand, they must learn to prize the freedom that comes with marginalization. Their only hope of long-term survival is canniness, a sense of mission, and a sense of community within their program and with their graduates. The hegemony is not only powerful and pervasive but also insidious; alternative educators must remain consciously in touch with their own criteria for good education and be prepared to reaffirm these criteria to themselves and others.

The Students. Students are what it's all about, the raison d'être of alternative education, and they must be honored. Learn to interpret their silences as well as their words, their body language, their absences and latenesses, and their "forgotten" homework. That is where resistance and low self-esteem are most manifest. While it is essential to be authentic with them, it is important to find ways of disagreeing without disconfirming them. Alternatives address the affirmation of students' perceptions, understanding, and worth. Whenever possible, share your deliberations with them, and let them teach you how to explain the school's ideology to subsequent generations of students. Make sure they understand that alternative programs proclaim hope for change and growth in a moribund system and society where hope has degenerated into the anticipation of pleasure from ephemeral objects and occasions.

It is essential to maintain contact with your alumni and to create situations for their participation. Produce a newsletter if you can. Alumni are important to reaffirm your hope and reenergize you. They are first-rate resources for surviving crises and in bearing witness to the value of the school.

Resources. No matter how modestly an alternative starts out, it is important to understand that as it develops, it will probably need more resources than were originally anticipated. Staff members of alternative programs must be deployed into positions where they can keep abreast of the policies and financial developments of the outer institution or educational system. This means that they should be active on key institutional committees as well as within the alternative itself. If the institution is unionized, they should be ready to participate in union activities. It is always wise to run for positions on the board of the larger institution in order to gain credibility as well as to have an overview of and input into institutional planning.

Alternative programs are frequently overlooked in planning. Sometimes this is an expression of administrative hopes that alternatives will simply wither on the branch and fall off. Since they are often political liabilities within institutions, alternative programs may be genuinely forgotten by those busy administrators who are supposed to represent them. One must be in place to signal the alternative's needs for a just portion of institutional resources. There is always institutional pressure on alternative programs to conform; this may be expressed by placing them on a par with other programs whose needs are totally different. Alternatives and their representatives have to walk a very thin line indeed, expressing their sameness in terms of their rights to equal resources and their differences in terms of how their needs should be met.

It is not a forgone conclusion that academic administrators or other teachers are delighted with alternative programs that are successful. This success cannot help but call into question mainstream educational practices. It is always wise to emphasize that there are "many roads to Rome." It is unwise, unless pressed against the wall, to confront mainstream education in one's institution. The vindictiveness of academics should never be underestimated, no matter how small the stakes may appear to be.

Because resources are managed by administrators and their assistants, it is important to understand the political value of working well with them. This could mean volunteering to do various things for the entire institution and offering administrators support when they need it. People hold administrative positions for long periods, and memories can be inordinately long. It is important to maintain a large and varied network within one's institution.

One should always be on the lookout for other resources, such as special governmental funding, developing fund-raising projects, and attracting human resources on a voluntary basis. All the while, though, it must be remembered that these are supplementary resources and that the alternative program has a fundamental right to resources within its larger institution.

In short, never apologize, never relinquish the field in a snit, and never expect anyone to hand you anything without your asking for it. Procuring resources for alternatives requires the instincts of a hustler, the sangfroid of a spy, and the bargaining skills of a horse trader.

Institutional Interface. A good rule of thumb is to avoid confrontation unless it is absolutely necessary. Always have an encore in mind; don't ever play your last card; and keep a last card beyond the encore and one even beyond that. It is important to be accepting of the outer institution on which you depend for resources without internalizing its values. One must always take the initiative of "translating" one's practices into institutional language. Conversely, one must never "translate" institutional practices into alternative language without close examination. Institutions will pressure alternatives to fragment themselves according to categories created for the expediency of administrative practices. Alternatives must resist such fragmentation where possible, maintaining internal practices of self-definition and using those structures appropriate to their ideology and praxis. All "translation" should be simultaneous and politically inspired, never penetrating beyond the point of institution-alternative intersection.

Survival. Act as if you're going to be around forever. I don't mean only the alternative; I mean the educational team. To be sure, there will be various attritions, and there should be. They must be explained to the external institution in the most positive light and with the clear message that while an alternative's ideology and praxis are its mandate, personnel are replaceable and the remaining staff is always prepared to welcome newcomers.

One way of surviving is by keeping up a public image. Volunteer to visit "feeder" schools or institutions. Get the scribes among you to write up your alternative, to present it at conferences, to publish accounts. Institutions are sensitive to external perceptions of them. Use this to your advantage by presenting as positive an image as you can, not just of the alternative but of the entire institution. Use the media when you can; any pretext will do. Get your students involved in the community and be sure to tell them to tell others about your program. They are your best emissaries, but they will go forth only if they feel important and trusted.

AS YOU CAN SEE, working for an alternative is a hard task, a bit like juggling. You must maintain your personal integrity, be a confirming colleague and educator, and keep an eye on the "outside" and potentially harmful world of your providing institution—not to mention the educational system. At the same time you must continually scheme for resources and survival. As you teeter on one toe with several bright globes in the air, you might from time to time wonder if it's worth it. If you love learning and learners, if you love the bustle of politics and the sound of engagement, if you dread boredom, and if you are determined to make a difference—you are probably ready to dream up an alternative educational setting where you live and breathe.

You are needed; we are waiting for you.

References

Aisenberg, Nadya, and Mona Harrington. *Women of Academe: Outsiders in the Sacred Grove.* Amherst: University of Massachusetts Press, 1988.

Altschuler, Alfred. *Developing Achievement Motivation in Adolescents.* Englewood Cliffs, NJ: Educational Technology Publications, 1973.

———, Diane Tabor, and James McIntyre. *Teaching Achievement Motivation: Theory and Practice in Psychological Education.* Middletown, CT: Educational Ventures, 1971.

Apple, Michael W. *Ideology and Curriculum.* London: Routledge and Kegan Paul, 1979.

Aronowitz, Stanley, and Henry A. Giroux. *Education under Siege.* South Hadley, MA: Bergin & Garvey, 1985.

Aronowitz, Stanley, et al., eds. *The Sixties without Apology.* Minneapolis: University of Minnesota Press, 1984.

Badgley, Robin. *Sexual Offenses against Children: The Report of the Committee on Sexual Offenses against Children and Youth.* Ottawa: Canadian Government Publishing Centre, 1984.

Barrett, M. *Women's Oppression Today: Problems in Marxist Feminist Analysis.* London: Verso Press, 1980.

Barrett, William. *Irrational Man: A Study in Existential Philosophy.* Garden City, NY: Doubleday, 1958.

Belenky, Mary Field, Blythe McVicker Clinchy, Nancy Rule Goldberger, and Jill Mattuck Tarule. *Women's Ways of Knowing: The Development of Self, Voice, and Mind.* New York: Basic Books, 1986.

Bernier, Normand R., and Jack E. Williams. *Beyond Beliefs: Ideological Foundations of American Education.* Englewood Cliffs, NJ: Prentice-Hall, 1973.

Bettelheim, Bruno. *Love Is Not Enough.* New York: Collier Books, 1965.

———. *The Informed Heart.* New York: Avon Books, 1971.

Biehler, Robert F. *Psychology Applied to Teaching.* Boston: Houghton Mifflin, 1971.

Blake, William. *The Viking Portable Blake,* ed. Alfred Kazin. New York: Viking Press, 1955.

Bogdan, Robert C., and Sari Knopp Biklen. *Qualitative Research for Education: An Introduction to Theory and Methods.* Boston: Allyn and Bacon, 1982.

Booth, Wayne C., ed. *The Knowledge Most Worth Having.* Chicago: University of Chicago Press, 1967.

Borton, Terry. *Reach, Touch, and Teach: Student Concerns and Process Education.* New York: McGraw-Hill, 1970.

Bowles, Gloria, and Renate Duelli Klein, eds. *Theories of Women's Studies.* London: Routledge and Kegan Paul, 1983.

Bowles, Stanley, and Herbert Gintis. *Schooling in Capitalist America.* New York: Basic Books, 1976.

Boy, Angelo V., and Gerald J. Pine. *Expanding the Self: Personal Growth for Teachers.* Dubuque, IA: William C. Brown, 1971.

Bricker-Jenkins, Mary, and Nancy Hooyman. "Feminist Pedagogy in Education for Social Change." *Feminist Teacher* 2, no. 2 (1987).

The Bristol Women's Studies Group. *Half the Sky: An Introduction to Women's Studies.* London: Virago Press, 1979.

Brodrib, Somer, and Micheline de Sève. *Women's Studies in Canada: A Guide to Women's Studies Programmes and Resources at the University Level.* Toronto: RFR/DRF (Ontario Institute for Studies in Education), 1987.

Brown, George Isaac. *Human Teaching for Human Learning: An Introduction to Confluent Education.* New York: Viking Press, 1971.

Bugental, J. F. L., ed. *Challenges of Humanistic Psychology.* New York: McGraw-Hill, 1967.

Bunch, Charlotte, and Sandra Pollack. *Learning Our Way: Essays in Feminist Education.* Trumansburg, NY: The Crossing Press, 1983.

Carnoy, Martin. *Schooling in a Corporate Society.* New York: David McKay, 1972.

————. *Education as Cultural Imperialism.* New York: David McKay, 1974.

Carr, John C., Jean Dresden Grambs, and E. G. Campbell, eds. *Pygmalion or Frankenstein? Alternative Schooling in American Education.* Reading, MA: Addison-Wesley, 1977.

Carriero, Mary E. *Modern Education: One Size Fits All.* South Hadley, MA: Bergin & Garvey, 1988.

CEGEP-Réalité. *Si CEGEP m'était conté . . . .* Sherbrooke, QC: Presses Cooperatives, 1972.

Clark, Donald H., and Asya L. Kadis. *Humanistic Teaching.* Columbus, OH: Charles E. Merrill, 1971.

Code, Lorraine, Sheila Mullett, and Christine Overall, eds. *Feminist Perspectives: Philosophical Essays on Morals.* Toronto: University of Toronto Press, 1988.

Conseil des collèges. *La réussite, les échecs et les abandons au collégial: L'état et les besoins de l'enseignement collégial. Rapport 1987–1988.* Québec: Gouvernement de Québec, 1988.

Conway, Jill K., Susan C. Bourque, and Joan W. Scott, eds. *Learning about Women.* Ann Arbor, University of Michigan Press, 1987.

Craig, Robert L., and Lester R. Bittel, eds. *Training and Development Handbook.* New York: McGraw-Hill, 1967.

Cross, K. Patricia. *Accent on Learning.* San Francisco: Jossey-Bass, 1976.

Culley, Margo, and Catherine Portugues, eds. *Gendered Subjects: The Dynamics of Feminist Teaching.* Boston: Routledge and Kegan Paul, 1985.

Curwin, Richard L., and Barbara Schneider Fuhrmann. *Discovering Your Teaching Self: Humanistic Approaches to Effective Teaching.* Englewood Cliffs, NJ: Prentice-Hall, 1975.

Dale, Roger, Geoff Esland, and Madeleine MacDonald, eds. for the Schooling and Society Course at the Open University. *Schooling and Capitalism.* London: Routledge and Kegan Paul, 1976.

de Beauvoir, Simone. *The Second Sex,* trans. and ed. H. M. Parshley. New York: Bantam Books, 1969.

Dennison, George. *The Lives of Children.* New York: Random House, 1969.

Dewey, John. *Democracy in Education.* New York: Macmillan, 1916.

_____. *Experience and Education.* London: Collier Books, 1938.

Dillon, J. Y. *Personal Teaching.* Columbus, OH: Charles E. Merrill, 1971.

Doyle, James A. *The Male Experience.* Dubuque, IA: William C. Brown, 1983.

Erikson, E. G. *Identity: Youth and Crisis.* New York: Norton, 1968.

Evans, Richard I., ed. *Carl Rogers: The Man and His Ideas.* New York: E. P. Dutton, 1975.

Farber, Jerry. *The Student as Nigger.* Richmond Hill, Ont.: Simon and Schuster of Canada Ltd., 1970.

Farnham, Christie, ed. *The Impact of Feminist Research in the Academy.* Bloomington: Indiana University Press, 1987.

Fox, Robert S., Margaret Barron Luszki, and Richard Schmuck. *Diagnosing Professional Climates of Schools.* Fairfax, VA: NTL Learning Resource Corp., 1975.

Frankl, Viktor E. *Man's Search for Meaning,* trans. Ilse Lasch. Boston: Beacon Press, 1968.

_____. *The Doctor and the Soul,* trans. Richard Winston and Clara Winston. New York: Random House, Vintage Books, 1973.

Freire, Paulo. *Education: The Practice of Freedom,* trans. and ed. Myra Bergman Ramos. London: Writers and Readers Publishing Cooperative, 1973.

_____. *The Politics of Education: Culture, Power and Liberation,* trans. Donaldo Macedo. South Hadley, MA: Bergin & Garvey, 1985.

_____, and Donaldo Macedo. *Literacy: Reading the Word and the World.* South Hadley, MA: Bergin & Garvey, 1987.

_____, and Ira Shor. *A Pedagogy for Liberation: Dialogues on Transforming Education.* South Hadley, MA: Bergin & Garvey, 1987.

Friedenberg, Edgar Z. *Coming of Age in America: Growth and Acquiescence.* New York: Random House, 1965.

Fromm, E. *Escape from Freedom.* New York: Farrar & Rinehart, 1941.

Frye, Marilyn. *The Politics of Reality: Essays in Feminist Theory.* Freedom, CA: The Crossing Press, 1983.

Galbraith, John Kenneth. *The Anatomy of Power.* Boston: Houghton Mifflin, 1983.

Gallagher, Paul, and Gertrude MacFarlane. *A Case Study in Democratic Education: Dawson College.* Montreal: Dawson College, n.d.

Gergen, Mary McCanney, ed. *Feminist Thought and the Structure of Knowledge.* New York: New York University Press, 1988.

Gilligan, Carol. *In a Different Voice: Psychological Theory and Women's Development.* Cambridge, MA: Harvard University Press, 1982.

———, Victoria Ward, Jill McLean Taylor, and Betty Bardige, eds. *Mapping the Moral Domain.* Cambridge, MA: Harvard University Press, 1988.

Giroux, Henry A. *Theory and Resistance in Education: A Pedagogy for the Opposition.* South Hadley, MA: Bergin & Garvey, 1983.

———. *Teachers as Intellectuals: Towards a Pedagogy of Practical Learning.* South Hadley, MA: Bergin & Garvey, 1988.

Goodman, Paul. *Compulsory Mis-education and the Community of Scholars.* New York: Random House, 1964.

———. *Growing up Absurd.* New York: Random House, 1969.

Goffman, Erving. *The Presentation of Self in Everyday Life.* Garden City, NY: Doubleday/Anchor Books, 1959.

Gradd, Gerald. *Professing Literature: An Institutional History.* Chicago: University of Chicago Press, 1988.

Graubard, Allen. *Free the Children: Radical Reform and the Free School Movement.* New York: Pantheon, 1972.

Grimshaw, Jean. *Philosophy and Feminist Thinking.* Minneapolis: University of Minnesota Press, 1986.

Gross, Ronald, and Beatrice Gross, eds. *Radical School Reform.* New York: Simon and Schuster, 1969.

Gross, Ronald, and Paul Osterman, eds. *High School.* New York: Simon and Schuster, 1971.

Hansen, Soren, and Jesper Jensen with Wallace Roberts. *The Little Red Schoolbook,* trans. from Danish by Berit Thornberry. New York: Simon and Schuster/ Pocket Books, 1971.

Harding, Sandra, ed. *Feminism and Methodology.* Bloomington: Indiana University Press, 1987.

Harvard Educational Review 42, no. 3 (August 1972). Special issue on alternative schools.

Havelock, Ronald G. *The Change Agent's Guide to Innovation in Education.* Englewood Cliffs, NJ: Educational Technology Publications, 1973.

Henry, Jules. *Culture against Man.* New York: Random House, 1963.

Hoffman, Edward. *The Right to Be Human: A Biography of Abraham Maslow.* Los Angeles: Jeremy P. Tarcher, 1988.

Holt, John. *The Underachieving School.* New York: Pitman, 1969.

———. *Freedom and Beyond.* New York: Dutton, 1972.

Holtz, Harvey, Irwin Marcus, Jim Dougherty, Judy Michaels, and Rick Peduzzi, eds. *Education and the American Dream.* South Hadley, MA: Bergin & Garvey, 1988.

Hooks, Bell. *Yearning: Race, Gender and Cultural Politics.* Toronto: Between the Lines Press, 1990.

Hunter College Women's Studies Collective. *Women's Realities, Women's Choices: An Introduction to Women's Studies.* New York: Oxford University Press, 1983.

Ignatieff, Michael. *The Needs of Strangers.* New York: Penguin Books, 1986.

Illich, Ivan. *Deschooling Society.* New York: Harper & Row, 1971.

_____, et al. *After Deschooling, What?* New York: Harper & Row, 1973.

Jagger, Alison M. *Feminist Politics and Human Nature.* Totowa, NJ: Rowman and Allanheld, 1983.

Jarrett, James L. *The Humanities and Humanistic Education.* Reading, MA: Addison-Wesley, 1973.

Jersild, Arthur T. *In Search of Self.* New York: Teachers College, Columbia University, 1971.

Jourard, S. *The Transparent Self: Self Disclosure and Well Being.* Princeton, NJ: Van Nostrand, 1964.

Karabel, Jerome, and A. H. Halsey, eds. *Power and Ideology in Education.* New York: Oxford University Press, 1977.

Karier, C. J., Paul C. Violas, and Joel Spring, eds. *Roots of Crisis.* Chicago: Rand McNally, 1973.

Kirschenbaum, Howard. *Advanced Values Clarification: A Handbook for Trainers, Counsellors and Experienced Teachers.* La Jolla, CA: University Associates Press, 1977.

_____, and Sidney B. Simon, eds. *Readings in Values Clarification.* Minneapolis, MN: Winston Press, 1973.

Konh, Shiu Loon. *Humanistic Psychology and Personalized Teaching.* Toronto: Holt, Rinehart and Winston, 1970.

Kozol, Jonathan. *Death at an Early Age.* New York: Bantam Books, 1967.

_____. *Free Schools.* New York: Bantam Books, 1972.

_____. *The Night Is Dark and I Am Far from Home.* New York: Bantam Books, 1976.

_____. *On Being a Teacher.* New York: Continuum Press, 1981.

Laing, R. D. *The Politics of Experience.* New York: Ballantine, 1960.

_____. *Sanity and Madness in the Family.* New York: Penguin Books, 1978.

Lasch, Christopher. *Haven in a Heartless World: The Family Besieged.* New York: Basic Books, 1979.

Leonard, George B. *Education and Ecstasy.* New York: Dell, 1968.

Lerner, Gerda. *The Creation of Patriarchy.* New York: Oxford University Press, 1986.

Lips, Hilary M. *Women, Men, and the Psychology of Power.* Englewood Cliffs, NJ: Prentice-Hall, 1981.

Livingstone, David, ed. *Critical Pedagogy and Cultural Power.* South Hadley, MA: Bergin & Garvey, 1987.

Mackie, Robert, ed. *Literacy and Revolution.* London: Pluto Press, 1980.

Mackinnon, Catherine A. *Feminism Unmodified: Discourses on Life and Law.* Cambridge, MA: Harvard University Press, 1987.

Maslow, Abraham H. *Eupsychian Management.* Homewood, IL: Richard D. Irwin/ Dorsey Press, 1965.

_____. *The Farther Reaches of Human Nature.* London: Penguin Books, 1966.

_____. *The Psychology of Science.* Chicago: Henry Regnery, 1966.

_____. *Towards a Psychology of Being,* 2d ed. New York: Van Nostrand Reinhold, 1968.

_____. *Religions, Values, and Peak-Experiences.* New York: Viking Press, 1972.

_____. "Humanistic Education vs. Professional Education." *New Directions in Teaching* 2 (1979): 3-10.

_____, ed. *New Knowledge in Human Values.* Chicago: Henry Regnery, 1959.

Matson, Floyd. *Within/Without: Behaviorism and Humanism.* Monterey, CA: Brooks/Cole, 1976.

Matthews, Michael R. *The Marxist Theory of Schooling.* Brighton, England: Harvest Press, 1980.

May, Rollo. *Man's Search for Himself.* New York, New American Library, 1953.

McLaren, Peter. *Life in Schools.* Toronto: Irwin, 1989.

Miller, Casey, and Kate Swift. *The Handbook of Nonsexist Writing,* 2d ed. New York: Harper & Row, 1988.

Minnich, Elizabeth, Jean O'Barr, and Rachel Rosenfeld, eds. *Reconstructing the Academy: Women's Education and Women's Studies.* Chicago: University of Chicago Press, 1988.

Morris, Van Cleve. *Existentialism in Education: What It Means.* New York: Harper & Row, 1966.

Morrison, A., and D. McIntyre. *Teachers and Teaching.* London: Penguin Books, 1969.

Moustakas, Clark. *Individuality and Encounter.* Cambridge, MA: Board A. Doyle, 1968.

———. *Teaching as Learning.* New York: Ballantine Books, 1972.

Natalicio, Luiz F. S., and Carl F. Hereford. *The Teacher as a Person.* Dubuque, IA: William C. Brown, 1971.

Neill, A. S. *Summerhill: A Radical Approach to Child Rearing.* New York: Hart, 1960.

———. *Freedom Not License.* New York: Hart, 1966.

Nelson, Lois N., ed. *The Nature of Teaching: A Collection of Readings.* Waltham, MA: Blaisdell, 1969.

Nemiroff, Greta Hofmann. "L'anglais au niveau du collège: Un doigt dans la digue." *Critère* (Montréal), no. 9 (janvier 1973).

———. "Women and Education." *McGill Journal of Education* 10, no. 1 (Spring 1975).

———. "The New School of Dawson College: A Humanistic Alternative." *The Humanist in Canada* (Autumn 1977).

———. "Women's Studies and Interdisciplinarity." *Canadian Woman Studies* 1, no. 1 (Autumn 1978).

———. "Women's Studies for the Work-place." *Canadian Woman Studies* 1, no. 2 (Winter 1979).

———. "Women as Persons: Self-Definition and Direction." In *Women as Persons/La femme en tant que personne: Resources for Feminist Research/Documentation sur la recherche féministe.* Toronto: OISE, 1980.

———. "Surviving Contradiction." In *The Sixties without Apology,* ed. Stanley Aronowitz et al. Minneapolis: University of Minnesota Press, 1984.

———. "Where Are Our Schools Going?" *Montreal Calendar* pts. I and II (January and February 1984).

———. "Psychiatric Malpractice: This Case Is about Power." *Phoenix Rising* (Toronto) (February 1985).

———. "Reflections on Recent Women's Conferences; or, Watch Out We Don't Sell the Farm." *Canadian Woman Studies* 6, no. 3 (Summer/Fall 1985).

———. "The Women's Chairs: Questions and Concerns." *Canadian Woman Studies* 6, no. 3 (Summer/Fall 1985).

———. "On Power and Empowerment." In *Women and Men: Interdisciplinary Readings on Gender*, ed. Greta Hofmann Nemiroff. Toronto: Fitzhenry and Whiteside, 1986.

———. "Canadian Women's Studies over the Last Decade." *Women's Éducation des Femmes* (Toronto) 7, no. 2 (Summer 1989).

———. "Beyond Talking Heads: Towards an Empowering Pedagogy of Women's Studies." *Atlantis* 15, no. 1 (Fall 1989).

———, ed. *Women and Men: Interdisciplinary Readings on Gender*. Toronto: Fitzhenry and Whiteside, 1986.

Nylen, Donald, J. Robert Mitchell, and Antony Stout. *A Handbook of Staff Development and Human Relations Training: Materials Developed for Use in Africa*. Washington, DC: National Training Laboratories, Institute for Applied Behavioral Science, 1967.

O'Neill, William F., ed. *Selected Educational Heresies: Some Unorthodox Views concerning the Nature and Purpose of Contemporary Education*. Glenview, IL: Scott, Foresman, 1969.

Osborne, Ken. *Educating Citizens: A Democratic Socialist Agenda for Canadian Education*. Brampton, Ont.: Our Schools/Our Selves, 1988.

Ozman, Howard A., and Samuel M. Craver. *Philosophical Foundations of Education*, 3rd ed. Columbus, OH: Charles E. Merrill, 1976.

Paley, Grace. *Later the Same Day*. New York: Penguin Books, 1986.

Parent, Alphonse-Marie, chairman. *Report of the Royal Commission of Inquiry on Education*. Quebec: Government of the Province of Quebec, 1965.

Pearsall, Marilyn, ed. *Women and Values: Readings in Recent Feminist Philosophy*. Belmont, CA: Wadsworth, 1986.

Perls, Frederick S. *In and out the Garbage Pail*. Lafayette, CA: Real People Press, 1969.

———, Ralph E. Hefferline, and Paul Goodman. *Gestalt Therapy: Excitement and Growth in the Human Personality*. New York: Dell, 1951.

Peters, Richard. *Authority, Responsibility, and Education*. New York: Atherton Press, 1967.

Postman, Neil, and Charles Weingartner. *Teaching as a Subversive Activity*. New York: Dell, 1969.

———. *The School Book*. New York: Delacorte Press, 1973.

Purpel, David E. *The Moral and Spiritual Crisis in Education*. South Hadley, MA: Bergin & Garvey, 1988.

Québec, Gouvernment de. *La pédagogie, un défi majeur de l'ensignement supérier*. Québec: Conseil Supérieur de l'Education, 1990.

Ravitch, Diane, and Chester E. Finn, Jr. *What Do Our 17-Year-Olds Know? A Report on the First National Assessment of History and Literature*. New York: Harper & Row, 1988.

Rice, A. K. *Learning for Leadership: Interpersonal and Intergroup Relations*. London: Tavistock, 1965.

Rich, John Martin, ed. *Readings in the Philosophy of Education*. Belmont, CA: Wadsworth, 1972.

———. *Innovations in Education: Reformers and Their Critics*, 3rd ed. Boston: Allyn & Bacon, 1981.

Rieff, Philip. *Fellow Teachers.* New York: Dell, 1973.

Robertson, Don, and Marion Steele. *The Halls of Yearning: An Indictment of Formal Education/A Manifesto of Student Liberation.* Long Beach, CA: Lizard Ventures, 1969.

Rogers, Carl R. *Client-Centered Therapy.* Boston: Houghton Mifflin, 1961.

––––––. *On Becoming a Person.* Boston: Houghton Mifflin, 1961.

––––––. *Freedom to Learn.* Columbus, OH: Charles E. Merrill, 1969.

––––––. *Carl Rogers on Personal Power.* New York: Delacorte Press, 1971.

––––––. *Freedom to Learn for the 80s.* Columbus, OH: Charles E. Merrill, 1983.

––––––, and B. Stevens. *Person to Person: The Problem of Being Human.* New York: Walker, 1973.

Roquet, G. Comité d'études des cours communs à tous les étudiants du CEGEP, *Rapport.* Québec: Conseil supérieur de l'éducation, 1970.

Said, Edward W. *Covering Islam.* New York: Pantheon, 1981.

Scott, John Anthony. *Teaching for Change.* New York: Bantam, 1972.

Shannon, Patrick. *Broken Promises: The History of Reading Instruction in Twentieth Century America.* South Hadley, MA: Bergin & Garvey, 1988.

Shor, Ira. *Critical Teaching of Everyday Life.* Montreal: Black Rose Books, 1980.

––––––, and Paulo Freire. *A Pedagogy for Liberation.* South Hadley, MA: Bergin & Garvey, 1987.

Silverstein, Shel. *Where the Sidewalk Ends.* New York: Harper & Row, 1974.

Simon, Sidney B., Leland W. Howe, and Howard Kirschenbaum. *Values Clarification: A Handbook of Practical Strategies for Teachers and Students.* New York: Hart, 1972.

Snook, I. A. *Indoctrination and Education.* London: Routledge and Kegan Paul, 1972.

Sobel, Harold W., and Arthur E. Salz, eds. *The Radical Papers: Readings in Education.* New York: Harper & Row, 1972.

Spender, Dale, ed. *Men's Studies Modified: The Impact of Feminism on the Academic Disciplines.* Oxford: Oxford University Press, 1981.

Spring, Joel. *Education and the Rise of the Corporate State.* Boston: Beacon Press, 1972.

––––––. *A Primer of Liberation Education.* Montreal: Black Rose Books, 1975.

Stanford, Gene, and Albert Roark. *Human Interaction in Humanistic Psychology.* New York: Free Press, 1971.

Sutich, Anthony J., and Miles A. Vich, eds. *Readings in Humanistic Psychology.* New York: Free Press, 1969.

Thibault, Gisele Marie. *The Dissenting Feminist Academy: A History of Barriers to Feminist Scholarship.* New York: Peter Lang, 1987.

Thompson, Claude W. *Humanism in Action.* New York: Pittman, 1972.

Tobias, Sheila. *Overcoming Math Anxiety.* New York: Norton, 1978.

Tomm, Winnie, ed. *The Effects of Feminist Approaches on Research Methodologies.* Waterloo, Ont.: Wilfrid Laurier University Press, 1989.

Troost, Cornelius J., ed. *Radical School Reform: Critique and Alternatives.* Boston: Little, Brown, 1973.

Wallerstein, Judith S. *Second Chances: Men, Women, and Children a Decade after Divorce.* New York: Ticknor and Fields, 1989.

Weiler, Kathleen. *Women Teaching for Change: Gender, Class, and Power.* South
    Hadley, MA: Bergin & Garvey, 1988.

Weinberg, Carl, ed. *Humanistic Foundations of Education.* Englewood Cliffs, NJ:
    Prentice-Hall, 1972.

Weinstein, Gerald, and Mario D. Fantini, eds. *Toward Humanistic Education: A Cur-
    riculum of Affect.* New York: Praeger, 1972.

Young-Bruehl, Elisabeth. *Mind and the Body Politic.* New York: Routledge and
    Kegan Paul, 1989.

Zahorik, John A., and Dale L. Bruebaker. *Toward More Humanistic Instruction.*
    Dubuque, IA: William C. Brown, 1972.

Index

ABOUT THE AUTHOR

GRETA HOFMANN NEMIROFF was a founding member of The New School of Dawson College, Montréal, Canada, in 1973 and was its Director/Co-director from 1975 to 1991. Currently on leave from The New School, she holds the Joint Chair of Women's Studies at Carleton University and the University of Ottawa. She is the President of the Canadian Women Studies Association. She has published numerous articles and stories and has edited two books on women in Canada.